The
Faith and Doubt
of Holocaust
Survivors

The
Faith and Doubt
of Holocaust
Survivors

Reeve Robert Brenner

THE FREE PRESS
A Division of Macmillan Publishing Co., Inc.
NEW YORK
Collier Macmillan Publishers
LONDON

The Free Press
A Division of Macmillan Publishing Co., Inc.
866 Third Avenue, New York, N.Y. 10022

Collier Macmillan Canada, Ltd.

Library of Congress Catalog Card Number: 79–6764

Printed in the United States of America

printing number

1 2 3 4 5 6 7 8 9 10

Library of Congress Cataloging in Publication Data

Brenner, Reeve Robert.
   The faith and doubt of Holocaust survivors.

   Includes bibliographical references and index.
   1. Holocaust (Jewish theology) 2. Holocaust,
Jewish (1939-1945)—Moral and religious aspects.
I. Title.
BM645.H6B73   296.3   79-6764
ISBN 0-02-904420-0

Dedication

This book is the product of three different stages.

The first—from concept
to research survey—is dedicated to
Gila Tikva, for joy and hope.
The second—the long period
of interviewing—I dedicate to
Neeva Liat, my creation;
Nurete Leor, the heart of the flame
bestowing light upon me; and
Noga Libi, illuminating my heart.
The third—tabulating and composing
each draft of the manuscript—I dedicate to
Eva.
And the entire work, which is this book,
I dedicate as a small token of love and honor to
my father—
Abraham Brenner
of blessed memory.
Czestochowa, Poland—1904
New York City—1906–1973
Netanya, Israel, 1973–1977

Contents

You can't just say, "God! that was some experience!" The very meaning of experience has to be radically changed. No other experience that man has endured can be placed alongside it, to compare with it, for the sake of comprehending it. Calling what we felt, saw, and suffered "an experience" simply will not do. We are totally different from what we had been.

Holocaust survivor who operates a
grocery store outside Tel-Aviv

We all have reason to be insecure. When the ultimate basis of our world is in question, we run to different holes in the ground, we scurry into roles, statuses, identities, interpersonal relations. We attempt to live in castles that can only be in the air, because there is no firm ground in the social cosmos on which to build. We are all witnesses to this state of affairs. Each sometimes sees the same fragment of the whole situation differently; often our concern is with different presentations of the original catastrophe.

R. D. Laing, *The Politics of Experience*,
Chapter 6

Preface

THE ORIGINS OF THIS BOOK, I believe, are rooted in my then recurring childhood dreams of being pursued by black-booted Nazi storm troopers through the side alleys, over backyard fences, behind the neat two-family buildings in the calm serenity of my Brooklyn neighborhood, nightmares which I thought then were dreadful beyond the imagination. It was only later, of course, that I understood that the reality happening to others, at the time upon which my evocations were based, were far worse, more grotesque and more evil than my most frightful images. These fears had been transmitted quite unintentionally to me by a cousin of my own age, brought to this country by my grandfather, having been snatched from the furnaces, to be my newest playmate. The newsreels at the local movie house of the marching German soldiers invested those dreams with concrete, verifiable particulars and grounded my childhood projections in an historical context.

The intensity of those inner feelings which in my youth were expressed in dreams never really abated. They may have even driven me to the formal postgraduate study of Judaism and Rabbinic ordination; to a U.S. Army chaplaincy tour of duty stationed in the Rhineland district and Nurenberg, Germany; to my first research project, "American Jewry and the Rise of Nazism" (under the instructorship of Dr. Martin A. Cohen, Professor of History, HUC–JIR); and to many hours of anguish treating and counseling Holocaust survivors. In the course of time, these elements became directed into an academic discipline, into which coalesced a series of gnawing questions.

For many years I had been bothered by the question, How have Holocaust survivors, those who have witnessed and have been the victims of the most brutal experience of our age, been changed by that experience? How has their thinking been changed especially on important questions, ultimate questions, religious questions, changed in their religious faith, ideology, and behavior? So many "experts" claim to know and speak for them. A certain theologian says "they" have been changed thus-and-so, categorizing them all as one. Another, himself a survivor, makes a different claim altogether. Those with vested interests —certain Jewish and Christian clergymen, for example—would rather not know or claim that regardless of how they may have been changed physically and emotionally, Jewish Holocaust survivors were not affected religiously at all. Certain other thinkers, some from the world of the academy, claim that overall the pious were transformed by what they underwent into atheists all. Everyone speaks for them, but no one has spoken to them; no one has previously asked the survivors themselves, especially in any unbiased, systematic way, dealing with all groups and communities and persuasions.

The research for *The Faith and Doubt of Holocaust Survivors* inquires into the manifold dimensions of the meaning and import of the Holocaust, the Nazi massacre of Jews during World War II, for survivors. It is particularly concerned with the effects of the concentration camp experience on the religious beliefs and practices of Jewish survivors. To understand its religious impact, one thousand Holocaust survivors—concentration camp survivors and others who survived outside the camps—were contacted according to random sampling techniques for a representative cross-section of the survivor community. Lists of survivors were secured from various Holocaust-related institutions and organizations, including Jerusalem's prestigious Yad Vashem, the Tel-Aviv–based organization of Nazi victims, and Kibbutz Lochamei Haghettaot. From these, 708 were willing to cooperate and be interviewed; 608 were interviewed by mail and 100 by personal interview.

Survivor subgroups were determined according to plausible and presumptive criteria, e.g., nonobservant, moderately observant, highly observant, ultra observant; survivors who believed in the traditional Jewish personal God, an impersonal Power, atheists, and agnostics; and similar categories, to see how each subgroup was affected by the Holocaust. Traditional articles of Jewish faith (messiah, chosen people, Torah as the word of God, Judaism as a true religion, etc.) were examined, and survivors were questioned to determine what these articles of faith meant to them in the light of their experiences and to see which survivors retained or relinquished these beliefs because of the Holocaust. They were asked more than a hundred questions concerning their religious beliefs and practices, their thoughts and ideas, at the designated time periods before the war, during the war, immediately after the war, and today. The results have been tabulated and analyzed in this book.

The generation of Holocaust survivors dwindles in number from day to day, and the time to ask these and other questions of the ultimate, that is, religious questions, may soon pass. There was therefore, from its inception to its conclusion, a sense of urgency connected with this research.

REEVE ROBERT BRENNER

New York, New York
Netanya, Israel
January 1980

Acknowledgments

It seems entirely appropriate here to disclose the identities of a few of those who helped shape the book. Professor Alan S. Zuckerman of Brown University; Dr. Saul Brenner of the University of North Carolina at Charlotte; Dr. Joyce Brenner of the Wurzweiler School of Social Work, New York, and Bar Ilan University, Tel-Aviv, Israel; Sharon Lerner; Dr. Martin Cohen of HUC–JIR; Professor Jacob Neusner, President of the Max Richter Foundation; Shalmi Bar Mor and others at Yad Vashem; Rabbi Eli Rosman; Kitty Moore of The Free Press; and the Holocaust survivors themselves, many of whom would prefer not to be identified by name, participated in the development and advancement of this work in more ways than I can acknowledge, much less hope to repay.

Phyllis Joffe spent an inordinate amount of time in Netanya, Israel, studying and correcting the manuscript and pruning the prose with a view to making it as readable as possible. She insisted I rework passages which were obscure and eliminate the words I believed I hadn't invented. She and Sy Joffe encouraged me in many ways.

Estanne and Dan Abraham of Netanya and New York nourished and upheld this project throughout its long course, cheered my determination, guided my efforts, and shouldered and supported the work in progress by many substantial and tangible acts of kindness. Their capacity to inspire is exceeded only by the range of their vision.

Above all the Abrahams and Joffes offered me the most precious gift of all: friendship. Except by my own friendship there is no way I can ever discharge my obligations to them.

The
Faith and Doubt
of Holocaust
Survivors

ONE

Introduction

THE HOLOCAUST IS A MIDNIGHT CALLER who never takes leave. It visited destruction upon the Jewish glaziers, plumbers, stove-builders, cobblers, and seamstresses of Lithuania and Latvia on the Baltic Sea and upon the Sephardic Ladino-speaking craftsmen of the Greek islands of Corfu, Crete, and Rhodes in the Mediterranean. It claimed assimilated bankers and grain merchants of cosmopolitan Odessa on the Black Sea as well as the highly unionized and politicized working-class Jews of Marseilles and Cherbourg. It brought death to the Jewish teachers, physicians, and attorneys of Paris, Berlin, and Vienna; to the self-employed clothiers and diamond dealers of Brussels and Antwerp; to the secondhand dealers and street traders of Amsterdam; and the beggars in the slums of the old ghetto of Rome. It appropriated Hasidic rebbes of Slovakia and Italian Jews barred from Fascist party membership. It carried away the culturally separatist Jews of Bucovina and Bessarabia, the Yiddish secularists of Charleroi and Ostend, the Neologs of Budapest, liberal Jews of Frankfurt and Warsaw, academics, Bundhists, labor Zionists and Communists, veteran army officers, and decorated war heroes.

The Holocaust is a fiend who refuses to make way, descending again and again like a persistent, indefatigable incubus upon the few who unaccountably were overlooked and to scourge their offspring and loved ones for the survivors' temerity to have escaped the earlier roundup. It acts as an avenging spirit, an angel of death who retraces his steps to reclaim stragglers. The Six Million, then, were not the only victims: Thousands of survivors dispersed in all the world remain living victims— and witnesses.

1

There are those who say that a survivor who is not a witness is not a survivor; he has perished with the rest for his failure to testify. According to this thinking survivors who have refused to cooperate in this and other surveys are to be discommended and censured. But perhaps, as Elie Wiesel has suggested, profound Silence is at least as appropriate a response to the terrors they endured and witnessed. The Silent should be understood and not rebuked: There is much to be admired in the determined stance of voicelessness. Besides, the Mishnah teaches, "Do not judge your fellow until you have stood in his place." Still, the respondents to this and similar studies on Holocaust survivors deserve our deepest gratitude for sharing their ordeals, experiences, and feelings with us.

The Holocaust is an abyss which never cries "Enough!" It bolted down six million men, women, and children during the span of a few short years; starved in ghettos, shot in ditches, gassed in camps, burned in ovens. And like a ruminating beast bringing back its cud, it continues to feed heartily and voraciously upon the few it earlier disgorged—and upon those whose lives they touch. The Holocaust is an ongoing engulfment preying upon its victims in mind and body. As a consequence of Holocaust-related disabilities, mutilation, "experiments," and illnesses—disease having run aggressively and unrestrained through the camps—many survivors' lives are still being cut short to this day: Their mental health and balance remain chronically constricted and impaired by all that they underwent. The Holocaust's capacity is unrelenting and limitless, a vastness that never ceases to consume.

Upon the conclusion of the war the victorious allies fully expected the persecuted remnant of European Jewry, seen not as members of a single folk or people but as disparate and unrelated refugees, "persons displaced by enemy action," to be repatriated each to his native land. But "repatriation," a word with the same root as "patriot," one who is zealous for his country, proved empty of meaning as pogroms, grisly footnotes to the history of the Holocaust, greeted the returnees. In Kielce in central Poland in early July 1946, a ritual murder accusation was believed by the local Christian population, and forty-one Jews who had barely escaped the Nazi hordes were massacred by the Poles as a posthumous offering to the Fuehrer, an endorsement of his Final Solution. Everywhere in Europe the hostility of local inhabitants made it evident to the Jews if not to the Allied Forces that repatriation was impossible. Europe, in truth, was to be free of Jews, judenfrei. Thousands of refugees, the remnant of the once great European Jewish communities, aspired to leave their inhospitable, blood-drenched native lands behind them, to escape their shadows forever into an unknown life.

They wished that the unspeakable memories of the civilized continent would also stay behind as unclaimed baggage. Now they found they were being repatriated from concentration camps to displaced person camps. For them liberation meant emigration. Of the four to five hundred thousand liberated Jews of Europe [1] only approximately fifty thousand decided to remain in Europe. More than ninety thousand made their way to the United States. Over fifty thousand found their way to other places, including Canada, South Africa, Australia, and Argentina. And between one hundred fifty and two hundred eighty thousand Jews, driven forward by the twin spurs of modern anti-Semitism and ancient memories, arrived in Palestine. There they outlasted British blockades and later, as Israelis, endured the ongoing ordeal of warfare with the surrounding Arab states.

For one person to be able to talk with another who has gone through such inhumanity and wickedness is an uncommon privilege. It is an indulgence, a bequest, and a trust. The dialogue becomes a most precious keepsake to be recorded for, and cherished by, all generations. Not to seize the opportunity when it comes may perhaps be judged a betrayal, surely more so than any unwillingness to talk on the survivor's part.

One would wish to ask numerous questions on scores of subjects, to identify which subjects are forbidden and when one is going too far, where we should tread lightly and when we should not tread at all. We would wish to hear from the survivors' own lips about their lives, their experiences, how they survived, and their feelings then and now: How did you re-establish your life and how do you spend your leisure? How did you begin your new family and how did you meet your husband or wife? How did you find other members of your family or village who also survived? How do you put the horrors you knew out of mind? How do you make new friends, and can you be friends with others who have not experienced what you have experienced or suffered what you have, others who are not survivors? How do you relate to your children and how do you see yourself as different from other parents? How do you earn a living and what are your politics? What books do you read? Can you read books on the Holocaust at all? And what are your ambitions, besides to be left to live in peace? And how do you feel you are different from others? Such an untidy tangle of questions begins at once to unravel in the mind.

This study attempts a systematic inquiry into the manifold dimensions of the meaning and import of the Holocaust's effect upon survivors. It chooses to focus primarily on religious questions, ultimate questions, Jewish questions, some as interesting as these, others probably less so, but not less important. We are especially concerned with how surviving European Jews construed and interpreted their Holocaust experiences and how they were affected religiously, in their faith and practices, by what they had undergone. But why should the Silent be willing to speak at all? And why should they agree to reflect on such questions as these?

That They Now Speak

Mute for so long, the survivors of the Holocaust were fully expected to carry their deepest secrets and innermost beliefs silently with them from internment to interment. Few thoughtful people, even among social scientists, were able to forecast their sudden "opening-up" and the rushing outpour of backed-up communicativeness that followed.

Something triggered a mechanism deep within them, releasing the restraints and obstructions and inducing survivors to disclose ardent, overpowering passions and sensibilities long concealed. The precise nature of that mechanism appeared enigmatic at first and initially difficult to decipher. It had been more than a quarter of a century, a relatively long period in the lifetime of a man, however short considering the span of Jewish history, since the German death camps in Europe were liberated. During the intervening years Israel's *shearit hapleita,* the Saved Remnant, were largely unwilling or unable to scrutinize their beliefs as related to their experiences. With new friends as well, and not only with trained interviewers, however tactfully they may have endeavored to create the right atmosphere, survivors were psychologically unprepared to review the Holocaust openly, except perhaps among themselves. And with fellow survivors there was no real need for spoken communication on their shared experience. Each knew the other had known the up-close meaning of atrocity.

Social scientists maintain that when interviewer and respondent are unknown to one another the dialogue has the best chance for success; individuals are more often willing to speak frankly to outsiders than to close friends and casual acquaintances. Nevertheless, previous attempts at interviewing survivors by this researcher and others had been met mostly with polite silence, skillful evasions, and occasionally with unconcealed, outright hostility. They anticipated the discomfort of others in their own presence; they were convinced that their stories would be seen as the ravings of the mad. The storyteller Elie Wiesel, himself a survivor and one of the foremost voices of the Holocaust generation, tells us further:

The survivors were reticent, their answers vague. The subject: taboo. They remained silent. At first out of reserve; there are wounds and sorrows one prefers to conceal. And out of fear, as well. Fear above all. Fear of arousing disbelief, of being told: Your imagination is sick, what you describe could not possibly have happened. Or: You are counting on our pity, you are exploiting your suffering. Worse: They feared being inadequate to the task, betraying a unique experience by burying it in worn out phrases and images. They were afraid of saying what must not be said, of attempting to communicate with language what eludes languages, of falling into the trap of easy half-truths. Sooner or later, every one of them was tempted to seal his lips and maintain absolute silence. So as to transmit a vision of the Holocaust, in the manner of certain mystics, by withdrawing from words.[2]

Despite the acknowledged need to bear witness, to tell the story, a need that contributed to their survival, for the largest segment of the past twenty-five years most survivors closed off the channels of introspection, barring their own innermost reflection on the destruction of European Jewry—which for them meant thinking about the implications of the torture and deaths of family and friends. Nor would they permit themselves the solace to be gained from verbalizing rationally and structuring theologically the beliefs they held as affected by that catastrophe. Elie Wiesel has said that they persisted in "surviving—not only to survive, but to testify. Victims elect to be witnesses." But to witness is not to reflect, necessarily. The one recounts, the other penetrates. The one provides us with a compendium of atrocity and numbing inhumanity, important as it is. The other offers insight into the human condition and the nature of existence. And given the enormity of the catastrophe, given the expectation that the depths of their recitation might correspond to the depths of their experience, there has been precious little of this. Notwithstanding the impressively long bibliography in some twenty languages of original survivor testimony, there is little evidence of religious reflection. If it has existed at all, it has failed to surface—perhaps as a consequence of their avoidance of introspection and their escape from sensibility. After the Holocaust, survivors found themselves charging through life, looking neither left nor right, least of all inside. If one could, best put it all out of mind.

Terrence Des Pres in *The Survivor* recognizes that fiction on the Holocaust offers "ideal lucidity." But with documents—and interviews as well—we deal with "the dense anguish of men and women telling as straightforwardly as they know how the story of what they saw and endured in their passage through the concentration camps. Their testimony is given in memory, told in pain and often clumsily, with little thought for style or rhetorical device." But as he points out elsewhere, they are certainly articulate enough to give clear accounts: "Through survivors a vast body of literature has thus come into being . . . this kind of writing is unusual for the experience it describes, but also for the desire it reveals to remember and record. The testimony of survivors is rooted in a strong need to make the truth known, and the fact that this literature exists, that survivors produced these documents—there are many thousands of them—is evidence of a profoundly human process. Survival is a specific kind of experience, and 'to survive as a witness' is one of its forms." "The experience they describe, furthermore, resists the tendency to fictionalize which informs most remembering." [3]

The opposing impulses to reflect and speak and to "withdraw from language into silence," each thwarting and contravening the other, demand resolution. The rope must be snapped to end this internal tug-of-war. The peculiar tension of the push and pull constituted a divergence with each side too dug in to let go on its own; each to winded to go on; the one unable to overcome the other.

Some students of the Holocaust have speculated that the relentless process of time itself and the accumulated experiences of living may perhaps provide an explanation as to why survivors are *now* willing to open up about their experiences and articulate their beliefs in theological terms: Time's own movement, as it soothingly and healingly pours over the jagged edges of the scar tissue which seals the internal wound, gently dislodges it, peeling away the impediment to speech that afflicted the Saved Remnant. Then again, time may have silenced by the very act of healing, forming a thick scar tissue over wounds.

It is quite true: Traumas may not be suppressed indefinitely. But the balm of inexorable time, however salubrious its effect, is but an inadequate palliative for anyone plagued with the ability to remember. It can hardly explain the *sudden* and *collective* readiness to break the seal of silence. Time's effect is diffuse, without focus, whereas the survivors' response has been precipitous.

There have been disclosures of one sort or another, of course: Biographies, diaries, documentary eyewitness accounts, novels, poetry, plays in different languages, as well as music and art composed by Holocaust survivors at various times during the course of the past quarter century. And they have not been exceptional. But the overwhelming number of survivors have remained virtually silent and uncommunicative on the *meaning* of their dehumanization—until now. Why now?

The 1962 Eichmann trial in Jerusalem's Bet Am, the National Building, recreating for a disbelieving world the grisly actualities of the German death camps, provided the stage upon which at least a few survivors were able to act out for themselves and others [4] as in a public psychodrama the previously repressed narrative of the concentration camp experience. For them perhaps, new pressures reopened unhealed wounds. But the greatest number of survivors were not called to open up in courtroom testimony. For them whatever vicarious release the Eichmann trial may have provided proved to be imperfect and impermanent at best.

Neither the passage of time nor the Eichmann trial offers adequate instruction. We shall have to look elsewhere for an explanation of the revelatory phenomenon.

The Six Day War

In his eyewitness account of the Six Day War, *The Tanks of Tammuz*, Shabtai Teveth observed the attitudes and disposition of the Israeli armed forces, Zahal, in May 1967, in its realization that "war was inevitable and that it would be a war for survival":

> I could sense the pent-up anger which permeated the brigade; an anger which could be traced back to the Nazi Holocaust. It was as if these men in uniform were saying: no more will Jews be driven out; no more shall they be beaten and slaughtered. . . . Time and again Israeli youth had meditated on what had happened, over there, in Europe. How was it possible to round up hundreds of thousands, even millions of Jews, to slaughter them like so many herds of cattle, without the Jews putting up a fight, without them even spitting in their murderers' faces? The answer to it came spontaneously in May 1967. The Jews of Europe had had no guiding and directing frame in which to act. The Jews of Israel do have such a frame—Zahal. Unto it have poured all the seasoned exiles from east and west. The reflexes from their sufferings in their dispersion, which in town prompted them to hoard sugar, incited them in Zahal to want war. Those who in Auschwitz had had their arms tattooed, while they stood helplessly before their torturers, were here turned into lions. To be precise, it was not so much Zahal the regular army which gave this focus, but Zahal as a taut, tight frame that included all the able-bodied and fit of the nation. In Zahal one got the impression that

the nation had taken a firm grip upon itself. When the Prime Minister [Levi Eshkol] was heard fumbling and stuttering in his speech to the nation on 28th May, a sergeant listening over his transistor while under a tank camouflage netting, was heard to say: "Levi, son of Deborah, let us do the talking!" [5]

It emerged from months of interviews of survivors that the symbolism here suggested, which links Auschwitz with the Six Day War, is both correct and appropriate. And the sudden "talking" of concentration camp survivors coming about as a consequence of the army of Israel "doing the talking" is the theory that most commends itself when one weighs all factors. Several Holocaust survivors during the course of many interviews spoke movingly to this very point. Here is a composite:

> Something happened to our psyches during the breath-taking weeks before the Six Day War in June 1967. It was a déjà vu; as though we had been there before. We all felt the long-buried, smothered but still smoldering emotions rising to the surface of our consciousness. I felt it within me as I know other survivors felt it within themselves.
>
> Once again we were stripped naked, turrets manned by SS machine gunners behind us, the *selector* of life and death standing before us. In the distance, black-smoking chimneys and flaming pits and crematoria. His motion to the left: the gas chambers and the death house; to the right, Hope. We ourselves had no control of our fate.
>
> But suddenly like in a dream, the nightmare was transformed into a lovely fantasy, a shared vision, in which we were advancing cloaked in military uniform and armed and proud—and self-reliant, don't leave that out. This time, not only did we recognize the danger, we were physically and emotionally prepared to confront it.
>
> But, strangest of all, while we stood poised at the danger in May, in my mind, like at the cinema, there were these flashbacks and Auschwitz rose in full recapitulation before me—and the connection was real, not reverie.
>
> Since the Six Day War—a day for each million, I wonder?—I've been more at peace with myself. I'm whole again; I find I am kinder, less moody, freer of speech, admitting to faults previously denied. My marriage has improved. I'm a better father.
>
> It was years of psychotherapy concentrated in a few short days and weeks. . . . I'm a new person, really.

The quotations here cited are hardly isolated ones. The Six Day War, theologians have observed, proved curative for almost all Jews: uniting world Jewry in the face of another threatened annihilation, another potential Holocaust; making Jewry robust again which was decimated and dehumanized a quarter-century ago; in addition, according to our findings, after the "breath-holding" and the war were over, dislodging and sweeping away in a rush the psychological barriers erected by the Holocaust survivor.

The Temple Wall was recovered and Jerusalem, the holy city was again made whole and along with it, perhaps symbolically, were the people made whole. If the Six Day War proved therapeutic for Jews generally, this second narrow escape in a lifetime may have been the needed catharsis for that portion of Jewry who are Holocaust survivors. The Six Day War opened the sluices in the dike of collective memory which had been restraining the backed-up waters of Holocaust survivors' unshed tears. Then apparently the Yom Kippur War (which took place when the largest part of these interviews had been concluded) opened the floodgates wider still. And now it can no longer be said that survivors are reluctant to "let it all out." In simple, measurable terms of survivor communicativeness, and on deep emotional levels as well, the time after the Six Day War may be qualitatively different from the time before.

Certain segments of Jewry, heretofore silent, perhaps for want of suitable analogies, perhaps for fear of being inadequate to the task, as Wiesel suggests, find that they are able to talk to one another again—about *these* recent existence-threatening episodes of war and, at long last, about *that* earlier near-annihilation. The Holocaust, François Mauriac tells us, marks the end of one era and the beginning of another. For all humanity. The Six Day War and the Yom Kippur War were not shared by all men; they were exclusively within the Jewish province, teaching Jews the significance of that new era in which so many have begun to realize and assimilate the message that each one is a fellow survivor. And each may feel himself obliged to probe the implications of that fellowship as well as the meaning of what they went through during that savage time.

Corroborating Evidence

The theory linking the Six Day and Yom Kippur wars with the research here undertaken, while based on imprecise evidence, is hardly mere supposition and unproven conjecture. There is interpretive evidence corroborating it. When the series of interviews underlying this study began, no inquiry regarding the survivors' willingness to share their thoughts and opinions with the interviewer was planned. It seemed more than sufficient that they were, by and large, cooperative, since their willingness meant that they would endeavor to clarify for a stranger that which was perhaps only partially lucid and comprehensible to themselves. These were deeply personal matters, as the following pages reveal. And so explicitly self-conscious a question as, in effect, "Why are you willing now to talk in depth when previously survivors were silent?" unwittingly diverts attention from the interviewee to the interviewer. Or such a question, however well-framed, could be taken to mean, "You know you shouldn't be discussing such things at all." A question touching directly upon the subject of a survivor's willingness to be interviewed was thought to invite the risk of cutting off or, at the minimum, reducing the effectiveness of the interview, if posed near the start of the session; or of leaving ill will and possibly regret—impairing follow-up potentialities—if asked at the close of the interview.

Nevertheless by the fifteenth in-depth interview it became apparent that the question whether the Six Day War held special significance for the Holocaust survivor could be evaded only to the detriment of the interviews and of the overall study as well.

The question, hastily improvised and used only in those cases—which proved to be the majority—in which the direction of the interview led naturally toward it, was posed in this way: Do you perceive any special significance which the Six Day War may have held for the Holocaust survivor as distinct from other Jews?

Despite the fact that the wording derived nearly extemporaneously from within the interview situation, the question turned out to be considerably suggestive. It was transparent that the interviewer was searching for some specific response. And to accommodate him the answer too may frequently have been a justification hastily invented.

Nevertheless it is still noteworthy that less than one in six (14 percent) thought the Six Day War held no special importance for the Holocaust survivor, whereas more than two-thirds (69 percent) thought that the Six Day War held greater psychological significance for the Holocaust survivor than for the average Israeli. Moreover, even for the former group the period of the Six Day War was felt to be informed by a peril of a different order from the previous wars, the Sinai Campaign of 1956 and the War of Liberation of 1948. Perhaps it is merely that one feels the impact of more recent crises most viscerally. A large portion of Holocaust survivors, however, spontaneously volunteered, as did the respondents quoted at length above, that they recognized an authentic similarity between the way in which they perceived the Six Day

War and the intensely charged anxiety of twenty-five years earlier. One Holocaust survivor, an Israeli college professor, quipped that "this research might not have even been given a title page much less become a book without the cooperation of the Arab armies which ought to be given credit somewhere in a scholarly footnote."

Surely, explanations for the long silence of survivors are not difficult to put forward, any more than reasons for their infrequent outcries. But reasonable theories accounting for their break with silence are far more difficult to provide. The theory here provided, offered by a significant number of survivors themselves, may commend itself to the thoughtful reader and account as well for their compliance with the rigors of the research project itself.

Israeli Society and American Society

After the victorious Allied armies lifted the shroud from Europe, the largest number of Holocaust survivors eventually made their way to Palestine, the land of their prayers, which extended as a haven its consolatory embrace and recalled them to their moorings. The vast reaches of the American continent received the second largest number. This study, however, was conducted in Israel not solely because many survivors resettled in the renascent Jewish state. The more critical consideration deals with the contrasting nature of the two societies in which survivors reside in the largest numbers. And inasmuch as this study proposes primarily to concern itself with theology, the religious backdrop of the particular society providing the sample survey, the universe from which the respondents are drawn, is of paramount importance.

In the case of American society as a whole, most empirical studies suggest that religious identification, however shallow it may prove overall, is highly esteemed. It is assuredly "the American thing to do." [6] According to the findings of Gerhard Lenski in *The Religious Factor*, today as before, "traditional religious groups continue to be viable and vigorous organizations." There is sufficient evidence that the established churches and synagogues enjoy considerable strength, especially from the "most urbanized and Americanized segments of the population." Moreover, Lenski reports, the "data suggests a pattern of increasing religious activity linked with increasing Americanization." [7] And Jews have generally conformed to the mores of the American majority by becoming "religious" Americans. [8] The fact that one belongs to an American synagogue or temple, practices home observances and rituals with one's family, or even professes belief in God may have as much to do with general American norms toward religion and group practices as with deeply held personal belief.

Not so in Israel. Apparently it is more by recollection than by practice that Israel is known as the land of faith. By contrast with American society, Georges Friedmann, the French sociologist, writes in *The End of the Jewish People?* that despite the four thousand synagogues and places of worship in a relatively small Jewish population of some two and one-half to three million; despite nearly four hundred rabbis whose salaries are paid by the state and confirmed by the powerful office of the Chief Rabbinate; despite the National Religious Party, religious kibbutzim, the large number of Yeshiva students and the seemingly anomalous sight of the Uzi-toting young troops wearing colorful kipot bobbypinned to the backs of their heads, Israel's population "has to a large extent abandoned its traditional beliefs and way of life." [9] And given the background and origins of many of the political, intellectual, and labor leaders, it may not be incorrect to assume that in Israel atheism—or at least agnosticism—and nonobservance are far more generally accepted and favored than in the United States. There is even the opinion expressed in certain skeptical circles that Israeli society puts on a pious face for the religiously oriented American Jewish community upon whose generous allocations it leans heavily to keep solvent.

At least one Israeli sociologist goes so far as to say, "There is no people on earth less religious than the people of Israel." [10]

In certain respects, therefore, the Israeli Holocaust survivor who keeps Jewish practices, attends synagogue regularly, and professes belief in God is behaving contrary to the more widely held norms of society and consequently must be making a genuine, conscious religious decision. Thus, the religiously observant Jewish survivor stands out more visibly from, and his conduct is more measurable and observable within, Israeli society.

In America being religious and professing faith receive societal approbation and commendation (a factor that renders genuine belief problematical). However, to be a more than perfunctorily practicing member of a minority faith-community whose observances make one appear different is often inexpedient and inconvenient and sometimes impossible. In this regard, American society inhibits religious faith and practice for Jews and further complicates an understanding of a survivor's genuine religious commitment.

In Israel, by contrast, the religious climate is far more neutral. The practicing Jew, even the ultra Orthodox Jew, does not stand out self-consciously. His is the majority faith. The Holy Days, public observances, and sacred occasions are his. He may practice his faith to the degree and extent his inclinations dictate. Or he may freely refrain from religious practice with no censure, ridicule, or reprobation, nor any imposed guilt feelings. In Israel alone, one's creed and one's natural religious disposition may be in full accord.

An even more crucial reason influencing the decision to focus on the survivors of Israel is the ethnic factor. The eldest son of an American Holocaust survivor joined his father when conversation was being casually prolonged after the conclusion of an exploratory interview preparatory to the Israel study:

Look, it seems to me that for a Jew the whole question of religion is essentially irrelevant. Let's assume that I no longer wish to be a Jew. How do I go about it? What do I do? If I were a Christian and wished no longer to be one, that would be a relatively simple matter to accomplish—although most Christians would undoubtedly disagree seeing that they no longer were what they claimed. Christianity is a matter of belief. One is a Christian because he believes in the divinity of Jesus, that Jesus is the Messiah; and in that belief there is salvation; and certain other doctrines. If one stops believing one ceases to be a Christian. Witness the Unitarians and the Universalists who recognized the fact and no longer call themselves Christians.

But how do I stop being a Jew? So what if I consider myself an atheist. Some of dad's best friends in shul are atheists. And I have certain doubts about dad himself. Doesn't mean a thing. I think there is a way to cease being a Jew if I should wish that and it is not connected with my belief in God or the Chosen People or the revelation of the Torah or the efficacy of prayer—or anything else you have in your questionnaire. It has to do with our people, its history and its destiny. It has to do with our tribe.

I stop being a Jew by some act—like intermarriage without making the family, especially the children, Jewish—an act which demonstrates that I no longer play a part in the perpetuation of the people. It has to do with people, not belief. And I'll do a lot of things I don't believe and go to shul with the other atheists for the sake of my people. Where else can I go in America to register my Jewish vote?

In America, and other countries with relatively large Jewish concentrations, Jewish observances and synagogue attendance tend to proclaim Jewish ethnic identity as much as, or perhaps more than, Jewish religious commitment.

The Israeli himself insists that the rituals and observances are today obligatory only upon the Diaspora Jew, not for himself. "In the Diaspora—where there is no Jewish sovereignty and the Jews, being in a minority, are obliged to fight tooth and nail for the very future of a Jewish existence it is incumbent upon Jews to bear the yoke of the mitzvot, even if they do not believe in them." [11]

By contrast, in the land of Israel a complete and secure Jewish life exists. One need not practice religious observances or express belief in God to proclaim one's Jewish identity. One can be a Jew without religion, merely by living in the reconstituted Jewish state, in the land with all its present associations and past memories. "One can be satisfied with the values of the Land—the language, work, the culture and the ethic that exist there." [12] It is only in Israel, therefore, that the religious element may be isolated from the ethnic variable. And the overlap be-between religion and purely ethnic identification, which can confound the analysis of the Holocaust survivor in America, is appreciably reduced, if not altogether absent, in Israeli society.

A fortuitous dividend from the decision to focus on Israel accrues from the diminutive size of the country and the relatively close proximity of its citizens. These considerations allow for the employment of standard sampling procedures and enables the researcher to track down for in-depth interviews individual respondents randomly spread over the entire expanse of the land. Because of Israel's geographical compactness there was no necessity to "cluster" survivors for accessibility (a convenient and legitimate sociological device but one which may affect a survey's reliability by disproportionately skewing the spectrum of responses and ultimately biasing the results beyond a tolerable level of error).

A study of Holocaust survivors in the United States, however necessary, could not, by virtue of the limited sources providing survivor rosters, afford as broad or varied a base to make accurate generalizations for the entire Holocaust community. In America the members of organizations like the Bergen-Belsen Survivors Association have become too homogeneous, that is, culturally alike, to be sufficiently representative of the entire community of survivors.

On the Objectives and Conduct
of the Research

In contrast with research that studies how diverse groups respond to problems of the ultimate—the purpose of life, the reality of death, good and evil, God's existence and comportment, etc., the subject matter or components of a religious ideology—our study inquires of *one* religious group and how some of its members confronted these issues of ultimate consequence, how they behaved and believed religiously. Particular attention is paid to how the Holocaust brought about religious change and what survivors thought about their religious tradition, its teachings and doctrines in the face of death.

Demographical considerations and data on the subject's educational background, birthplace, and sex were not deemed unimportant and they are not overlooked in this work. But this research was undertaken primarily to find out how survivors of the catastrophe behave religiously and what they believed over the course of some three decades and at certain stages in their life histories. These periods have been designated as before, during, and immediately after the Holocaust, and today. Especially are we interested in how survivors were changed by their Holocaust experiences, and why. Our study therefore does not begin by asking is a Polish Jew more likely to have been affected religiously by his concentration camp experiences than a German Jew, a man more than a woman, the better educated more than the less, and the like. It will endeavor to answer these questions and others further on. And it does not fail to ask who is more likely to have been changed religiously, a concentration camp survivor or one who survived in other ways in Europe. But it first and foremost focuses on how survivors who were observant or nonobservant, devout or atheistic, traditionally minded or theologically radical responded religiously to the physical and emotional ravagings of the Holocaust, and if they responded by changes in religious beliefs and practices, how and why.

Crucial for this research is the Kantian distinction on how the mind functions between intellect, whose quest is knowledge, and reason, whose pursuit is meaning. Both researcher and reader exercise the former faculty: We seek to know how others were inspired to search for meaning, what conclusions that search brought, and what truths may be determined in connection with their search. Unlike theirs, the results of our pursuit may be verifiable if the research adheres to certain methodological criteria. The survivors in this survey, however, utilized the latter capacity: They, in exercising reason, sought not verifiable truth but unverifiable meaning to make sense of their experiences. And reasoning for meaning serves a very urgent need particularly in extremity, as Viktor Frankl has taught us.

Hannah Arendt, in *The Life of the Mind*, tells us that reason (as in their search for meaning) and not intellect (as in our search for truth), that is, what the survivors were thinking and not what we are thinking, takes priority—except, perhaps, when we too by inquiring of their thinking do so to find meaning in our own lives. And then we are as they. Arendt writes:

> The need of reason is not inspired by a quest for truth but by a quest for meaning. And truth and meaning are not the same. To expect truth to come from thinking signifies that we mistake the need to think with the urge to know. Thinking can and must be employed in the attempt to know, but in the exercise of this function it is never itself; it is but the handmaiden of an altogether different enterprise.[13]

Nor was this study undertaken to provide answers to complex theological, sociological, and historical questions. Its intention was rather to find out before the generation passes away and the questions are past asking what survivors of the most brutalizingly inhuman conditions thought then and think now about God, the Jewish people, and the religious doctrines they had been brought up to believe. The survey population—all survivors of the Holocaust—is not composed of scholars who have spent their lives researching and reflecting upon the issues raised by these questions, although a few, mostly surviving rabbis, undoubtedly have. This survey asks respondents—average human beings except for what they underwent—to select from multiple choices the answers that came closest to their own thinking on numerous extremely difficult subjects touching upon Judaism, their Jewish identities, the Holocaust and their Holocaust experiences, and the like, questions that should require a lifetime to answer.

But these survivors do not have a full lifetime ahead to ponder the measure of these imponderables, nor is there any reasonable argument sufficiently compelling to have them discontinue the pattern of adjustment in their daily lives to seek such answers. Better that these near-victims try to live in peace. Regrettably, peace for some was momentarily interrupted by this research. Despite the emotional pain it induced, many survivors apparently welcomed the incursion of this survey into their lives. And apparently they were happy too when the interruption was concluded. For some, painful memories were jarred loose, again rising to the surface of their consciousness, once more stirred up by the various questions. For some it was cathartic; for others simply painful; for none merely routine.

One might have expected that much more of the survivor population, survivors of the worst traumas of their, or perhaps any, lives would refuse to cooperate. Against cooperation were stacked an impressive array of factors: the length of the questionnaire itself—some ten type-filled pages—and the time it took to complete it. The questionnaire was in Hebrew—not their mother tongue regardless of the years spent in Israel, and they had the option of writing answers in any language they preferred. One hundred of the 708 who willingly cooperated—of the total one thousand contacted—were further inconvenienced by the presence of a stranger in their homes discussing personally these matters touching upon sensitive nerves with little opportunity aside from cigarettes, tea, and coffee breaks to regain composure when necessary.

We can only guess as to the reasons nearly three hundred survivors had failed to return the questionnaire—or returned it unanswered. Perhaps some agreed with the appraisal of the questionnaire offered by the Orthodox Mizrachi party's newspaper Hatzofeh (the *lookout*). A front-page story called it "mischievous and provocative." (Of those whom the questionnaire offended or to whom it brought distress, we sincerely beg forgiveness and plead that the study nevertheless had to be conducted.) We are on more certain ground in trying to understand the motivation of the 708 who responded:

1. A strong need to cooperate: "If I don't answer the questionnaire on my Holocaust experiences and opinions, who will?" And "No one else can know what I know." "When we are gone no one will know what we thought and felt and believed unless we take the trouble." "We must force ourselves to answer them or someone else will answer them for us and we'll have only ourselves to blame."
2. The Yad Vashem return address. Yad Vashem is Israel's prestigious Holocaust research institution, which lent authority to the project and induced a large proportion of survivors to cooperate who might otherwise have not. (For the influence of Yad Vashem on the survivors' willingness to take part in this study, see Chapter 5, "Seven Theological Questions.")

One thousand survivors were selected from the survivor lists of those residing in Israel. Yad Vashem was the main source for these rosters. Kibbutz Lohamai Haghettaot (Fighters of the Ghetto) and the Tel-Aviv–based Irgun Artzei Isurai Hanazim Lesheavar (the Organization of Former Prisoners of Captive Nazi Lands) made available their membership and survivor listings as well. From these organizations the random sampling was drawn. With the assurances of anonymity, 708 agreed to answer the questionnaire. Of these, one hundred were interviewed personally, and the rest were interviewed by mail. As for the questionnaires returned by mail, in the space of the few late months of 1970, little else could match the elation brought on by the arrival of the day's mail sack bestrewn with the modest, uniform, glossy brown envelopes. One such envelope was delivered seven years too late for the tabulations.

But a quickening of an entirely different order was experienced when, at an imprecise, mysterious moment during the course of an interview, a certain pitch of intensity was reached. The color on the cheeks of the respondent altered—some chalking pale like a death mask, others turning blood red. And a rush of inspired narration came upon the speaker like a seizure, transporting him or her, the researcher, and whoever else happened to be within the call of the voice, away to wherever the vision was taking us, as though of its own accord. This occurred so frequently one began to wait for it, hope for it, and sense when the moment was approaching.

The number of Christians who had been classified as Jews and interned as Jews by the Nazis and who survived the camps is not known. The fact that "Jewish Christians" formed a not insignificant group before the war can be seen from the Nazi need to promulgate the Nuremberg racial laws and in the existence of Christian churches in the Jewish ghettos. The Nazi mind understood the difference between ethnic identity and religious affiliation but chose to ignore it in its racial persecutions.

According to Jewish law there is no distinction between religious affiliation and ethnic identity: A child of a Jewish mother even if converted to Christianity is Jewish. And a convert to Judaism, regardless of the matter of race, becomes part of the ethnic community. But the former may indeed see themselves as Christians of Jewish descent. After the war those who survived and remained Christians were not likely to settle in Israel. And the few who did reclaim their religious heritage for whatever reasons, including marriage to a Jew, were so small in number they would not appear in our study. It was unlikely many were reached by this random sampling.

One questionnaire was returned by such a survivor with the notation that the survey does not apply to her, seeing that she was Christian before the war and did not keep Jewish religious practices then. Even if reached, they might not have been willing to admit to their previous religious affiliation and therefore refrained from returning the questionnaire. They are simply an unknown.

Survivors spoke and wrote in Hebrew, Yiddish, occasionally German or English, and often a combination of several languages. The largest majority spoke in Hebrew. Tape recordings and note-taking were routine procedures during the session. Each interview was written up in English immediately upon its conclusion. The author's translations were rendered freely but as carefully and faithfully as possible. The attempt was made to be always conscious of the spirit and tenor of the accounts, their expressions, and connotations as well as plain meaning.

Occasionally, as when Polish was written, translations were made first into Hebrew and then into English. Shalmi Barmor at Yad Vashem was particularly helpful with translations, especially from English to Hebrew, of the questionnaire. All interview translations were done by the author, as were all the mailed questionnaires written in Yiddish, German, and Hebrew. In addition, most of the other translations appearing in this book, including those from Jewish sources, the Bible, prayer book, and Talmud, were rendered by him. Any mistranslation or misunderstandings and misrenderings are entirely his own.

Although not a single survivor's words have been discarded or discounted, the very best, most interesting, revealing, and representative quotations for each conviction and opinion were selected. The foremost consideration was the ability to convey expressively what others felt. The particularly impassioned and well-spoken survivor statements were most frequently chosen and rendered into English with a view to preserving their uniqueness. But the voice of one survivor is never less important than any other's, regardless of his or her gifts of expression. Throughout, we have had a profound respect for the distinctive original voice of survivors. Nevertheless, we have not hesitated to edit the translations for the sake of grammar and syntax and to endeavor to communicate their passion and elegance. The spoken words of survivors, wherever and however uttered, will always haunt humanity. And the bare statistics of these pages must not be allowed to coarsen our perceptions of what they underwent. As is clear throughout, survivors held strong and informed opinions on various subjects related to this study. It is remarkable then that these self-revelations were not more frequently self-serving memoirs. Relatively few were pompous and turgid; most were open, forthright, and intelligent. These are a remnant of a civilized Jewish world that was. And we will have achieved our objectives if we can take our stand within their own perspectives and provide, with this volume, the religious dimension of the survivors' experience.

Experimental and Control Groups

The findings of this research which appear in the forthcoming pages apply to Holocaust survivors alone, but there is no denying that there may be many parallels among other Jews living in Israel and elsewhere. Until similar studies are conducted we simply cannot speak of the affinities or incongruities in the thinking of survivors with that of the rest of Jewry. We cannot even speak of the differences in the impact of the Holocaust on the religious faith and behavior of survivors against the Holocaust's effect upon other Jews who, to a greater or lesser extent, were also influenced in their religious ideology and identity by the Nazi annihilation of European Jews. We do not know the answers to the question, What *has* been the religious effect of the Holocaust upon all the Jews, the average Jew and not the professional theologian, academic or rabbi alone? We can at least speak now, however, with some authority of the faith and doubt of Holocaust survivors.

In this book the term "Holocaust survivors" refers to the entire European Jewish community consisting of former concentration camp internees and every other Jew who passed all or part of the war years in the Europe of Nazi hegemony. Only those Jews who escaped from Europe before the Nazi wall of fire arose were not encompassed by our study. With this exception, ours may be considered a survey of the survivors of all European Jewry. Nevertheless it is necessary to distinguish between concentration camp survivors and other survivors to determine whether the Holocaust brought about a difference in religious behavior and attitudes between the two survivor groupings. Are the Jews saved from the furnaces who have returned to life from the concentration camps in some way different from other European Jewish survivors? Will a survivor's confinement in one of the several kinds of Nazi camps be more likely or less likely to effect changes in his or her religious behavior and faith?

In social science the experimental group that represents the individuals who have undergone the unique experience under study is contrasted with the larger control group to measure how they were affected by that experience. Thus the new immigrant ought to be considered within the experimental group and the native-born within the control collective. Or one single variable or factor may be manipulated for the experimental group and then the ensuing behavior is observed and compared with the control group to understand the effect of the variable— that is, whether the presence or absence of the factor produces a measurable difference between the groups.

It may be thought that the concentration camp experience provides the salient variable distinguishing a small segment of the survivor population from the majority. As a consequence of German efficiency in rounding up European Jewish communities, however, the reverse is more probably true: The experimental group is larger than the control group. Although precise figures are unavailable and perhaps beyond recovery, most surviving European Jews were for varying lengths of time interned in various types of Nazi concentration camps, including detention or internment camps, transit and exchange camps, and annihilation or death camps where crematoria were installed.

In our study survivor rosters composed of, and distinguishing between, former concentration camp internees and non–concentration camp survivors were utilized for random sampling purposes. They produced a higher than two-to-one ratio of former concentration camp against non–concentration camp populations. But inasmuch as the original survivor rosters were not compiled by survivor organizations and institutions with a view toward representing correct proportions reflecting the entire survivor population, neither should the two-to-one ratio be construed as a precise reflection of all Holocaust survivors. Comparisons between these two subgroups with regard to religious change in faith and practice will be drawn and analyzed below in Chapter 2 on religious behavior.

Pre-Holocaust escapees represent another population which, although falling outside the primary scope of this work, warrants at least a brief comparison with Holocaust survivors. An assessment of the major theory concerning their makeup may not be inappropriate here, in view of the cluster of impressions about them assimilated during the course of this research.

One might suppose that escapees constitute a group virtually identical with Holocaust survivors. Their countries of origin; their economic, social, cultural, and educational backgrounds; even their pre-Holocaust migratory histories, it is suggested, are similar. The single distinction is that, in whatever way they may have endured—and chance alone explains it—they were able to get out before the gates of Hell were erected and before the continent of Europe was transformed into an escape-proof charnel house shut off from the rest of the world.

This theory argues that it will not do to assume that the very fact that a certain small percentage of Jews managed to leave Europe "in time" demonstrates that they are different in kind from concentration camp survivors. It denies that some additional variable must be sought to account for their "foresight," such as greater intelligence, education, or political acumen. Accordingly, pre-Holocaust escapees are not considered to be of a different order from nonescapees. The two sets of near-victims are essentially alike; it is sufficient to acknowledge that the former are by and large more fortunate than the latter; the latter in turn more blessed than six million others. The opposing theory, however, that pre-Holocaust escapees and nonescapees are indeed fundamentally dissimilar, is more plausible.

Even conceding momentarily the well-recognized distinctions (in education, affluence, influence, etc.) between East and West European Jewish communities and comparing instead East European escapees with East European nonescapees and Western escapees with their counterparts, survivors themselves acknowledge, what is evident to any objective observer, that the escapees, regardless of geography, were for the most part wealthier, better connected with local officialdom for the strategic deployment of their wealth, better educated, better informed, and politically more sophisticated than nonescapees of the same community. Not that membership in this "Jewish elite" assured escape; it merely offered greater opportunity for such. The result was, just as in other times in advance of impending catastrophes, that a greater percentage of upper-class Jews, however meager their number overall, managed to flee than their more humble brethren.

Survivor rosters of Yad Vashem and the various survivor organizations were not compiled with the view to providing researchers proportional geographical representation. We are on reasonably firm ground in making East–West [14] distinctions as they bear upon religious change, inasmuch as survivors registered their country of origin during the course of their interview. In our study, 81 percent of survivors were from East European countries (including the areas of the present-day Soviet Union), and 19 percent were from the West. (The distinctive features of the areas of survivor origin are examined in the chapter on religious behavior, particularly as they relate to education and religious change.)

This study has also directed its attention to the relationships between religious change and:

1. the number of years spent in camps
2. the types of concentration camps endured, such as work camps, death camps, etc.
3. the experiences of survivors of one particular camp as compared to others, for example the notorious Auschwitz, Treblinka, Buchenwald, Maidanek, etc.
4. the loss of spouse and children
5. the age and sex of the survivor

Our preliminary investigations, subsequent interviews, and statistical measurements failed to warrant justification for any of these correlations.

It is not necessary to dwell at length upon them, but a number of noteworthy disclosures relative to Holocaust survivors may be appropriately reported here. They came about as an informational spinoff of the investigation of religious change. For one thing, it has long been known that in camps women, children, and older people were invariably the first to be destroyed, whereas able-bodied men were often conscripted as slave laborers under death-inducing conditions. Since men were generally more valuable alive than women, this may account for the survivor population randomly interviewed having been composed of more than twice as many men as women, 69 percent to 31 percent.

Regarding the current age ranges of the survivors in our study, it appears that the nearly four decades since the Holocaust have leveled all distinctions between survivors and the rest of the population. At the time the study was conducted, a scant 6 percent were over seventy years of age. That is, they were thirty-eight or older in 1939, the year of the war's outbreak; 24 percent were between sixty and sixty-nine years old, or between twenty-eight and thirty-seven in 1939; 38 percent were between fifty and fifty-nine years old, or between eighteen and twenty-seven in 1939. And 32 percent were between forty-five and forty-nine years old, under eighteen but over thirteen, at the war's commencement. Even though they may have observed most of the commandments in their childhood, those under forty-five were deliberately omitted from consideration for this study, inasmuch as they would have been under thirteen at the time and, except for some girls who were considered to have reached their religious majority a year earlier, were "not obliged to practice Judaism" in the same way as an adult (that is, they were not Bar or Bat Mitzvah). One and one-half million is the accepted number of Jewish children destroyed in the Holocaust.

Ideally, in pursuing empirical knowledge the skilled researcher remains throughout an impartial, unaffected observer, a detached scientist, who like a camera approaches his subject free from impressions and predispositions, his film neutral until properly exposed. In this work, no deliberate attempt was made to distort the lens or focus or to create special effects.

Any and all obliquities that may appear are entirely unintentional and are the sole responsibility of the cameraman-author. Nevertheless, no Jew can possibly remain at an emotional distance or ought to attempt to extricate himself from his own passionate, personal involvement with the intimacy of his people's ordeals to deal only "factually" with a subject that strikes echoes of anguish in one's heart. Nor was there an attempt by the author to do so. A main concern throughout was to avoid the kinds of categorization that interfere with the humanity of its members.

This work was designed to investigate and probe the mind of the survivor: his or her opinions, attitudes, feelings, beliefs, and ideas. Of necessity it would be conducted and presented as a work of objective social scientific research. But one thing was quite clear well before the survey was conceived: If it is given at all, it is given alone to the power of literature—what Lawrence Langer calls the literature of atrocity,[15] which assuredly admits the nonfiction literature of survivor attestations in the forthcoming pages—and not to statistics and numbers on those same pages, however important they may be in satisfying our need to know, to provide entree to their souls.

TWO

The Religious Behavior of Holocaust Survivors

U NTIL ITS GRINDING PROGRESSION WAS HALTED, and rarely slipping a cog, the super-efficient German death machine contrived its grisly solution. Only a miniscule fraction of European Jewry managed to evade or endure it. Six million, variously estimated at between 30 and 40 percent of the entire Jewish people at the time, could not. The survivors were, in the words of one of them, condemned to life. All the inmates of the inferno—death camps, forced labor camps, and foredoomed ghettos—experienced protracted terror. They witnessed mass murder, which, frequently before their despairing eyes, swept away members of their immediate families: husbands, wives, children, parents, and siblings mercilessly torn from their sides. Those who miraculously outlasted the ordeal and eluded the terrible fate that befell the others subsequently endeavored to return as much as sanity permitted to the formidable task of normal living. Among the questions this research explores are these: To what extent does this include participation in the religious life of the community? And what has been the Holocaust's impact upon the religious faith and religious practices of the individual survivor? Will a survivor become less or more religiously observant after the Holocaust? Perhaps from these and other questions we may also learn generally how radical personal tragedies, such as those connected with wars and natural disasters, sustained and shared by relatively large numbers of a particular religious group, affect religious attitudes and religious behavior.

25

Ethical Commandments
and Ritual Commandments

An American Jewish chaplain who attended the first post-Holocaust memorial Yizkor service on the festival of Shavuot in a Bavarian displaced persons camp observed that the officiating rabbi, himself bereaved, instead of comforting the survivors over their losses, said, "Observe the Sabbath." "I thought at first how unfeeling," the chaplain remembered, "and then I began to sense the wisdom of an ancient therapy." [1]

Judaism is based largely on the observance of a set of prescriptions, or mitzvot (commandments). Traditionally, all mitzvot are equally binding, although they are not all of equal importance. And even if the two components are, at bottom, inseparable, in cases of conflict the ethical commandments generally take precedence over the doctrinal. Notwithstanding the importance of the ethical commandments, and many survivors themselves affirm that moral considerations motivate ritual behavior, the Jew is quite obviously identifiable, and judged "religious," by the doctrinal or ritual commandments he or she observes, rather than the ethical norms. This, then, provides one reason why our scaled inventory of Jewish observances, as shown in the accompanying form, focuses on the doctrinal to the exclusion of the ethical commandments and why our study does not research moral behavior.

It is regrettable that moral behavior must lie outside the scope of this study and that a "morality scale" as a corollary of a scale for Jewish observances has not as yet been devised and developed to assess various acts for the weight and rank of their ethical content. We should very much wish to apply such a scale to measure, as systematically as possible, the impact severe catastrophes, such as the concentration camp experience, have on moral behavior and moral sensitivity.

Obviously, it is far more difficult for people to acknowledge that they violate moral conventions than to admit that they disregard religious observances. Moreover, whereas certain lapses in moral behavior *during* confinement in a camp may be regarded as excusable and be freely divulged, permanent changes, carrying over after the liberation into the present, would not be readily disclosed, assuming that they are even consciously recognized by the survivor.

From personal narratives, journals, and written accounts, it is common knowledge that certain immoral acts were indeed committed in the camps by inmates, victim to victim, for which survivors confess they were deeply mortified. It couldn't be otherwise. "At Auschwitz," Elie

Wiesel writes, "one breathed contempt and indignity: a crust of bread was worth more than divine promises, a bowl of soup transformed a sensitive human being into a wild animal. Principles, disciplines and feelings only feebly resisted the implacable laws of Maidanek."

The first entry of the remarkable *Unknown Diarist of Lodz Ghetto,* kept in four languages in the margins and flyleaf of an old French novel, was dated May 5, 1944.[2] It was one of the few entries written deliberately in English by the anonymous diarist, presumably an unfamiliar language to his twelve-year-old sister. The diary—speaking to us from beyond the grave—was undoubtedly begun as an act of contrition and penitence for what under the circumstances was felt to be an unspeakable crime:

> I committed this week an act which is best able to illustrate to
> what degree of dehumanization we have been reduced—namely
> I finished up my loaf of bread at a space of 3 days, that is
> to say on Sunday, so I had to wait till the next Saturday
> for a new one [the ration was about 33 ounces of bread a week].
> I was terribly hungry. I had a prospect of living only from
> the resort soup [the soup ladled out to forced laborers] which
> consists of three potato pieces and two decagrams [three-quarters
> of an ounce] of flour. I was lying on Monday morning quite
> dejectedly in my bed and there was the half loaf of bread of my
> darling sister . . . I could not resist the temptation and ate it
> up totally. . . . I was overcome by a terrible remorse of conscience
> and by a still greater care for what my little one would eat for
> the next five days. I felt a miserably helpless criminal . . .
> I have told people that it was stolen by a supposed reckless and
> pitiless thief and, for keeping up appearance, I have to utter
> curses and condemnations on the imaginary thief: "I would
> hang him with my own hands had I come across him."

Such disquieting, self-indicting, intimate memoirs and confessional chronicles suggest that while moral *behavior* may have temporarily deteriorated—infected and contaminated by the brutalizing conditions attending deportation and confinement—moral *sensitivity* probably was not impaired. Internees who retained their mental capacities recognized right from wrong but, understandably, could not always keep themselves from "the ultimate degradation—acting like beasts in a jungle not of our making."

At the end of May the Unknown Diarist turned his hand to a

highly literary Hebrew in which he laments pitifully: "Despair increases steadily as does the terrible hunger, the like of which mankind has not yet suffered. With complete assurance we may say that they [the Germans] have not left us even a jot of that which is called body or soul . . . but shall we survive? Is it possible to come out of such unimaginable depths, of such unfathomable abysses?"

The diarist of the Lodz Ghetto, his beloved sister, and his entire family could not. Others, a tiny fraction, barely survived. And to his final question, "Is it possible to come out of such unimaginable depths?" we may respond with an unconditional answer: certainly not psychologically and spiritually intact. But to what extent, this research asks, were these inevitable, even if not predictable, psychological and spiritual changes manifested in religious terms, as religious behavior and religious faith?

Religious Practices

To answer this question with regard to religious behavior (religious faith will be examined in later chapters), Holocaust survivors were surveyed in connection with their observance of twenty Jewish religious practices (commandments)—18 for men, 16 for women—at different periods of time (see p. 29 for the survey and p. 32 for a glossary of commandments). Three sequential time periods or stages were established to disclose by intervals the changing patterns of religious behavior of Holocaust survivors:

Stage 1. The time "shortly before the Holocaust" which designates the base period and draws our attention to what was normal religious behavior previous to the upheaval. From this period, subsequent increases or decreases in religious observances may be observed at a glance. This was the time in Europe prior to the Nazi war of Jewish annihilation and before "the brutal and abrupt removal of a person from most environmental stimuli which had formed the conditioning framework of his everyday life," [3] when it was still possible for a Jew to practice his religion in relative freedom. For each European country and Jewish community the time varied in accordance with the German schedule of invasion.

Stage 2. The time "just after the Holocaust," whether in displaced persons camps, shelter houses of Europe or, for others, in Palestine. (The stage "during the Holocaust" is omitted here for reasons explained below.) "The period," as one survivor perusing the schedule put it,

COMMANDMENTS	BEFORE HOLOCAUST	AFTER HOLOCAUST	TODAY	NEVER
1. Observes dietary laws at home				
2. Observes dietary laws outside home				
3. Observes shaatnez (separating linen and wool fabrics)				
4. Fasts on Day of Atonement				
5. Fasts on the Ninth of Av				
6. Lights Hanukkah candles				
7. Observes Passover Seder				
8. Prays daily				
9. Attends synagogue on Sabbath				
10. Attends synagogue on festivals				
11. Attends synagogue on Day of Atonement				
12. Observes the Sabbath				
13. Observes the Sabbath (without use of electrical switches)				
14. Observes the Sabbath (without use of automobile)				
Men Only				
15. Wears tzitzit (fringed garment)				
16. Wears peot (earlocks)				
17. Daily use of tephillin (phylacteries)				
18. Keeps head covered				
Women Only				
19. Attends mikveh (ritual bath)				
20. Kindles Sabbath candles				

"when I had just begun to think about trying to pick up the pieces of my life and retrieve may sanity. When my responses to the world were visceral—and bitter, and yet a time when, after living in a madhouse of death for so long, I would have given everything I possessed, which meant then the remainder of my 69 pounds, to taste one drop of sensible, conventional living—although I knew it never really could be the same again."

This was the period when the acutely felt after-effects of the camp experience converged with the period of the first opportunity, if the will remained alive, for return to previous patterns of religious observance and religious activity.

Stage 3. The present (that is, the early 1970s, when the study was conducted), a time sufficiently distant from the Holocaust to provide the survivors with the opportunity to assimilate its implications and attempt to normalize their lives. By selecting a third time period we may ascertain which changes were lasting and perhaps permanent and which were temporary and transitory.

The Commandments

Not only in our time but always, Jewish tradition has distinguished among the commandments and never has accorded identical value to them. The Talmud suggests a scale of priorities among the commandments in terms of the dominant consideration of preserving or saving life—a subject which will be returned to and expanded upon in connection with the sacrifice of the Six Million and the creation of the State of Israel. Saadiah ben Joseph Gaon, the tenth-century scholar and author, not only differentiated between the rational and dogmatic commandments but clearly claimed superiority for the rational in his *Beliefs and Opinions.*

In the Decalogue the mitzvot are divided into two categories governing man's relationship with God (ben adam la-Makom) and with man (ben adam la-chavero). Jewish tradition classifies the hundreds of theoretically obligatory commandments—usually referred to as the 613 (taryag) mitzvot—as edot (doctrinal precepts), mishpatim (ethical precepts) and hukim (inexplicable divine decrees). Within the teachings of Scripture, Talmud, and Codes, the ceremonial laws are indiscriminately interfused with the ethical imperatives and are considered no less divine and binding. Whereas they may be all equally binding, however, they are not accorded equal importance; and when they are in conflict there are criteria provided for choosing between them. Only a small fraction of the world Jewry believes that they are all God-given mandates not to be classified in any order of priorities or relative importance. As early as the Talmudic period Jews were already distinguishing among the various commandments in terms of "weightiness" and were being exhorted not to neglect a "light" one any more than a "weighty" one: "Be heedful of a light precept as of a weighty one, since you cannot know the reward granted for each precept." [4] Many Jews have accepted the commandments as a theoretical structure, valid metaphysically, but they are nevertheless subject to selectivity in the particular. The German Jewish theologian Franz Rosenzweig (1886–1929) drew a further distinction between universal legislation (Gesetz) and personal commandments (Gebot): The commandments are not superior to laws, but they speak to the innermost heart and move one to performance.

The commandments may also be classified according to their "heaviness" or difficulty, that is, the time and conscious effort required to perform them, as well as how they call attention to their practitioner. A number of commandments are kept by nearly all Jews, such as ritual circumcision (brit mila) upon the newborn male, and hardly convey information on one's religious predilections. Certain commandments are performed by all observant Jews; others identify the assiduously observant alone. Peot are worn almost exclusively by Hasidic Jews, one of the subdivisions of the ultra or extremely observant, and serve as a useful shorthand for their identification. A Jew who fasts on the Ninth of Av (Tisha b'Av) which marks the destruction of the first and second Temples in Jerusalem will not fail to observe the fast of the Day of Atonement, the most solemn occasion of the Jewish calendar. A Jew who observes the dietary laws outside the home does not fail to observe them in the home. And one who observes the biblical prohibition against wearing clothing made of linen and wool (shaatnez) will be certain to keep virtually all the remaining mitzvot (peot being the obvious exception).

Who Is Observant

In our study, the *nonobservant* survivor was one who characterized himself or herself as having kept no more than five of the most universally observed Jewish religious practices (see Table 1). Generally such a survivor observed these few commandments to a limited degree: observance of minimal kashrut, in the home, that is, following to some measure the dietary laws, such as abstaining from pork products; celebrating in some minimal way the festival of Passover, which broadly speaking may be set forth as observing the Passover Seder, with at least a family meal consisting of a number of appropriate symbolic foods and wine, even without reciting from the Passover Haggadah (Hebrew for narration); observance of the Hanukkah holiday by lighting can-

TABLE 1. Criteria for Degrees of Observance

COMMANDMENTS	NON-OBSERVANT	MODERATELY OBSERVANT	HIGHLY OBSERVANT	EXTREMELY OBSERVANT
1. Observes dietary laws at home	X	X	X	X
2. Observes dietary laws outside home		X	X	X
3. Observes shaatnez				X
4. Fasts on Day of Atonement	X	X	X	X
5. Fasts on the Ninth of Av			X	X
6. Lights Hanukkah candles	X	X	X	X
7. Observes Passover Seder	X	X	X	X
8. Prays daily			X	X
9. Attends synagogue on Sabbath		X	X	X
10. Attends synagogue on festivals		X	X	X
11. Attends synagogue on Day of Atonement	X	X	X	X
12. Observes the Sabbath		X	X	X
13. Observes the Sabbath (without use of electric switches)			X	X
14. Observes the Sabbath (without the use of automobile)			X	X
15. Wears tzitzit (fringed garment)				X
16. Wears peot (earlocks)				X
17. Daily use of tephillin (phylacteries)			X	X
18. Keeps head covered				X
19. Attends mikveh (ritual bath)				X
20. Kindles Sabbath candles		X	X	X

Glossary of Commandments (Mitzvot)

1. **Dietary Laws** (Kashrut, Hebrew for kasher meaning fit or proper). Laws of the Bible and Talmud prohibiting certain foods from the diet of the

Jew: animals and fowls not slaughtered ritually, and humanely, or found defective in one of their vital organs, and other regulations restricting the eating and drinking practices, habits and customs of Jews. Most Jews observe some degree of kashrut by at the very least abstaining from pork products, a prohibition the violation of which in Israel today entails an effort similar to the cost and effort of finding a kosher butcher elsewhere. Jewish tradition considers the prohibition against various other forbidden, "unclean" animals as equally binding. These include fish without fins or scales, such as shellfish, and birds which are not traditionally known as "clean," and certain wines, etc. Flesh torn from a living animal and certain parts of "clean" beasts, meat from which the blood has not been extracted by a special salting process, meat and milk foods intermingled or eaten in proximity are all designated as unfit, that is, unkosher.

2. **Shaatnez** (a word likely of Egyptian origin meaning a mingling of fabrics). The Bible (Lev. 19:19; Deut. 22:11) prohibits the admixture of wool and flax in a garment worn by a Jew except for certain priestly garments and fringes (tzitzit). Jewish commentators offer various explanations for the prohibition against the mingling of fabrics. Clothing today is for the most part clearly labeled as to contents but a Jew who indicates studied compliance with the shaatnez legislation is generally extremely observant. The law also forbids the wearing of a woolen garment sewn with linen threads.

3. **Day of Atonement** (Yom Kippur). The most solemn occasion of the Jewish calendar, Tishri 10, while categorized formally as a festival in the Bible (Lev. 23:26–32, where it is described as the Sabbath of Sabbaths) is strictly observed as a day of fasting, self-affliction, cleansing of self of all sins (Lev. 16:30). Most Jews mark the occasion with fasting for all or at least some part of the day and synagogue attendance, particularly for the impressive evening service, Kol Nidre (all vows).

4. **Ninth of Av** (Tisha b'Av). Fast day commemorating the destruction of the First and Second Temples in Jerusalem. Dirges (kinot) are recited in the synagogue. The day also marks the anniversary of other Jewish calamities including the 1492 expulsion of the Jews from Spain. A moderately observant Jew today will not fast and will more than likely be oblivious to the day's occurrence.

5. **Hanukkah** (Hebrew meaning dedication). An eight-day festival commemorating the successful revolution of the Maccabees in 165 B.C.E. against the excesses of Antiochus Epiphanus and the rededication of the Altar of the Second Temple following its desecration. The festival was instituted for eight days in commemoration of a cruse of oil which miraculously burned for that period, and Jews kindle lights each of the eight nights to celebrate the event. Hanukkah is one of the most popular Jewish holidays, particularly for youngsters. The rabbis stressed religious values to diminish the military aspect of the festival. However, in the State of Israel, the military character has been reemphasized.

6. **Passover** (Pesach). The springtime pilgrimage festival commemorating the Exodus of the children of Israel from Egypt, hence its designation as the "festival of freedom." It is also known as "the feast of the unleavened bread" (matzah) in the Bible (Lev. 5–6). Passover is a seven-day festival in Israel (eight days elsewhere). Both first and last days are holy days on which all work is forbidden. Special dietary laws apply the entire period of the festival. The most popular festival of the Jewish calendar is simultaneously agricultural (marking the beginning of the barley harvest) and historical (referring to the passing over or sparing of the children of Israel from the plague of the first born and their subsequent liberation from Egyptian bondage) in origin. The seder (order) ceremony, which features the recitation of the Haggadah narrative and festive meal of symbolic foods and beverages, is the most important home ceremony of the year. Jews of almost every background and persuasion observe the festival with some form of special seder family meal.

7. **Sabbath** (Shabbat). The weekly day of rest for Jews, which is observed from Friday before sunset until after nightfall Saturday. According to its biblical origin (Gen. 2:1–3), it is a memorial of the seventh day of God's creation of the world as well as of the liberation from Egyptian bondage and of God's covenant with Israel (Exodus 31:16–17). The commandment of the Decalogue (Exodus 20:8) enjoins: "Remember the Sabbath day, to keep it sacred." In the home candles are kindled, generally by the woman of the household, and the man recites the Kiddush Prayer acknowledging the special character of the day, over a cup of wine, before the Friday night meal, which is prepared of the finest foods possible. Synagogue services including readings from the Torah and Prophets as well as prayers signal the importance of the day. And the Sabbath is terminated after nightfall with valedictory benedictions over wine, spices, and candle to distinguish (Havdalah) between the Sabbath day and the secular character of the rest of the week. Certain types of action are considered an infringement of the day, and the extent to which they are observed often determines the extent to which the Jew is thought of as observant.

8. **Tzitzit** (fringes). The Bible commands the wearing of fringes or twisted cords appended to each of the four corners of a garment (Deut. 22:12 and Numbers 15:38). A special garment of this sort is worn by male Jews during the day in keeping with the biblical precept. The continuous wearing of the fringed garment beneath one's outer clothing points essentially to extremely observant behavior.

9. **Peot** (Hebrew, literally corners). Earlocks worn by male Jews in keeping with the literal interpretation of the biblical injunction (Lev. 19:27) not to round the corners of the head or mar the corners of the beard. Allowing the hair around the ear to grow long is now characteristic of ultra observant, Hasidic Jews.

10. **Tephillin** (phylacteries). Two black leather cases fastened to leather straps

which contain scrolls of parchment on which are written four portions of the Bible. They are bound to the arm and head by the Jewish male of thirteen years of age and older during the weekly morning service at home or at the synagogue. The injunction to wear them is based on four paragraphs in the Bible: Exodus 13:1–10, 13:11–16; Deut. 6:4–9, 11:13–21. Many Jews are introduced to the practice at their coming of age (Bar Mitzvah), but only the highly and extremely observant Jews continue to "lay" tephillin daily the rest of their lives.

11. **Covering of the Head.** The prevailing custom among the extremely observant is to keep their heads covered at all times, whereas others would cover their heads only while praying or eating. The covering of the head finds its source not so much in Jewish law as in custom, which in time assumed the force of the law.

12. **Mikveh** (Hebrew for gathering or collection, especially of water). Ritual bath used mainly by the post-menstruous woman for the ritual of immersion.

dles at least one of the nights; fasting on the Day of Atonement for however long one deems appropriate; and attendance at the synagogue on that day. Even a fuller observance of these five commandments was considered insufficient to transpose one to the category of an observant Jew.

All others were considered *observant*.

The observant survivors were futher designated as *moderately observant* if these five commandments were kept as well as at least one of the following: observance of dietary laws outside the home; attendance at the synagogue on the Sabbath, at least occasionally; and on the festivals occasionally as well; observance of the Sabbath in some general manner; and, for a woman, kindling of the Sabbath candles.

A *highly observant* survivor was one who kept all nine of these commandments, or ten for a woman, and at least one of the following: fasting on the Ninth of Av (Tisha b'Av); daily prayer; observance of the Sabbath without using electrical switches; without riding in an automobile; and, for men only, the daily use of tephillin (phylacteries).

Extremely or ultra observant survivors kept all of these fourteen commandments or, if a woman, fifteen, and additionally, at least one of the following: observes shaatnez; wears tzitzit (if men); wears peot (if men); keeps head covered (if men); attends mikveh (if women). Except for the wearing of peot, which distinguishes the Hasidic Jew from his fellow ultra observant, most ultra observant were found to have kept all the commandments of our schedule.

Not merely or necessarily the quantity of commandments, therefore, but the quality or character of the mitzvot one keeps distinguishes among contemporary Jews. The keeping of certain commandments elevates or transfigures a moderately observant Jew into a highly observant one, and others, due to their special performance difficulty, bring one to the domain of the extremely observant. Similarly the disregard of certain commandments relegates one accordingly from one category of observance to another. This is what is meant in our study by religious "change" in religious observances.

These particular clusters of Jewish practices were chosen for providing natural divisions depicting the various groupings of observant Jews. The divisions enable us to speak in the pages that follow of increases and decreases in the number of commandments on a scale from nonobservant to ultra observant.

There is no way to determine today by survey procedures just how observant European Jewry was prior to the Holocaust. We do assume that a much larger number of observant Jews lost their lives than nonobservant Jews. Entire communities of East European Jews, traditionally observant and believing, were murdered during the Holocaust. Proportionately fewer escaped. Central and West European Jewish communities were not nearly as densely populated before the war nor "as religious," and a greater percentage managed to survive the devastation or escape before it. These assumptions may, of course, be subject to different interpretation, if not outright dispute.

The survivor population, in Israel and elsewhere, therefore, is not qualitatively the same—although six million fewer—as the European Jewish community before the Holocaust; nor is the survivor population religiously identical to those who did not survive. Rather, of the three pre-Holocaust groupings, the Six Million were probably the most religiously observant; the European Jewish population taken as a whole somewhat less religiously observant; and the survivor community probably composed of Jews who were the least religiously observant of the three. We must be careful here not to confuse Holocaust survivors generally with concentration camp survivors specifically. Concentration camp survivors were overwhelmingly East European in origin. Relatively fewer Western Jews were interned; relatively fewer still survived the camps. Undoubtedly the Nazi schedule of invasion in each country (and the problems they encountered) contributed more than any other factor to the religious make-up of the survivor population.

Religious Behavior Before the Holocaust

Despite the assumption that the survivor community before the Holocaust was the least religiously observant, our study reveals that fewer than half, only 45 percent, could be classified as nonobservant (keeping five or fewer Jewish religious practices; see Table 2). And a full 55 percent could be classified as observant—a substantial figure when one bears in mind the probability that the Jews in Europe overall and the Six Million in particular were even more observant.

Still more revealing is the inquiry into the distribution of the survivors who were, according to the extent and intensity of their practices, religiously observant before the Holocaust. One might expect that the more commandments there were to keep, the fewer would do so. But the reverse is closer to the facts: 45 percent of the Jewish population that was observant prior to the Holocaust claimed to have kept all, or nearly all, of the practices and was consequently classified as ultra observant; 30 perecent was classified as highly observant, and 25 percent was classified as only moderately observant.

A large majority of the survivors categorized as nonobservant before the Holocaust was also found to have acknowledged keeping at least a few Jewish religious practices, such as conducting a family Seder and lighting the Hanukkah candles. Many affirmed by some religious act, such as briefly visiting the synagogue or observing a modified fast, the arrival of the Day of Atonement. Still others recited the Kaddish, the Jewish prayer for the dead, on the anniversary of the death of loved ones in Europe. Even granted that in Europe, as elsewhere in the diaspora, the ethnic factor played a part in determining religious practices; *whatever else may be said concerning the Jews of Europe before the catastrophe one generalization applies: They constituted a religiously observant community.*

T A B L E 2 . Observance and Nonobservance Through Three Stages

	BEFORE HOLOCAUST	AFTER HOLOCAUST	TODAY
Nonobservant	45%	66%	57%
Observant	55	34	43

Religious Behavior After the Holocaust

Upon the conclusion of the war the devastating after effects of the catastrophe were still being experienced by all survivors. Nevertheless, it was again possible to practice Judaism if the will remained. We have referred to this period as Stage 2, and our study reveals that a sizable abatement occurred in the Holocaust community's religious observances. While before the Holocaust 55 percent of the survivors could have been classified as having been observant, at Stage 2, only 34 percent may be so designated. The decrease, which is more than one in five, enlarged the ranks of the nonobservant population to a full 66 percent after the Holocaust. Whether or not this was because of the Holocaust will be addressed further on.

In the breakdown according to the extent and intensity of religious practice, it emerged that the ultra observant, while still remaining the largest subgroup among observant Jews, at the same time sustained the severest attrition, from 45 percent to 39 percent. The moderately observant received the ensuing increment to 33 percent, while the highly observant stayed virtually the same, decreasing negligibly from 30 percent to 28 percent.

Fewer Holocaust survivors after the war remained religiously observant. And for those who remained observant there was a marked diminution in the intensity of their practice.

Religious Behavior Today

Today, three decades after the Holocaust, the observant/nonobservant proportions, as reflected by the responses in Stage 3, have seesawed by 9 percent from Stage 2. The observant community has increased by 9 percent at the expense of the nonobservant community, constituting a partial return to Jewish religious activity. The survivor population then, in the matter of religious observances, has virtually reversed its pre-Holocaust ratio of 45 percent nonobservant, 55 percent observant.

At present, Holocaust survivors are 43 percent observant as against 57 percent nonobservant. The 38 percent of the community of survivors who were observant prior to the Holocaust and had relinquished their religious behavior in Stage 2 or 3 were partially offset by the 14 percent "returnees," that is, observant survivors who after relinquishing their observant behavior in Stage 2, became observant again in Stage 3; and the latter were augmented by the 19 percent of the nonobservant population that has also become religiously observant today.

TABLE 3. Observant Survivors and Their Degrees of Observance Through Three Stages

	BEFORE HOLOCAUST	AFTER HOLOCAUST	TODAY
Moderately observant	25%	33%	34%
Highly observant	30	28	22
Ultra observant	45	39	44

When we again examine the breakdown according to the extent and intensity of religious practices, it appears that the ultra observant not only remained consistently the largest category of observant Jews but recaptured nearly all its pre-Holocaust appeal (see Table 3). Of all observant survivors today, 44 percent are ultra observant; 22 percent are highly observant, and 34 percent, nearly the same as in Stage 2, are moderately observant.

Over the course of the three stages or three decades, a tendency toward polarization among observant survivors has occurred so that, in the main, they have become increasingly either minimally observant or extremely observant. Through the years, the middle ground, described as highly observant, progressively lost its membership to the moderately observant group.

Survivor Population and Israeli Population Contrasted

How does the survivor community compare to today's Israeli population as a whole? The available studies, unfortunately, fail to provide precise information. But one research project appears somewhat relevant. A question asked by a team of Israeli social scientists from the Israeli Institute of Applied Social Research concerning religious observances ("keeping of commandments") was put to some 1,170 individuals of the adult Jewish population of Israel. In all, 15 percent claimed to observe all, and 15 percent most, of the commandments. These figures correspond with 18 percent in our study of all survivors who are today ultra observant and 9 percent of all survivors who are highly observant (totaling 27 percent in our study of Holocaust survivors, as against 30 percent of the general Israeli population).

Unfortunately, the information concerning the largest group is not especially useful: 46 percent chose the answer "I observe tradition to some extent," far too vague a response for our purposes. Perhaps, however, it may be reasonable to speculate that approximately one-third of these observe six or more of the commandments of our study and may consequently be considered moderately observant, in which case it is also to be assumed that two-thirds of these kept five or fewer of the commandments and should be classified as nonobservant.

Since 24 percent of the 1,170 declare themselves totally nonobservant and since we have arbitrarily assumed a two-thirds to one-third ratio of the 46 percent, allowing for 15 percent observant and 31 percent nonobservant, the 55 percent nonobservant total (24 percent plus 31 percent) accords well with the 57 percent nonobservant of our study.

If these calculations can be supported (and bearing in mind that they are no more than speculations), then there are sufficient affinities between the general Israeli population and the Holocaust population to wonder whether the two communities have influenced each other mutually, equally, or whether one has had greater impact upon the other in religious as well as other matters. It is maintained by some Holocaust survivors that the survivor community is to a large extent responsible, subtly as well as overtly, for the religious behavior of all Israel. In a personal interview, Yehuda Bauer, historian at the Institute for Contemporary History at the Hebrew University, said that the Holocaust population "in the matter of its special influence due to its special history, is today running the country," that is, it is to a large extent determining policy in all areas, religious and secular.

Eight Patterns of Observance

The breakdown into three sequential time periods or stages of religious observance allows for eight patterns of Jewish religious practice to develop for the survivors. The percentages refer to the distribution of survivors within each of the corresponding patterns:

. 1. An observant Jew prior to the Holocaust resumes [5] his religious behavior subsequent to liberation and remains observant to the present.

OBSERVANT —— HOLO- CAUST —▶ OBSERVANT —— 25 YEARS —▶

—▶ OBSERVANT: 26%
   (referred to as OOO)

2. An observant Jew prior to the Holocaust resumes his religious behavior subsequent to liberation but during the intervening years between then and the present ceases to be observant.

HOLO-   25

OBSERVANT——— CAUST ——►OBSERVANT ——— YEARS ——►

——► NONOBSERVANT: 2%

(referred to as OON)

3. An observant Jew prior to the Holocaust ceases to be observant subsequent to liberation but during the intervening years between then and the present becomes observant again.

HOLO-   25

OBSERVANT—— CAUST ——►NONOBSERVANT —— YEARS ——►

——► OBSERVANT: 8%

(referred to as ONO)

4. An observant Jew prior to the Holocaust ceases to be observant subsequent to liberation and remains nonobservant to the present.

HOLO-   25

OBSERVANT—— CAUST ——►NONOBSERVANT —— YEARS ——►

——►NONOBSERVANT: 19%

(referred to as ONN)

5. A nonobservant Jew prior to the Holocaust remains nonobservant subsequent to liberation and stays that way.

HOLO-   25

NONOBSERVANT—— CAUST——►NONOBSERVANT—— YEARS —►

——►NONOBSERVANT: 35%

(referred to as NNN)

6. A nonobservant Jew prior to the Holocaust remains nonobservant subsequent to liberation but during the intervening years between then and the present becomes observant.

HOLO-   25

NONOBSERVANT—— CAUST ——►NONOBSERVANT—— YEARS —►

——► OBSERVANT: 4%

(referred to as NNO)

7. A nonobservant Jew prior to the Holocaust becomes observant subsequent to liberation and becomes nonobservant again.

HOLO-   25

NONOBSERVANT—— CAUST ——► OBSERVANT ——YEARS ——►

——►NONOBSERVANT: 2%

(referred to as NON)

8. A nonobservant Jew prior to the Holocaust becomes observant subsequent to liberation and remains observant to the present.

HOLO-   25
NONOBSERVANT —— CAUST —► OBSERVANT ——YEARS —►
—►OBSERVANT: 4%
(referred to as NOO)

At this juncture we must again be reminded not to assume that it is the Holocaust itself which provides the principal explanation for religious change. Rather, these eight patterns of change and the percentage of survivors traveling through each of these three-steps can only claim limited value in their disclosures on the effects of the Holocaust. They are more biographical than explanatory. Nevertheless, our attention is drawn to several interesting findings relevant to the Holocaust community.

The Formative Years

The two largest categories of the eight patterns of observance (OOO and NNN) may be interpreted as a reflection of the extent and durability of religious training received during the formative years. They suggest the likelihood of the retention by survivors of their pre-Holocaust religious behavior regardless of the upheavals in their personal lives. Of all survivors, 26 percent remained observant Jews throughout their lives, and 35 percent similarly stayed nonobservant through the Holocaust ordeal to the present. That is, 61 percent recorded no changes whatever in their religious behavior over the course of some three decades. An additional 10 percent were changed only temporarily, for a total of 71 percent.

Put in even more graphic perspective: If we momentarily disregard the nonobservant Jews and examine the observant community exclusively (Table 4) we find that of all Jewish survivors who were observant

TABLE 4. Patterns of Change in Observance, Observant Survivors

Before Holocaust	After Holocaust	Today	
Observant	Observant	Observant	48%
Observant	Observant	Nonobservant	3
Observant	Nonobservant	Observant	14
Observant	Nonobservant	Nonobservant	35

TABLE 5. Patterns of Change in Observance, Nonobservant Survivors

BEFORE HOLOCAUST	AFTER HOLOCAUST	TODAY	
Nonobservant	Nonobservant	Nonobservant	77%
Nonobservant	Nonobservant	Observant	9
Nonobservant	Observant	Nonobservant	4
Nonobservant	Observant	Observant	9

before the Holocaust, 48 percent remained consistently observant through the Holocaust ordeal to the present. Adding to this the 14 percent who ceased to be observant in stage two (after the war) but then became observant again, we find that 63 percent retained or returned to their earlier religiously observant behavior.

By the same procedure we find that when we disregard the observant Jews and examine the nonobservant Jews exclusively (Table 5) the likelihood of the retention of one's previous nonobservant behavior is even greater: 77 percent remained nonobservant throughout the three stages. And if we add the 4 percent who became observant only briefly in Stage 2, our total is 81 percent—which may be interpreted as another substantiation of the overriding significance of the influence of one's formative years.

We may gather from these findings that *over the course of the years from Europe through the Holocaust to the present in Israel, the observant Jew was more likely to modify his Jewish behavior than the nonobservant; the latter proved more consistent throughout the three stages:* 38 percent of all Jews who were observant before the Holocaust became nonobservant, whereas approximately half that proportion, 19 percent, or just fewer than one of every five previously nonobservant survivors (8 percent of all survivors) are today living in Israel as observant Jews—for reasons not yet examined.

How should these figures be interpreted? Since there is no reliable way of ascertaining the proportion of religious change that might have been expected of European Jewry, or of any other population for that matter, in the course of an ordinary lifetime, there is similarly no way to predict, or to evaluate for comparison, the extent of religious change to be expected from the extraordinary life experiences of the Holocaust survivors.

It may, for example, be convincingly maintained that the 38 percent of observant Jews cited above who became nonobservant is a considerable figure, appreciably beyond what normal living would have brought about naturally and spontaneously.

And surely even less predictable is the smaller but perhaps more notable progression of 19 percent, nearly one in five, of the nonobservant who "went the other way" and became observant during the course of the years. This development was hardly foreseen and requires further investigation.

These findings may be set in more moderate perspective and still retain their significance. The two directly contrasting patterns of religious behavioral change are those numbered 4 (ONN) and 8 (NOO). The first discloses that of all Holocaust survivors 19 percent ceased to be observant Jews after the Holocaust. By comparison only 4 percent of all survivors first became observant after the Holocaust, a relatively small but prominent and important subgroup whose views will not be overlooked because of its size.

Later we shall consider the survivors who specifically and consciously attribute the modifications in their religious behavior to the Holocaust or the concentration camp experience itself. But for now it is sufficient to note that *during the years of the Holocaust nearly five times as many observant European Jews relinquished their religious practices as nonobservant Jews took upon themselves the "yoke of the commandments."*

When Religious Changes Occurred

Without attributing to the Holocaust itself sole accountability for the development, it emerged that *the most numerous changes in religious behavior among Holocaust survivors are recorded at Stage 2, just after the war,* having occurred during the Holocaust years: 33 percent of all survivors recorded changes in religious observances (from observant to nonobservant or from nonobservant to observant) at Stage 2—after experiencing the Holocaust.

On the other hand, 16 percent of all survivors modified their observances in the years between the Holocaust and the present time in Israel. That is, fewer than half the Stage 2 changes were recorded at Stage 3.

We may infer therefore that the period of the war and the Holocaust (the years of the Holocaust but not necessarily the Holocaust itself) exerted a greater impact upon the survivors in the matter of religious observances than their experiences living in the State of Israel.

Apparently, the experiences connected with living in Israel may be interpreted as having had little religious impact. Patterns 2 and 6 converge in a particular way to draw our attention to this. We are not ascribing to Israel, the land or the nation per se, responsibility for the existence or the lack of religious influence, it merely provides the context or setting for either instance. In Israel only 2 percent of all survivors ceased being religiously observant, and only 4 percent may be said to have become religiously observant sometime during their years as Palestinian residents and Israeli citizens. This, along with other similar findings, shows that the land of Israel provided a slight if any positive influence in the matter of Jewish religious observances.

When we shift our perspective and concentrate exclusively upon the survivors who were nonobservant in Europe (Stages 1 through 2), however, we find that a more impressive percentage of survivors were in fact influenced during their years in Israel in becoming observant Jews. Almost one in ten (9 percent) nonobservant survivors became religiously observant, whereas only 3 percent of the observant Jewish survivors relinquished their Jewish practices while living in Israel. Seen in this light, *for certain Holocaust survivors life experiences in Israel may be regarded as having had an affirmative effect in the matter of religious observances.*

In point of fact, *for survivors who were nonobservant before the Holocaust the experiences associated with living in Israel proved as influential in bringing about change in the direction of increased religious observances as those of the Holocaust years.* Precisely the same number of Holocaust survivors (9 percent) became observant during the years between the Holocaust and the present time in Israel as became observant during the period of the Holocaust. There is, of course, no way of knowing how many of these, nearly one of every ten survivors, would have become observant anyway, for various commonplace reasons: intellectual, psychological, or spiritual motivations; marriage to an observant spouse; or the influence of some other person. And for them it may be that the Holocaust actually postponed the inevitable progression.

While the Israel years, for survivors who were observant before the Holocaust, proved of virtually no consequence in bringing about a rejection of religious observances (3 percent), by contrast the Holocaust years brought profound adverse changes in the religious lives of these survivors. More than ten times as many observant survivors gave up their religious practices during the genocide period (as recorded in Stage 2) as did later.

Patterns 3 and 7 are particularly revealing in this regard: 14 percent reverted to observant in Israel after having become nonobservant after the war, whereas hardly any (4 percent) reverted to nonobservant in the new state subsequent to having become observant upon the conclusion of the war. Perhaps it can correctly be inferred that the experience of living in Israel is more likely to bring the survivors back to earlier religiously observant behavior than to have them resume their nonreligious behavior.

In short, life experiences in Israel seem to have propelled a segment of the survivor community to become religiously observant. But the Holocaust years influenced a far greater number of observant survivors, more than one in three, to relinquish their religiously observant behavior.

Religious Change and Three Observant Categories

A final factor not to be overlooked in the context of changes in religious practices pertains to the three classes of observant Jews subdivided earlier in this chapter.

It is significant that *the observant Jewish population relinquished or retained its religious behavior in direct relation to the intensity of its previous practice. The more intensely observant the more likely to remain observant; the less intensely observant the greater the likelihood of becoming nonobservant.*

Patterns 1 and 4 are most revealing in this regard, inasmuch as they represent the largest pre-Holocaust observant groupings—the one composed of observant Jews who remained observant; the other observant Jews who became nonobservant.

Among formerly observant survivors, 23 percent had been ultra observant, 32 percent highly observant, and 45 percent moderately observant. The proportions among observant survivors who retained their religious behavior throughout the three decades were 61 percent for the ultra observant, 30 percent for the highly observant, and 9 percent for the moderately observant.

Contrary to the widely held opinion of religious polarization—that after an enormous catastrophe the "most religious" become the "least religious" in a radical reversal—our study conveys the case for the retentive strength of the assiduously observant and the holding power of religious upbringing.

The eight patterns of change or stability in Jewish practices disclose the biographical and historical progression of the survivor community's religious behavior. But they do not provide the root causes, motivations, and explanations for their development nor the reasoning and justification, if any, in those instances of no change. Most important, we cannot yet determine when modifications in religious behavior should be attributed to the Holocaust or when to developments unrelated to it such as marriage, immigration, education, personality factors, or entirely unspecified reasons. Similarly, the figures emerging from the eight patterns of change fail to distinguish the degrees of change specifically attributable to the Holocaust among the moderately observant, the highly observant, and the ultra observant nor the crossings from one of these categories of religious observance to another. These will be examined later on in this chapter. Moreover, the differences between concentration camp internees and European Jews who survived the Holocaust outside the camps must also be scrutinized.

Survivors Changed, Survivors Affected

One of the leading motivations for undertaking this work arose as a response to the lack of any systematic knowledge concerning the Holocaust's influence and effect upon the religious observances of survivors. Our inquiry focuses essentially on two distinct but connected questions, the first general, the second quite specific:

1. How many survivors today explicitly acknowledge that the Holocaust experience affected or influenced their religious observances? And what were the specific consequences of that effect and the nature of the group affected? Conversely, what is the percentage of survivors who claim the Holocaust had no influence upon their religious practices? And what do they all say about themselves?

In grouping those survivors whose religious observances were affected by the Holocaust we included those whose religious practices were in fact changed due to the Holocaust by a significant (i.e., a sufficient number of changes to effect transition from one category to another: e.g., from ultra observant to highly observant or from nonobservant to observant) increase or decrease of the number of observances kept.

The "changed" category, besides being subsumed within the "affected" category, was given independent status as well, in the following question.

2. How many survivors claiming changes in their religious behavior attributed the reasons for them specifically to their Holocaust experience? What were the consequences of the changes and the nature of the group that changed? And what do these survivors say about themselves?

After the first part of the interview was completed and the survivors indicated the religious observances they had kept at the three stages in their lives, prior and subsequent to the Holocaust, as well as today, two further questions were asked of the survivors.

Question 1. If there were changes in your religious observances ("keeping of the mitzvot") in any of the three time periods, were the changes

a. entirely or essentially due to the Holocaust?
b. to a large extent due to the Holocaust?
c. due only in small measure to the Holocaust?
d. brought about by the Holocaust only temporary ones?

Question 2. If there were no apparent changes or very few changes in your religious observances ("keeping the mitzvot") at any of the three stages, do you believe the Holocaust

a. strengthened or reinforced your religious practices (that is, the mitzvot you keep)?
b. strengthened or reinforced your lack of religious practices (that is, your nonobservance of the mitzvot)?
c. had no influence whatsoever on your religious observances (that is, in keeping the mitzvot)?

Survivors Unaffected by the Holocaust

Survivors who selected (a) or (b) of Question 2 were classified as having been affected by the Holocaust in their religious behavior. The selection of (c) designated the respondent as not having been affected.

We will first examine the effect/no effect sector of the survivor population. Several representative comments from survivors who maintained they had not been affected in their religious practices by the Holocaust are appropriate here:

> The Holocaust was an aberration, a prolonged but unreal
> nightmare which is over and I keep it that way—over. It had
> nothing to do with anything, except history and politics. Certainly
> in no way is it connected to my religious behavior or beliefs. The
> Holocaust was a detour in the pathway of the progress of
> civilization and the Holocaust was a detour in my personal life.
> I am back on safer ground now and I'll never even glance
> down that horrible road again if I can help it. . . .

I consider myself a nonreligious secular Jew. I was brought
up that way and will no doubt remain that way. That does
not mean I feel no religious obligations but they are ethical and
humanistic responsibilities toward my fellow man and to Israel my
country, and to world society generally—and even to the
Jewish people. But the traditional ritual Jewish practices are not
part of my life. I never really considered keeping "kasher" or
attending synagogue; nor has the Holocaust impelled me in any
way to reconsider my nonreligious ways. Instead, today, if I
am influenced at all Jewishly, it is by Jewish humanistic and
universalistic values and that is what I was like, my family, and I,
before the Holocaust as well.

———◆———

My beliefs have been affected by the Holocaust but not the
mitzvot I perform. It is still necessary for me to be a Jew, now
more than ever before, and the only way to be a Jew is to do what
Jews do. Before the Holocaust, and since the Holocaust to this
very day, you could not tell from my religious behavior what I
have undergone, what the Holocaust has done to me, but in
my soul where my beliefs reside there has been a tremendous
transformation. My faith has been crushed and I am nearly a
nonbeliever. . . . You may say I've been changed philosophically,
and religiously in connection with beliefs about God, but not
changed at all where for a Jew it counts most—in actions.
In this respect I'm still a pious Jew.

———◆———

When I say the Holocaust has no effect upon the mitzvot I keep,
I'm not saying the Holocaust has no effect on my life. In truth,
the Holocaust touches my life in ways unlike anything else I've
ever experienced, but it has no effect upon the kind of Jew
I am. The Holocaust is all around me searching me out everywhere
except for my religious practices and yiddishkeit. These are
separate and apart from the Holocaust. . . . Instead, I see myself
as changed by the Holocaust psychologically and emotionally—
in the manner I relate to people, in the way I see myself as a
person, in the way I treat my wife and kids, especially my kids.
And since many survivors are like I am, psychologically changed,
therefore it's a social or social-psychological not a religious
phenomenon. The Holocaust is to be studied primarily by
sociologists and not theologians.

For any one of these or various other reasons, fully half (52 percent) of all survivors questioned were able to declare of themselves that the Holocaust has had no effect at all upon their religious behavior—an astonishing revelation considering what was thought to be the religious implications of the Holocaust and the supposition that it reached each and every survivor with the greatest impact in all dimensions of their lives. Moreover, it is not sufficient to point out merely that every second survivor remained entirely unchanged in the matter of religious observances despite his ordeal. The unaffected survivors could not even bring themselves to say, along with one of the selections offered, that the Holocaust affected them to the minimal extent that their previous behavior, or the rationale for their previous behavior was "reinforced" by their experience.

Half the survivors in our study were simply not influenced one way or another by the Holocaust in the matter of their religious behavior. Similarly, half the survivors—and not necessarily the same survivors, were not influenced in the matter of religious beliefs. Nevertheless, this still leaves 48 percent of all survivors, a rather large segment of the survivor population, to study for whom the Holocaust had an effect—for some, a great effect—with regard to religious observances.[6]

The statement that half the survivor population remained unaffected religiously by the Holocaust, although correct according to our research, may ultimately prove quite misleading nonetheless. The size of the statistic must be judged by the nature of the survivor community. It should be borne in mind that prior to the Holocaust years 45 percent of the total survivor community was nonobservant (see Table 2). An expectation of religious change from these nonpracticing Jews, which is tantamount to an expectation that they become observant to some degree, or that they should in any way be affected religiously, is far more improbable than the converse: observant Jews relinquishing their religious practices. There is simply no reason to expect that a nonreligious Jew should be affected religiously. Moreover, a nonpracticing Jew is far less likely to allow that he has been affected religiously by the Holocaust experience even to the minimal extent of seeing his nonreligious behavior or beliefs reinforced or confirmed by the catastrophe. He would be more inclined to deny any connection with religion whatever.

Not surprisingly, when we separate for comparison purposes two pre-Holocaust communities, the observant and the nonobservant subgroups, to ascertain which was affected least by the Holocaust experience, we find that 44 percent of the former as against 61 percent of the latter declared the Holocaust irrelevant to their religious behavior. This means that 56 percent of the observant and 39 percent of the nonobservant communities were in fact affected in their religious behavior by the Holocaust. The pattern therefore continues to develop which, not unexpectedly, will bring us to the conclusion that *an observant suvivor was the more likely to be influenced religiously by the Holocaust than his nonobservant counterpart.*

Nevertheless, we cannot maintain the more observant, the more affected. Among Jews who were observant prior to the Holocaust, the ultra observant were the least affected by their Holocaust experience: 51 percent declared themselves untouched by the Holocaust in the matter of religious observances. On the other hand, fewer than half of either the highly observant or the moderately observant were similarly unaffected by the Holocaust: 63 percent of all highly observant Jews declared themselves affected, and, providing us with no consistent ascending or descending scale, 57 percent of all moderately observant Jews were likewise affected by the Holocaust.

A study of the consistently ultra observant, a subgroup of the larger population which was ultra observant prior to the Holocaust, may also be illuminating. Of the survivors who remained ultra observant throughout the three stages, 71 percent claim that they were uninfluenced by the Holocaust in their religious practices. And the remaining 29 percent maintain that they were affected only insofar as the Holocaust reinforced and strengthened their ultra observant behavior. Too few even to register statistically were the consistently ultra observant survivors for whom the Holocaust "weakened" religious behavior. These few survivors spoke of continuing their strict religious practice all their lives but with diminished enthusiasm or with attenuated faith. With few exceptions, the *ultra observant Jews were highly motivated and undoubtedly strongly predisposed to view the great catastrophe as either unrelated to, or a confirmation of, their religious predilections.*

Survivors Affected but Unchanged

A study that attends exclusively to survivors who were changed religiously by the Holocaust and disregards those survivors who were unchanged but "merely" affected in more subtle ways, oversimplifies and distorts its findings by overlooking an important dimension of the Holocaust's impact.

When we turn our attention to survivors who were affected but not changed by the Holocaust, we place in consideration members of the survivor community whose religious practices, or the resolve and rationale behind them, were strengthened and reinforced or whose non-observance was reconfirmed. There are also those instances alluded to above in which no changes occurred sufficient for a shift in category but the survivor maintains that his or her Jewish practices were "weakened" by the Holocaust experience.

There are, additionally, cases of survivors who gave up or took on a single religious practice because of the Holocaust. They were, therefore, not changed statistically, i.e., by a sufficient number of practices to be classified as having "changed" from one category to another. But their emotional investment in the single changed religious observance may have been very great. This may also be partially attributable to the fact that in Judaism, as has been pointed out previously, not all mitzvot are equally regarded.

There is the case, for example, of the highly observant survivor of the Sachsenhausen Concentration Camp who gave up only one single observance, the daily use of tephillin, and was consequently "unchanged" according to our criteria. Although he registers only in the "affected" classification in that his religious practices, however "weakened," were on the whole unchanged, nevertheless for him, inwardly, a significant transformation indeed occurred. He gave up no other Jewish practice, but he sees himself as "getting even with God" by no longer donning tephillin, a form of rejection of God for "His having rejected my family and all Jews." The discontinuance of one important religious observance, apparently, was sufficient to proclaim his bitter resentment of God's deportment, and there was no need to abandon the rest. The abandonment of the practice of tephillin features prominently in survivor narrations:

> I was in the Lodz ghetto and knew Romkowski the head of the
> ghetto, not well, but to say hello to. He cared very much for
> all the children. One day I went out to look for food. My little
> sister was very hungry and cried for something to eat. But
> there was nothing at all to be had. I ran from place to place looking
> everywhere, anywhere there had been some food to be had
> previously. Nothing at all. I returned home empty-handed.
> I walked slowly, afraid to rush back empty-handed, thinking
> how could I tell my little sister that I could bring her nothing
> to eat. I didn't know what I'd say but it turned out I didn't have
> to explain a thing to my little sister. She was gone when I

arrived. They had come for her and taken her away while I was gone. I too would have been taken to my death then had she not saved my life by sending me on the fruitless task of trying to locate something to eat for her all over the ghetto. That errand kept me alive. But I never saw her again.

It's been twenty-five years or more since then but no day passes by without my thinking about that day, without my thinking about the room's emptiness, my sister's little belongings on the floor, a doll, a torn sweater, one window a trifle open with the curtain drawn and sucked outside by the draft, the table empty of food, a book from which I had been reading to her opened to the page I was up to and was to continue to read to her after I returned with something to eat. And my tephillin. I could never bring myself to wear tephillin again. The blue velvet bag was there on the table and I have a picture in my mind of my sister, before being taken away, touching it once, quickly kissing it, as she had often done piously, religiously, lovingly, with me in the room watching approvingly as though kissing it was itself a religious act and at the same time, since it was my talit and tephillin which she saw me—her older brother whom she loved and who protected her—wear at prayers, it was as though she was kissing me when she was bringing it to her lips devotedly. I cannot look at tephillin without remembering that scene, without tears and without despair. I simply cannot look at another pair of tephillin.

Another survivor who does not show up in our classification as having been changed religiously is the Polish Jew who spent three years in Auschwitz, during which time all his family was lost. He retains a sufficient number of religious practices to remain the moderately observant Jew he was prior to camp internment. But his one expression of rejection or rebellion is, curiously, invested in making a point of smoking cigars on the Sabbath, "regardless of the fact that I am not much of a smoker the remainder of the week. It is my way."

There are other survivors who, within the contours of our definition, are classified as having remained unchanged in religious behavior. Rather than rejection or rebellion, they have taken upon themselves some "religious" duty. Most often, it is a single all-consuming objective, an ever obsessive mission, which they readily acknowledge as not a religious practice in the traditional sense. They, nevertheless, consider themselves as having been "religiously changed" by it: the hunters who have devoted themselves to tracing and pursuing escaped Nazis; Holocaust researchers, archivists, and historians; fund raisers for these and related causes; unsalaried workers for survivor organizations; and others caught up in similar activities are included among them. They claim to look upon themselves as fulfilling a "Holocaust mitzvah." And they appear in our study within the category of survivors affected religiously by the Holocaust.

One prominent survivor interviewed in September 1946 by the psychologist David P. Boder—who subsequently published his post-war interviews in a book appropriately entitled *I Did Not Interview the Dead*—spoke of his consuming religious passion immediately after his liberation from a concentration camp:

> I returned to my native Wiesbaden . . . and I was still very sick,
> very weak. . . . And so I, as a Wiesbadener, was inspired to
> rebuild anew the House of the Lord, which served as a holy place
> for my parents and for the oldest rabbi of Germany, Rabbi Doctor
> Leo Kahn—may he rest in peace. I consider it almost the task
> of my life to rebuild the house in which my father and my mother
> —may they rest in peace—have stood, the house in which I
> was confirmed, the house in which my sisters and brothers
> worshipped for decades. And to rebuild it again as it was.
>
> I consider it my life work to rebuild this house for the sake
> of the dead, for those who shall not return anymore, and for those
> who were able to leave this country in time, so the Word of God
> may spread over all the world, a memorial to all who knew
> Wiesbaden and who once lived in Wiesbaden.[7]

A Netanya survivor active in the Organization of Former Prisoners of Captive Nazi Lands also spoke of his need to build a synagogue as a Holocaust memorial. He related his experiences some three decades after the previous citation.

> I was taken to Auschwitz in the very last roundup from the
> Lodz ghetto, which was liberated immediately thereafter by the
> Russians. And then I was swept along with the German retreat
> after a matter of a few days at Birkenau, which saved me. What
> saved me all along was my trade as a blacksmith, my brother too,
> a family trade of generations, which was why we survived the
> selections. We were taken there by train in stalls meant for pigs.
> It took fourteen days. We were squeezed like folding chairs

into these tiny stalls without food, without water, our mouths kept open for the falling snow to enter.

During the march with the German retreat, many, many were shot and left dead on the road along with dead and mutilated German soldiers and others, no telling who. And wherever we arrived, not only was there no place for us, but other Jews were added to our group from Dora to Ehrlich, Klein Ehrlich, Northausen, and so on and on and on.

Much later at one point the Germans broke rank and ran away leaving the Kapos in charge, and at night seven of us, my brother included, sneaked off to the forest at a prearranged distraction. One of our group was shot dead on the second day. The rest of us hid and dug up potatoes to eat. We ate them raw. I was by far the oldest at thirty-three, and I was swollen and bloated from beatings. I received one terrible beating in Auschwitz from a townsman who failed to recognize me at first and then, after beating me, scolded me for not telling him who I was. I lost my left eye from it. It was clear we couldn't survive any longer in the forest. Our wanderings were aimless and the patrols were everywhere. I was also getting sicker and sicker and more swollen. So I said to my brother and the others that the next jeep I see on the road I'm going to go out to it and if it's the Germans they will shoot me. And you will all know to run and hide. But if they're the other side and I am received well, come out yourselves and be saved. A while later a jeep appeared and I staggered out of the forest towards the road. In the jeep was an American officer and a Polish civilian. I don't remember much what happened next because I awoke in an empty Folk Deutsch house with others. Dysentery wiped us out, because we weren't used to eating. And many, many died.

When I recovered, circumstances took us to Regensberg, especially to be with other Jews and to form a kind of kibbutz. Amcha? Amcha? we asked one another, identifying ourselves as Jews. There I dedicated myself to building a synagogue in memory of my father who was a gabbai of the synagogue as well as a blacksmith. I sought out a carpenter, who built an ark to my specifications as close to the way our own shul's ark looked as I could remember. A sefer [scroll] torah had been brought along by a Jew from Russia. Then I got all the other craftsmen I could find, a seamstress for the cover and another man for the ner tamid [eternal light], and I built a whole synagogue

singlehandedly for my father. I had to do it. The synagogue
still stands there in Regensburg today, and I keep in touch with
it as best I can. I forgot to tell you, when I went back to my
home in Lodz and knocked at the door of my house, the Poles living
there said, "What, you're alive? Too bad." And then they threw
me out of my own house. The police said find another room
somewhere else. I left the same day.

These and similar cases fall within the framework of survivors who were
affected in their religious practices but not changed by the Holocaust.

There are, additionally, a very small number of survivors who attribute the total change in their religious behavior to one specific experience they believe to be unconnected, or only remotely related, to
the Holocaust. Nevertheless, they have been included in our statistics
in the affected *and* changed categories. For one thing, it is nearly impossible to distinguish between direct and indirect Holocaust causality,
and, more to the point, the event cited and the change in category
occurred within the time frame of the Holocaust years. There were
numerous unusual and extraordinary experiences connected with the
Holocaust but not precisely "of" the Holocaust. One survivor, a former
Auschwitz inmate, related one such experience to which he attributed
the abandonment of all his religious practices:

> After liberation when the struggle to regain our health became
> the single most important task, bars of soap were at a premium.
> We needed them to keep clean and fight infections and
> psychologically to scrub away the stench of death all around us.
> Contact with the dead had to be washed away.
>
> Well, one day a storage bin of soap was discovered, which had
> been overlooked previously. We were all happy and excited about it.
> But somehow the Orthodox rabbis heard about this bin of soap
> and decided the contents were not kosher enough for Jews and
> prevented all of us from gaining access to it. This was not soap
> made from human fat, mind you. This was from some other
> substance, perhaps animal fat, and it could very well have come
> from an unkosher animal. I don't know. But in any case, we
> weren't allowed to use it. We were deprived of decent soap for so
> long by the Nazis and we were further deprived of it by the rabbis.
> They heaped cruelty upon cruelty. They said food was for
> health but soap was not as essential. From that time on I lost
> all my respect for rabbis and my will to practice Judaism in the
> same way I had before the war.

When a survivor registered modifications in religious behavior due to the Holocaust there is of course no way of knowing whether the changes might not have come about at a later date in any event. There is also no way of knowing when a survivor becomes predisposed by the cumulative effect of many savage Holocaust experiences to have the very next incident in life, however peripherally related to the Holocaust, trigger a change in religious behavior. The survivor from Auschwitz observed, "I may not have stayed religious even without the bin of soap incident and the stupidity of the rabbis, but I know that for me it was the final crucial blow."

Biographies of Affected Survivors

Corresponding to the brief autobiographical sketches recorded a few pages earlier of survivors for whom the Holocaust had no effect upon their religious behavior are the following six statements. They are representative if not "typical" autobiographical fragments in which survivors endeavor to clarify how and why they *were* affected by the Holocaust.

To tell the truth I was not much of a Jew in Europe. More than this, I'm ashamed to admit I wasn't a very nice or moral person either. During the time I spent in the camps I was even worse. I behaved like an animal, but I also must point out that that is why I was able to survive. I'll admit it to you confidentially, but I'd rather not admit it to others openly, that I played along and cooperated with our enemy and haters in the camps. I felt I had no choice. I was a kapo. I had to be in order to live. And eventually, through much guile, rose to a prominent and influential position in the camp which enabled me to eat relatively well and keep myself better than the other Jews. I'm not particularly proud of the way I behaved and how I treated some of my fellow Jews. And yet I believe I learned a sense of humanity. I often hoped during those years that I'd survive and then try to be a decent person and live a good life and make up for some of the things I did. But as for being an observant or religious Jew, I began to feel the opposite, whenever I gave the matter some thought, that I'd never do any of those foolish things that we Jews do. The rituals, I mean. I'd never have any part of that, which is meaningless nonsense. How anyone can live through the concentration camps and still be an observant religious Jew is beyond me. I just do not understand it. The camps convinced me that all the good Jewish practices in the world are of no value. Man is not going to be changed and made good by them and God doesn't seem to care. This is what I learned in the camps.

———◆———

I suppose I'm one of those unusual Jews who looks upon the Holocaust as concrete proof of God's greater intention for mankind and particularly for the Jews. It was a message from God to all Jews that they are a unique people, chosen by God to be His special beloved people and it also taught that the rest of mankind is made up of wild savages. The message to the Jew was that he should keep the Torah and all the commandments, and if and when he fails to do so the savages will be unleashed against him.

I was very religious and highly observant before the Holocaust, of course. And I came from a very religious home, but the Holocaust convinced me that there is only one way for the Jew to be and that is to keep the commandments. I see the Holocaust as a sign from God to that effect. God doesn't do anything without purpose and the Six Million was too tremendous a slaughter to take lightly and to suppose that it was for nothing. It was ridiculous to suppose it had no meaning.

The Holocaust had a message. The Holocaust was saying that Jews who keep the mitzvot are doing the right thing and Jews who do not are doing the wrong thing, a terribly wrong thing, but that we will all suffer and be punished alike, the innocent and guilty together, until we all become religious and observant Jews. We Jews are all responsible one for the other.

———◆———

It would be a gross error to assume because I recorded no changes above [in the three stages], that the Holocaust did not alter my religious behavior. On paper there may appear to be no modifications because I was just as observant before the Holocaust as afterwards, at least outwardly. But to be entirely honest I'd have to say that I was transformed by the Holocaust and it *is* reflected in my religious behavior above all else, regardless of appearances. It shows up most in my religious practices. And I think it shows up here, in religious practices, for most Jews.

Before the Holocaust I was a simple observant Jew. Today I'm an observant Jew but very complex, not at all simple. Due to the Holocaust, I can now say that every single religious practice

I keep—and I keep most— is because of what I have undergone and
witnessed and experienced during those terrible years. I observe
the mitzvot now because of the Holocaust, specifically because
of the Holocaust. I have now a clear reason in my mind and
very deep motives for practicing Judaism—whereas before it was
not as clear. Besides everything else, it's my revenge against Hitler
and the Nazis . . . it is spitting on their graves. My way of getting
even is by practicing my religion with fervor and enthusiasm.
Serving God and the Jewish people and carrying on my father's,
my grandfather's and ancestors' traditions.

I made a lot of decisions about my life during the years I was
in hiding—hiding out in forests, in Christian homes, trying to
pass myself off as a Gentile—and later when I finally was caught
and brought to Buchenwald.
    One of the decisions was that I'll never "serve the Lord with
gladness nor come before Him with singing." I'll never serve God
by performing for Him, by observing the commandments of
Judaism. It was a very conscious decision on my part. I actually
asked myself should I become a religious Jew or not, should I
do this or that when it is all over. I wasn't a religious Jew up to
that time in the late 1930s but I had often thought about it, that
I should become observant, like my brother who died years
ago did right after the war. And many times I had come almost to
the point of resolving to do so. But then, during those dreadful
years, my final decision which I have kept to this day was not
to serve God because He really doesn't want me to and because He
let it all happen. It proved I was right all along in my behavior and
my belief. There was not outward change, of course; it was all
inside. But the Holocaust convinced me not to become a religious
Jew.

I can't answer your inquiries in a simple way with a simple
answer and I am confused even when I try to explain what I do
and what I believe to myself. How much more difficult to explain
to someone else, to another person, a researcher, what has happened
to me and what the consequences have been, and how my life
has changed.
    I am an observant Jew. I keep the mitzvot and I always
have, but here is the difference and the change. Whereas before I

kept them with happiness and joy like my rebbe and all of us,
his followers, were supposed to do; afterwards and today I just
go through the motions. My heart is not in it. I'm no less observant
but it's different. And I know that the camps are responsible
for this.

◆

I answer your survey question in the following manner: No.
There weren't apparent changes or very few changes in my religious
observance at any of the three stages. Yes to choice A: I do
believe the Holocaust strengthened and reinforced the mitzvot
I keep. I can also say that the mitzvot I keep are the same as I
kept before the war, but I keep them much more intensely and
regard them much more seriously. I've grown up as well as older
because of my experiences so close to death. The Holocaust has
matured me in my religious thinking and attitudes. I am more
convinced than ever that being a religious Jew is the right way
to behave. I am a much stronger Jew because of the Holocaust
than I was before. So, I believe, are many others like me.

Temporary Changes in Religious Behavior

Just under half of all survivors claim to have been influenced in their
religious behavior by their Holocaust experience. The smallest group,
4 percent, indicated that the impact upon them was of a transitory
nature and within time they reverted to their prewar attitudes and
behavior.

Survivors whose religious practices were modified temporarily either
by increase or decrease after the Holocaust were not registered among
survivors who changed their religious behavior inasmuch as the changes
were not lasting or permanent. Instead, these survivors were included
in the effect classification as having been influenced by the Holocaust.

The number of observant survivors in this category was more than
twice that of nonobservant survivors. That is, *it is more than twice as
likely that an observant survivor who gave up his religious practices
would become religiously observant again than a nonobservant survivor
who took upon himself the commandments immediately after the Holocaust would return to his previous nonobservant behavior.*

Characteristic of survivors who temporarily gave up religious observances is the one who explained that her immediate emotional re-

sponse upon learning the truth of the tragic fate of her husband and children after her release from Maidanek death camp was that of sinking into a deep depression, which obliterated all her customary concern for other people as well as her faith in God and the practices of her religion. For several years the depression persisted, but gradually she came out of it. Although she has never really gotten over the tragedy, she has learned to live with it; she has reconciled herself to the events of her past and has resumed her life as best she could. She has remarried and has become a participating member of the Israeli community and once again a moderately observant Jew.

A Polish-born survivor who escaped from camp to a forest where she joined the partisans before being recaptured remembered her feelings of a quarter-century ago:

> I was liberated just a few days before Rosh Hashana 1945 and
> I went to shul. It was unbearable. I stayed to say Kaddish in
> the women's section with other survivors but I couldn't take it.
> And Passover and Hanukkah were even worse. I couldn't control
> my memories and I couldn't control my tears. My mind would
> leap back to my brothers and parents and to the happy celebrations
> of the holidays we all had shared and the meals we had together
> before they were murdered by the Germans. It was more than I
> could stand. For a long time I couldn't practice Judaism again
> as I previously had. But I forced myself to go to the synagogue
> for Yizkor, the service for the dead, three times a year and at the
> high holy days and that helped me gradually to resume practicing
> Judaism again almost as I had previously. The memories are
> still very powerful, very hurtful, and there are certain things
> I still can't bring myself to do and probably never will. But I
> have resumed most of my Jewish observances. The memories are
> the worst part—even today.

Another survivor who, by contrast, temporarily took up rather than gave up religious practices after the Holocaust is also typical in what she has to relate:

> I had to do *something*, I felt, something Jewish, after the Nazi
> era was over, because being Jewish was the reason why the Nazis
> murdered so many of us in the first place. So I began, for the
> first time, to be observant for a while. Not fanatic, just a few
> things I had never done before, like going to the synagogue on the

Sabbath and lighting candles and other things, including fasting
on Yom Kippur, of course, which I never gave up. But as for
the rest, I didn't continue them. I don't know why. Perhaps if
I hadn't come to Israel I would still be somewhat observant. In
Israel it doesn't seem as necessary and not doing it doesn't make me
feel irreligious or that I am a bad Jew or ungrateful to God that
I survived. I still on occasion go to the synagogue and sometimes
do other things as well. It carries over from then but generally,
I admit, it just didn't become a part of me.

Modern Mitzvot

Also classified with the affected rather than the changed subgroup were
the survivors, not large in number, but commanding our attention for
representing attitudes expressed in diverse ways by survivors of the
various other categories as well, who insisted that their previous traditional religious observances had been "replaced" by other, contemporary,
mostly state-oriented observances. One Mauthausen survivor spoke
heatedly to this point:

> You've got it all wrong. You've got the wrong set of values and
> you've got the wrong set of Jewish mitzvot on your list. That's
> the old list of observances; I keep a new list of observances
> incumbent upon the modern Israeli Jew after the Holocaust.
>   The old simply do not apply in our day and age any longer;
> not after Auschwitz and after the establishment of the state.
> When the Jew comes on aliya [immigration] to Israel there are
> new religious obligations and these obligations are just as binding and
> just as revealed by God and just as pleasing to God—more so,
> I would submit—than putting on tephillin in the morning or
> going to mikveh to be cleansed of menstrual flow. . . .
>   I'm not a Canaanite. I'm a Jew and I observe Jewish
> commandments, but I observe more relevant ones. I observe
> mitzvot more important for the survival of the Jew: I vote in the
> elections and work for a good candidate. One that can do good
> for the country. That's a mitzvah. And when you take it seriously
> it's not all that easy. I pay my taxes. I serve in the army. I'm
> involved with the tzofim [young scouts]. I helped get a kibbutz
> started. I have been among the volunteers teaching new immigrants
> from Eastern and Oriental countries. These are all mitzvot.

And perhaps another mitzvah is my study of today's Torah, that is, modern politics, especially in the Middle East, not only by reading the Prophets for ancient history about Nebuchadnezzar, King of Babylon, or King Sennacherib or the Pharaohs of ancient Egypt but by reading about Anwar el Sadat and Hussein and modern Egypt.

Survivors Affected and Changed

We have previously recorded representative biographical statements and made several observations concerning the *unaffected* portion of the survivor population. The six autobiographical statements above provide reasons survivors offered for having been *affected* in their religious behavior by the Holocaust. We are now able to turn our attention to this latter group of survivors to conduct a breakdown into the various affected (but unchanged) subgroups, make some observations about them, and determine more precisely how they were affected by their Holocaust experiences.

Survivors who were permanently affected with regard to their religious behavior by the Holocaust fall into four possible categories:

1. observant Jews who felt the Holocaust reinforced their religious behavior
2. observant Jews who felt the Holocaust weakened their religious behavior
3. nonobservant Jews who felt the Holocaust reinforced their irreligious behavior
4. nonobservant Jews who felt the Holocaust weakened their irreligious behavior

In the aggregate, survivors who claimed to have been permanently affected in their religious behavior by the Holocaust constitute less than half the entire survivor population, 44 percent. The negligible 4 percent for whom the Holocaust's effect was not lasting has been excluded from this group.

For 65 percent of this segment of the survivor population the Holocaust's impact worked against Jewish religious practices by either weakening the observant Jew's religious behavior or reinforcing the nonobservant Jew's irreligiosity. For the remaining 35 percent, the Holocaust's impact was such that it favorably supported or encouraged the survivor to practice Judaism by either strengthening an observant

Jew's religious behavior or, less frequently, by impelling a nonobservant Jew towards the commandments.

Because of their similarities as well as the large size of their populations, the two groupings that were subdivided earlier—the survivors who remained consistently observant throughout the three stages and their counterparts, survivors who remained consistently nonobservant throughout the three stages (Holocaust survivors of three-steps 1 and 4)—warrant special attention. For example, 70 percent of the consistently nonobservant (NNN) as against 65 percent of the consistently observant (OOO) remained uninfluenced in their religious behavior by the Holocaust. And 26 percent of the former (NNN) as against 28 percent of the latter (OOO) claimed their earlier behavior was reinforced. Finally, 4 percent of the former (NNN) as against 7 percent of the latter (OOO) claimed to have had their observances weakened[8] by their Holocaust experiences. The two populations, therefore, constitute mirror opposites of each other, besides being alike in their respective consistency.

When we divide for comparison the affected segment of the survivor population into two communities, the one observant and the other nonobservant before the Holocaust, we find that *an observant survivor was more than twice as likely to be affected negatively than positively by the Holocaust in the matter of his religious behavior.* For 70 percent of the affected observant community the Holocaust had an adverse influence, and for 30 percent the Holocaust had a beneficial, favorable influence.

The affected nonobservant survivors were, by contrast, far more evenly divided. As to the influence of the Holocaust upon their religious practices, 57 percent maintained that the Holocaust reconfirmed and reinforced their irreligious behavior, while for the remaining 43 percent the Holocaust provided an encouraging influence which favorably disposed them toward Jewish observances.

These last figures are decidedly unforeseen and somewhat astonishing inasmuch as they disclose that a *nonobservant survivor who claimed to have been affected by the Holocaust in his religious behavior was almost as likely to become inclined toward Jewish precepts and prohibitions as disinclined toward them.* One might have expected that the nonobservant survivor would almost without exception find in the Holocaust experience justification for his nonreligious behavior should he ever admit at all to being affected in a religious way.

The affected category is by far the largest, as it includes both survivor subgroups—those who were changed as well as those unchanged in their religious observances by their Holocaust experiences—although all of the latter felt their practices were either reinforced or weakened. Of this category, 70 percent, however deeply affected they may claim to have been, emerged from the impact of the Holocaust unchanged in their religious practices, while the remaining 30 percent of all affected survivors were, in addition, significantly changed by it.

In the section above entitled "Eight Patterns of Observance," *our findings disclosed that 29 percent of all survivors had changed their religious behavior from the time prior to the Holocaust.* Of these, 21 percent were observant Jews who relinquished their religious practices after the Holocaust. And the remaining 8 percent were nonobservant Jews who took upon themselves the regimen of Jewish precepts and prohibitions. When next we consider the various subgroups of survivors who *consciously attribute the changes to their Holocaust experiences* we shall begin to come to grips with one of the seminal motivations for our inquiry, irrespective of abstract tallies, computable measurements, or the size of the populations.

The Reliability of Survivor Testimony

During the course of the gathering of data it soon became evident that when survivors who had *changed* in their religious behavior were being questioned we were on far firmer ground for expecting accurate and reliable responses than when survivors who claim to have been *affected* by the Holocaust were being investigated.

For the most part the affected category is composed of respondents genuinely aware of the Holocaust's influence upon them. But the claim of being affected can also be invoked by the doubtful and embarrassed survivor who, not wishing to appear indifferent to the Holocaust, responds that his previous religious behavior has been strengthened or weakened. He would rather not acknowledge being totally unaffected by the catastrophe seeing pejorative implications, perhaps callousness or insensitivity, in that classification. The affected category may have inadvertently included a number of these. Even the most careful interviewer may encounter considerable difficulty distinguishing between the respondent who realizes his religious behavior has been genuinely affected by the Holocaust and the one who merely asserts as much at the time of the interview and for the sake of the interviewer. We have, therefore, on frequent occasions throughout this study, qualified our affected subgroup with the phrase "claimed to have been affected," or "maintained

they had been affected." The survivors who *were* changed by their
Holocaust experiences also "claim" or "maintain" as much, of course.
But they had to be aware, were they not reasonably precise and well
grounded as to the details of their lives, that their observable religious
behavior could readily call attention to any discrepancies or exaggera-
tions. Moreover, as has been pointed out by Des Pres and others, survivors are possessed of a special inner calling to testify rigorously and
unerringly to the strict facts connected with the Holocaust phenomenon.[9]

Survivors Changed by the Holocaust

In this section the survivors who were changed by the Holocaust—and
not "merely" affected—will be separated and studied. Their personal
reflections and observations are the most pertinent and compelling of
all, and their responses to the Holocaust the most radical and visceral.
Consequently, they are being given attention well out of proportion to
their number. Not that their number is necessarily small or insignificant,
but we are particularly interested in these members of the Saved Remnant both as single individuals and as co-sufferers. In addition to cal-
culating their statistics, and remaining always aware that it would be
presumptuous to attempt to fathom the depth of their experiences, we
shall be carefully attuned to each one's unique story of catastrophe and
transformation and never regard them as mere digits or measurable data.

It has already been shown that *approximately three of every ten
survivors changed their religious behavior from what it had been prior
to the Holocaust.* Our survey also reveals that *71 percent of these survivors attributed those changes to the impact of the catastrophe; 29
percent saw no connection between their change in behavior and their
Holocaust experiences.*

When we divide the changed segment of the survivor community
into those who were observant and those nonobservant before the Holocaust, we find that 74 percent of the former ascribed to the Holocaust
the reasons for their discontinuance of religious practices, and the remaining 26 percent set down grounds other than the Holocaust, such as
marriage, immigration, the army, and education, for discarding their
previous religious behavior.

With regard to nonobservant survivors who became practicing Jews,
64 percent attributed the cause to the Holocaust; the remaining 36 percent became religiously observant from other causes.

It is therefore of considerable significance to learn that *the formerly observant Jew is more likely to attribute the change to the Holocaust than the nonobservant Jew who became observant.*

A closer, more detailed look at these survivor subgroups yields the following information: 56 percent of all formerly observant survivors stated that their religious changes were due *entirely* to their Holocaust experiences; 28 percent advanced the Holocaust as the *main* reason for their changes; and 16 percent offered the Holocaust as but *one of several* crucial explanations for their religious changes.

Most significant is the disclosure that 76 percent of the formerly observant survivors who asserted that their religious changes were entirely or mainly due to the Holocaust proved to have been either ultra observant or highly observant Jews. A moderately observant Jew would be less likely to view the Holocaust as sole justification for relinquishing Jewish practices. In fact, 80 percent of the entire category of survivors who viewed the Holocaust as one of several reasons for their religious change were moderately observant Jews. *Consequently, the more intensely observant, the more frequently the Holocaust is associated with religious change.*

A survivor of many concentration camps, labor camps, and death camps, who had been ultra observant spoke of his religious life before the genocide period:

I used to have a very personal, intimate relationship with God.
I thought everything I did and every move I made God knew and
was right there and He was participating in my life every step
of the way. You see, at that time I felt God took an active interest
in me and knew my thoughts and I'd speak to Him not just
frequently but all the time. We had an ongoing dialogue, or at
least He'd hear me speaking to Him and He'd respond, I then
thought, by allowing good to be happening to me and my family
and bad to my enemies because I had been an observant Jew
and because of the mitzvot I had been doing, and in that way serving
Him. He was always around me individually. I didn't think
whether or not He was also around anyone else. And His job was
to watch how punctiliously and perfectly I had been practicing
each mitzvah and with how much fervor and exactitude and
kavanah [devotion] I'd had and how much my heart was in it.
So I would never miss an opportunity to do a mitzvah and I'd
never do a mitzvah by rote or as a matter of course because
He'd be there just above me, watching and admonishing and

saying, "tut-tut-tut" about those inner bad thoughts I might
have or any unwillingness I might have doing the mitzvot. That's
the kind of person I was, and that's how observant I was then.

Then the Nazis came, and where did He go? God was no
longer near me. Disappeared. And I am no longer the
person I was. I don't do mitzvot that way any longer. It's all gone.

Concerning the nonobservant survivors who became religiously observant because of their Holocaust experience, 77 percent stated that the
Holocaust was *entirely* responsible for their religious changes; 12 percent advanced the Holocaust as the *main* reason and 12 percent offered
the Holocaust as but *one of several* crucial explanations for their
religious changes. And, although the actual size of this group of
survivors is not sufficient for proportional analysis, it appears that as
many formerly nonobservant survivors became highly or ultra observant as became moderately observant. These formerly nonobservant survivors are deserving of further study, but we may tentatively suggest
here that *when the Holocaust inspired a nonobservant survivor in the
direction of Jewish observances he would very likely travel the entire
route to become an assiduously religious Jew.*

We may summarize a portion of our findings thus far by pointing
out that our research upholds the popular notion that generally *when a
European Jew underwent a religious transformation and became either
observant or nonobservant, the Holocaust was more than likely to be
the reason.*

Viewed exclusively from the perspective of survivors who were
changed in their religious behavior by the Holocaust, we find that 74
percent had been observant Jews who relinquished their religious practices. And the remaining 26 percent were nonobservant survivors who
became observant by reason of the Holocaust. It must be acknowledged
that the latter, despite appearances, is more than a moderate figure: *Not
one of ten or one of twenty but one of every four survivors who
changed his or her religious behavior because of the Holocaust was a
nonobservant Jew who became religiously observant.*

One Bergen-Belsen survivor, a teacher in Tel-Aviv, who attributed
his becoming observant to the Holocaust offered a similar observation:

I and a number of survivors I know have become observant and
good religious Jews because of the Holocaust. And it seems
singularly impressive to me, the number of Jewish survivors who
had formerly been nonobservant and because of the Holocaust

became observant. I expected in advance that many observant Jews
would give it all up, and in a way I don't blame them at all. The
number of observant Jews who became nonobservant is important,
of course. But to me, far more striking and important are those
who became observant even if the number is smaller. It is
connected with the idea of polarization and radicalization and of
giving things up. For example, if a concert pianist undergoes a
traumatic experience which may cause him to give up the piano
and become a nonmusician like the average man on the street
it is not terribly astonishing. It is rather expected and happens all
the time. But when the average man on the street undergoes a
traumatic experience and will feel the need to push for a direction
to express his feelings by polarization, and by some extreme act,
he doesn't suddenly decide to devote his life to becoming a
concert pianist. That's not how he becomes polarized. He can go
in many directions and express his feelings in many different ways.

With regard to observant Jews whose lives are entirely caught
up with their observances like the pianist his piano, when
traumatized and polarized they are far more likely than not to
give up the mitzvah system in a 100 percent reversal and complete
flip-flop. But the nonobservant Jew, were he to be traumatized
and polarized, there's no earthly reason to expect that he'd
become observant. He's just as likely to become political: a socialist,
for example, or a humanist or anarchist. Or a vegetarian for that
matter. Or what have you. Or if his particular reaction must be
a religious one, he could even become a "believing Jew" but not
necessarily an observant Jew. Or he can convert out of Judaism
altogether. He could make a religious decision and become a
Christian.

So the Jews who became observant even if fewer in number
tell us far more about Judaism and about Jews than the other
Jews who gave everything up.

Jewish survivors who converted to Christianity—they would hardly
have come to Israel after the war except perhaps years later for mis-
sionary activity—and Christians who became Jews were omitted from
our study, even though a number of the latter more than likely appeared
on our survivor rosters and two who married Jews were in fact contacted inadvertently. The converts were not suitable candidates for
our study, as they were not Jews during Stage 1, before the Holocaust.
Child of the Holocaust by Jack Kuper is a particularly useful book for

sensitive insights into the mental anguish leading a youngster to conversion to Christianity.[10] David P. Boder's *Topical Autobiographies of Displaced People,* a massive sixteen-volume work in manuscript form, is helpful for survivor interviews of converts to Judaism during the time they were displaced persons after the war.[11]

Biographies of Changed Survivors

The profiles and personal accounts that follow are of survivors who changed dramatically in their religious practices. They were selected from numerous other reports for arbitrary reasons, primarily for their subjective appeal. But they do include representative narratives and memoirs of both formerly observant and formerly nonobservant survivors, some of whom had undergone their transformations gradually and others rather suddenly.

The first three are autobiographical accounts of survivors who became observant; the three following are of survivors who became nonobservant:

> Most people who know me probably believe that I became religious and began to keep the commandments because of my marriage after the war. But I think that one of the reasons for my marriage was that I had resolved to become religious and needed the help of a good woman who could guide me.
>
> My wife and I were both inmates of Buchenwald, and my wife's father, on several occasions when I was very weak, actually saved my life. I was a perfect stranger to him and his daughter at the time, and he took care of me. He brought food for me and watched over me like I was his own child. He was very religious and devoted to Jewish tradition, and he was like an angel and he saw to it that I received my share of food when I was very vulnerable and that no one would take anything away from me.
>
> All my family was gone. His wife and other children were also killed. All he had left was one daughter, and he acted like a father to me until the day he died about two weeks before we were liberated.
>
> One day, with his encouragement, I started to become religious and I found that God was near to me because of this man's piety and goodness. He also taught me about God, that God had a purpose in what was going on around us in the camp which we could not comprehend, but we should all become good practicing Jews. He never pressed me or urged me to change

but I came to him one day and said I wanted to be observant like
he is. Then he proceeded to teach me everything I know. He'd
talk to me for long periods of time whenever he was able, even
sometimes at considerable risk, so I would know and not remain
an ignorant Jew, an *am haaretz*.

I don't want to go into everything, but he sacrificed his life
for mine, actually and literally, he gave his life for mine. When
I married the daughter—it was not exactly arranged but it was
settled quickly—I became religious firstly because of my
father-in-law's help in teaching me what a Jew must do and by
his exemplary life, the life of a pure and holy man, one of the
thirty-six great righteous men on earth—everyone who knew
him realized this.

The second reason is that everything that happened to me
and other Jews in the camps showed me God's purposes and that
He intends for us to follow His teachings.

———◆———

You must remember what I went through and what I saw:
monstrous things with my own eyes in the camps and out, infants
being dashed to death and other young people starved. And yet
I escaped and lived. I had to interpret that fact for myself.

Others say, How could you be religious and keep the
commandments after what God did to you and all the Jews and
how He let the Nazis murder us like flies?

I can only speak for myself and try to understand what
happened to me personally. Time and time again I survived the
appel, the selection. I'd pray to God and He would hear me.
And I made vows that if I would survive this selection I'd eat only
kasher after I was set free. And when the next came I'd say if
I will survive this selection I will keep the Sabbath 100 percent.
And if I'd fool them into thinking me healthy and strong when
I was weak and nearly dropping, and should have been selected
for death, I'd vow to do more, be a still better, more observant, Jew.

I never went back on my word. And in this way I became
a religious Jew, keeping the commandments and living a Jewish
life. And my wife, when she was alive, would even go to mikveh
and preserve the purity of family life.

During the long death march, when so many others fell
aside, and I kept promising so many vows to God, I had resolved
to be a very pious Jew. And I am that today, as you can see.

———◆———

I was not observant before the Holocaust and I was not observant after the Holocaust, but I am observant today because of the Holocaust. And because of my nine-year-old son.

My own home, as I was growing up, was not observant. If anything, it was anti-Jewish primarily due to the influence of my father who was an atheist and a strong opponent of religion generally. He was a good socialist and very politically motivated. He was a very important official. A lot of good it did him!

If today I do observe these few commandments [fasting and attending synagogue on the Day of Atonement, observing Hanukkah and the Passover seder, lighting Sabbath candles and attending services on certain holidays], I do so in order that my son will be exposed to the traditions and will experience the feelings which I was deprived of when I was a child growing up in Europe, feelings of deprivation which I began to understand during the Holocaust years and which surfaced in a substantial way, and with considerable intensity, when my own son came along and I had to consider what I was going to do for him to help him come to appreciate his Jewishness. I didn't want him deprived like I was by my parents. Now that I am responsible for a child's upbringing, the Holocaust has especially obligated me to teach Judaism and to set an example for him, because naturally there is a considerable difference between teaching commandments and living them.

The strange part is that during the Holocaust in the camp Lisowice, then in Poland, all believing and practicing Jews appeared ridiculous to me in the light of what was going on all around us. And yet I envied them. And now it is precisely because of the Holocaust, and because of them, that I make the special effort to have my son brought up experiencing tradition.

◆

It happened very gradually to me but not imperceptibly. In fact I was very conscious all the while and simultaneously conscience-stricken and guilt-ridden. At the time there was a sense of liberation and freedom from compulsion and duties. But it came about very slowly.

Of course, hiding out in the fields, in the forests, on farms, does not lend itself to keeping religious practices in the first place—but that's not the reason I gave up all Jewish ordinances, with no thought to resume. I gave up permanently. I was fifteen in 1941, and was sent by my mother to run away to save myself.

And my mother also made it clear that I would have to pretend not to be Jewish and learn never to give myself away. That is why I cursed the evidence on my flesh and feared to be seen without trousers or relieving myself. And for a while I despised my origins out of fear.

Fortunately my Polish was good and I did not look particularly Jewish. I was fairer even then than I am now. So I was lucky and survived, although I was in danger every day and was on the verge of being caught several times. I was very small for my age and looked much younger, and sometimes people would pity me and have sympathy for me for a short while, although they may have believed it endangered them. Many times I wished I was not Jewish, especially when I saw other Jews hunted like animals in the forest. I'd keep my distance from them so as not to be identified with them. I was younger and I challenged God to justify His having created Jews and at times believed we were cursed and punished for what we did killing Christ. And the German soldiers looked like Greek gods to me when I was so little.

Still, while I was giving up everything, I could never bring myself to eat pork even though I went hungry often. I knew that after the war, whatever else I might do, I'd never be a religious Jew again.

------◆------

You would never believe it from seeing me now but in the camps I was the most religious of all—apart from the Hasidim, of course. But that didn't last long. I was as observant as one could be in the camps. I was the one to tell others when the time had come to celebrate Passover or Tabernacles or Rosh Hashana. And I fasted in the camps, mind you, not only on Yom Kippur but, in the beginning at least, on Tisha b'Av and Asarah b'Teveth. And I helped smuggle in matzah and conducted a little seder at great risk to my life.

All right, others did this too, but I was frum, pious. And I encouraged others to be observant. It may have also been my own form of defiance, a response and reaction to my captors. I was even more religious in the camps than previously in that before I went my own way with the other religious Jews of my town, not trying to influence others to be religious. But in the camps I was zealous for being a good Jew and I inspired others to do what they could and be as religious and keep as much as they could.

I sometimes even tempted fate. I would stand right before a

guard or a trustee and I'd daven [pray] and all the other Jews
around would see me and witness it, seeing my act of defiance.
But of course I'd look the other way and pretend I was occupied
with something else whenever the guard would peer around
towards me.

Then I gave it all up. Everything. Everything disappeared
at once: the rituals, the symbols, the celebrations. I reversed
myself and stopped practicing Judaism altogether when we were
liberated. At first I was defiant against the Nazis and I said my
prayers and practiced faithfully and scrupulously in the camps.
Then afterwards I was defiant against God and gave up everything
just as scrupulously and defiantly and with finality. I don't even
go to the synagogue on the High Holy Days and I don't fast
on the Day of Atonement. It is not an exaggeration to say I
hardly know when they arrive.

I believe I really lost it all in the camps, but I kept it up
because it was my nature, very stubborn, and it was my way of
getting even, of striking back at the Nazis and their henchmen. And
maybe it was also my way of preserving my sanity. But today
because, because who knows why? . . . the camps, the destruction
changed everything.

———◆———

I was in Auschwitz for two years and fully expected that if
and when I'd be free I would resume being the kind of Jew I had
been prior to the war. Not that I gave it much thought at any
time during those years. That's not what I had on my mind. What
I did think about, what kept me going, were dreams of what
life could be, its pleasures: food, home, women, a bed, warmth,
and cleanliness. These things and not religion kept me going. I
didn't feel the need to practice Judaism, nor to daven the traditional
prayers. But it never occurred to me during those years that I
wouldn't pick up where I left off and be a religious Jew again
after liberation. Not a fanatic Jew. I never was that. But in some
ways religious at least.

After liberation I spent several months in the camps of the
allies and I had the opportunity to attend services and to eat
kasher food and practice my religion again. I even became friendly
with an American rabbi who was an army chaplain.

At first, for reasons I didn't understand, I couldn't even bring
myself to the synagogue. It just seemed such a fraud . . . I
knew services were being conducted and I could go if I wanted

to but I just couldn't bring myself to it. After some weeks I finally went. And I admit the old rabbi said some very wise things about how and why we must be observant and keep the Torah now more than ever because of the great loss we all sustained. And I agreed in principle but I couldn't do it in practice. I could not go to services again. It was no longer in me. And I just don't keep anything any more. After everything that happened to the Jews it seems pointless and even dishonest and I can't be religious ever again.

The Camp Factor

Although undoubtedly a greater proportion of Jews who were never camp internees survived the war, one must not be misled into assuming that they were in every case better off or spent more tolerable years than their counterparts in concentration camps. In fiction, Jerzy Kosinski's *The Painted Bird* [12] dispels in grotesque imagery and graphic detail such a misapprehension. It also must not be thought that placement in private industry could avert death or delay it. Working conditions were those of the maximum exploitation of slave labor, which brought about a higher death rate than even the camps themselves. For example, the manpower turnover in the I. G. Farben Bunawerke artificial rubber plant at Monowitz near Auschwitz was 300 percent yearly!

By any index or calculation, whether within the camps or outside, very few Jews withstood and outlasted Hitler's Europe. Nevertheless, it can be said that those Jews who were concealed by non-Jews through the war years; those who masqueraded and successfully passed themselves off as Christians; those who fought with partisan bands in the forests; and others in various circumstances who eluded detection and capture were able to increase their chances of survival. Perhaps, too, they witnessed fewer atrocities and suffered fewer deprivations. And for the most part, as a collective, if not from individual to individual, they endured the period in less brutal and ravaged conditions.

Inasmuch as the privations and hardships were somewhat less odious for these survivors, should we therefore expect a smaller percentage of them to change their religious behavior and religious faith? And should we expect fewer changes of them? One theory connects the intensity of oppression with the likelihood of religious change. Another theory sees oppression as a catalyst for igniting religious faith and religious behavior.

Proving a corrective to both these theories, our survey fails to dis-

close any appreciable differences in religious behavior and attitudes between concentration camp survivors and other survivors. Nor have we
discerned any connection between the intensity of the Holocaust ordeal
and religious change. A concentration camp survivor of particularly
brutal conditions was no more likely to give up or assume religious behavior or faith than other victims of the Holocaust.

The survivors' own unmatched accounts of daring and endurance
are studded with expressions such as "what happened in the camps,"
"what we went through in the camps," "during the time of the camps,"
and "when I was a katzetnik," a slang designation for a prisoner in a
Nazi death camp. From them one rarely hears "during the Holocaust,"
or "what I experienced in the Holocaust." The exception is the expression "during the war," but even these words are heard less frequently.
One may infer from these phrases that the camp is the significant
variable. And it is quite true, of course, that the world of the death
camp was another world entirely, one handed over to demons. Survivors
themselves often say "it was not of this world."

The train arrived on the new Planet and stopped. The doors
were shoved apart and humanity drained out of the cattle trucks
on to the vast platform.

Night was all around, swathing the destination in black. No
screams here, no speech. The Site of Silence. Soundlessness was all
around, engulfing the outflow of humanity from the cattle trucks.
The different laws governing here were instantly tangible; the air
was different; the platform lights here shed a different glow.
Night here had an essence all its own. Night here was at the beck
and call of an omnipotent sovereign, a sovereign supreme over
the Planet. Night muffled, stealing inaudibly on tiptoes to envelop
you, inaudibly, so as to keep from trespassing upon the terrifying
silence reigning supreme.

No speech, here. Demons but glancing at you and you are
converted; instantly made to feel you are no longer you, but an
all-of-you, totally transmuted into a focus of glowing intent;
intent upon the bidding of the eye glancing at you.

[He] stood among his people, and saw the captive denizens
of the Planet: all one—round-headed, hairless. Livid, rounded
skulls; and the garb—pants, shirt, and the little cap perched on
the skull-tip—all one, light-coloured and striped.

The Stripees were just as soundless—like fish. Swimming,
too, across the platform like fish in an aquarium—swift, nimble,
and as soundless. Not at a walk, but darting, back and forth.

The Demons standing apart, their glances activating the little fish to dart, to flutter, soundlessly.

Stripees took to arraying the importees in rows, and the newcomers instantly obeyed, just as voicelessly. An execution swift and silent, until, from among the Demons, one approached, to move his finger right then left—a finger-dialect the Stripees were completely at home with. In a darting race they snatched at the newcomers, classifying them, right, left, nimble and voiceless.

The newcomers recalled having witnessed something similar in the previous world. . . . That, however, had been in the human world, where life had gone on, with people around to scream and weep and tear at their hair. But what was the connection with this world of the Hereafter? With this Afterlife Planet? What was going on here? Life was nothing but a dream here—or, rather, death was.

The mute ritual now over: of the humanity riding from the other world, about fifty per cent had suffocated in the cattle trucks; of the remaining percentage, forty were stood to the left, ten to the right.[13]

If the world of the concentration camp is indeed the pivotal factor and the singularly grotesque variable, should we not have expected to find that the effects of the camp upon former "stripees" were appreciably different from the Holocaust's effects upon those who were never inmates? It has already been acknowledged that certain placements were as inhuman as some camps. But should we not nevertheless find in the aggregate evidence that the impact of the various camps was by and large more severe upon the religious faith and religious behavior of inmates? The answer, apparently, is that we should not.

Tables 6 and 7 are instructive for the differences in religious change between concentration camp survivors and those who survived the war in places other than in the camps. The table concerning religious faith shows that the negligible distinctions between former camp inmates and other survivors that do appear are countervailed elsewhere down the column. And precisely the same percentage (47 percent) of each survivor population reports no changes in their religious faith as a consequence of the Holocaust.

Table 7, dealing with religious behavior, reveals that no more than a percentage point or two separates the survivor groupings throughout the schedule, so well matched are they.

The findings that concentration camp survivors were somewhat (7

T A B L E 6. Changes in Religious Behavior, Concentration Camp Survivors and Others

RELIGIOUS BEHAVIOR	CONCENTRATION CAMP SURVIVORS	NON–CONCENTRATION CAMP SURVIVORS
No changes due to Holocaust	51%	58%
Changed by Holocaust		
Became observant due to Holocaust	6	4
Became nonobservant due to Holocaust	14	12
Temporarily changed due to Holocaust	4	4
(o-n-o 2%)		
(n-o-n 2%)		(o-n-o 4%)
Affected by Holocaust		
Holocaust reinforced observances	8	6
Holocaust reinforced nonobservances	9	8
Holocaust weakened observances	6	4
Holocaust weakened nonobservances	2	4
	100%	100%
	(N 452)	(N 192)

Note: 64 survivors chose not to respond.

percent) more inclined to record changes in their religious behavior may simply be understood as an aspect of the East–West factor discussed below: A higher percentage of East Europeans were camp inmates. And East European Jews were more inconstant and unsettled, the more subject to change in all matters.

Resumption of Religious Behavior

Not to be overlooked, however, is another theory, which presented itself during the course of interviews with those survivors who spoke of changes in their religious behavior. It is that whenever religious behavior was discontinued during the Holocaust, never to be resumed, while *at the same time* faith remained intact, overstated and exaggerated explanations for the phenomenon should not be sought. Once religious behavior is interrupted for a relatively lengthy period and *for whatever*

TABLE 7. Changes in Religious Faith, Concentration Camp Survivors and Others

Religious Faith	Concentration Camp Survivors	Non–Concentration Camp Survivors
No changes due to Holocaust	47%	47%
Changed by Holocaust		
Gained faith in God due to Holocaust	4	6
Lost faith in God due to Holocaust	14	18
Affected by Holocaust		
Faith strengthened	13	8
Faith weakened *	18	18
Reinforced nonfaith	3	3
	99%	100%
	(N 442)	(N 228)

Note: 38 Survivors chose not to respond.
* Includes Survivors whose faith changed from belief in a personal God to belief in an impersonal God and those whose faith was temporarily affected by the Holocaust but never fully returned to its previous certainty.

reason, its recommencement is almost always a problematic, even formidable, undertaking.

The determinant factor, therefore, may be not so much the grinding dehumanization of the camps as the comparatively trivial and frivolous difficulty of recovering and reviving one's past religious patterns of behavior once brought to a halt: The rigorous routine has been fractured; the regularity of the habit has been not so much discredited as discon-

TABLE 8. Religious Behavior Before the Holocaust and the Concentration Camp Experience

	Non–Concentration Camp Survivors	Concentration Camp Survivors
Observant (55%)	28%	72%
Moderately observant	24	76
Highly observant	37	63
Ultra observant	26	74
Nonobservant (45%)	32	68

nected. Faith may be carried on whether in the camps or exteriorly; religious practices were far less feasible for inmates than for others during the Holocaust years. A Kfar Saba survivor of Treblinka who operates a modest restaurant made the following observation:

> My religious beliefs didn't change during the war in spite of the experiences I had in the camps. In fact I think most Jews stayed as religious as always in their hearts and minds. But in Treblinka, where I was brought from Warsaw, there was no possibility to continue observing the mitzvot, none whatever, except perhaps on rare occasions to be reminded of a holiday and some synagogue melodies. I loved Kol Nidre and sang it often during the year, and it helped me remember how it was at home, and in the synagogue, with cantor and rabbi, just reminiscences to hold on to and to help pass the time and to escape from the present horrors back into the past. That, yes.
>
> In our hearts we were good faithful Jews in the camps— and after as well. But once you get out of the habit of doing the commandments: tephillin, daily prayers, blessings over food and drink, attending synagogue, once you stop it all, it is very hard to begin again. I tried. It feels so false, so artificial, and I can't. It's not so much the camps and the influence of the camps but the long period of the camps and the war when the opportunity was not there to do the usual natural everyday things; it's hard to resume afterwards and to start again.

Education and Observance, East and West

In Chapter 1 it was pointed out that four-fifths of the survivors in our study population were of East European origin. And it is common knowledge that Western Jews were more likely to have been "irreligious" than Eastern Jews before the Holocaust. Only 13 percent of all pre-Holocaust observant Jews of our sampling were of Western origin, whereas twice as many, 27 percent, who were nonobservant before the Holocaust came from Western countries.

Also not unforeseen are differences in the educational attainments, both secular and religious, as between West and East European survivors surveyed. West European Jews were generally better educated secularly than East European Jews; the latter far better educated religiously than their Western coreligionists. For example, 15 percent of all

West European Jews received only the minimal elementary school education (or less), whereas more than twice as many East European Jews, 37 percent, were similarly minimally educated. Further, 55 percent of all West European Jews achieved an equivalency to a high school diploma, as compared to 41 percent among East European Jews. And while 30 percent of all West European Jews held academic degrees above high school, the percentage is only 22 percent for East European survivors.

In Jewish education, however, the figures are for the most part reversed. A full 47 percent of all Western survivors recorded that they had no Jewish education whatsoever—four-fifths of these were survivors who were nonobservant before the Holocaust—but 26 percent of all East European Holocaust survivors recorded that they had failed to receive even an elementary-level Jewish education.

The European Heder was an elementary school providing a religious education for Jewish youngsters. Of East European Jewish Holocaust survivors, 51 percent completed Heder or its equivalent, as compared to 36 percent among West European survivors.

The Yeshiva was a more advanced Jewish educational institution; and beyond the Yeshiva, the Metivta (or the Yeshiva which was a Metivta), prepared prospective rabbis with highly intensified Talmudic educations. Among East European survivors 20 percent indicated that they had received a Yeshiva education, and 3 percent went beyond to the Metivta; 12 percent of the survivors of the Western European Jewish community were Yeshiva-trained, and 5 percent indicated that they had gone beyond to the Metivta. The latter figure may at first appear unusually high, but in the more educationally minded and affluent West an observant Jewish family would have been more likely to encourage and have the means to enable a willing candidate to pursue higher Jewish education—perhaps even leading to ordination as rabbi and perhaps a career in the rabbinate—than a similar Jewish family in Eastern Europe.

Contrary to most intuitive conjectures, *East European survivors were far more likely to change their religious behavior than Western survivors. East European observant survivors relinquished their Jewish practices after the Holocaust nearly three times as often as Western observant.* And proving as volatile within the nonobservant Jewish community, East European survivors became observant after the Holocaust at almost the same high rate, more than twice that of their Western counterparts. Perhaps it is the differences in educational levels that account for the differing stability in religious behavior.

T A B L E 9 . Educational Levels and Effect of Holocaust on Observance

	No Ans.	Completed No More Than		Completed Academic
		Elementary School or Equivalent	High School or Equivalent	Degree Above High School
Observant survivors who remained observant	1%	51%	40%	8%
Observant survivors who became nonobservant	3	47	34	16

	No Ans.	No Jewish Education Whatever	Completed Heder	Completed Yeshiva	Completed Metivta
Observant survivors who remained observant	2%	6%	57%	32%	3%
Observant survivors who became nonobservant	16	26	37	16	4

The importance of the educational factor for religious change is underscored when consistently observant survivors are contrasted educationally with survivors who gave up their observances after the Holocaust. When these two subgroups are compared in the matter of secular non-Jewish education, no striking contrasts are discernible except that survivors who became nonobservant were slightly better educated (see Table 9).

In the matter of Jewish education, however, the differences are striking. The survivors who remained observant had received a far better Jewish education (see Table 9).

Significantly, the pre-Holocaust observant survivors who had no Jewish religious education whatever were more than four times likely to become nonobservant as to remain observant. And should the very high figure of 16 percent No Answer in the former group be properly included, that ratio undoubtedly would be still further increased. Except for the small percentage of survivors who completed Metivta the contrast remains consistent through all Jewish educational levels. In short, *among survivors, there is a definite correlation between Jewish education and the retention of religious behavior.*

The ironies which abound are apparent. On the one hand we have shown that Jewish upbringing and education seem to lead to the greater likelihood of the retention of religious behavior. The East European received a better Jewish education than his Western cousins and co-religionists. Nevertheless, the East Europeans were more likely to abandon their religious practices and, assuredly, although the matter is best explored elsewhere, the least devout, least religiously educated among them changed the most.

The Jewish Bargain

Religious change is multidimensional and multidirectional: It denotes finding as well as losing faith, the strengthening and weakening of beliefs, becoming observant and the discontinuance of religious behavior. Returning to previously held convictions, overcoming their provisional or partial estrangement as well as the immutable abandonment of belief and practices, all fall within its scope, as these chapters disclose.

Survivors for whom the camps were seen as the place not only of physical annihilation but also of the death of spirituality are attended to in this study. Similarly, considerable stress has been laid upon the numbers who cite the camps as the instance of their faith and the motivation for their religious practices. But invariably Jews do not speak of their "spiritual birth" in the camps as certain Christians do, as is seen in Alexander Solzhenitsyn's record of the Soviet penal system. There are no Jewish survivor accounts corresponding to what Solzhenitsyn recalls when he was released from his Gulag slave labor camp in 1953: "Only on the threshold of the guardhouse do you begin to feel that what you are leaving behind you is both your prison and your homeland. This was your spiritual birthplace, and a secret part of your soul will remain here forever, while your feet trudge on into the dumb and unwelcoming expanse of *freedom*." [14]

No equivalent stab of regret pierces the Jewish heart upon liberation from parallel slave labor camps—and certainly not from the death camps. Not a single Jew of our study, even among those who "became religious in the camps," looks back longingly upon that period or feels that the freedom on the other side of the furcated barbed wire swastikas and inbent swan-neck cement poles was or is, by contrast, a spiritual wasteland. The interned Jews accurately saw themselves as caught like one of many disease-carrying insects in a network of tightly woven Nazi spider webs spun to isolate and devour the contagion. And in the minds of former inmates then as now, that area there, beyond the entanglement, constituted real, tangible, hallowed grounds, hardly "un-welcoming," for the hope it offered them of reunification with loved ones and for the beckoning of a different sort of homeland.

Few survivors felt that if the voice of God is to be heard at all it would be heard through the bitter struggle of a painfully tormenting existence. There has been no tendency to turn the celebrated Browning poem upside down and declare that because all's wrong with the world God's in His heaven, that only out of the depths can man call upon the Lord. Des Pres reminds us that the belief in salvation through pain is Christian, not Jewish.[15]

The few became religious in the camps with the intention of carrying their newly discovered faith forward with them into freedom. One Bnei Brak resident, a former Belzec inmate, observed that "God has chosen a way to instruct and discipline us to believe in Him and to keep the mitzvot afterwards, if we should live through the horror."

The intensity of their religious fervor may have been ignited there. And there is no denial that, as Des Pres suggests, "the ordeal of survival" can be "at least for some, an experience of growth and purification,"[16] but for them the camps were nevertheless totally and unredeemingly evil. Instead, Jewish survivors who became observant as a direct consequence of their camp experiences tend to speak of the bargain with God which they made when they were within the camps and to characterize their bargain as a kind of spiritual investment: "God, I pleaded, save me. Let me outlive all of this and I promise I will now become a good Jew. I will give up the sinful behavior of my past and become also a good person. I will serve You and keep Your mitzvot and You will not be sorry You let me live. Save me." Another survivor struck his bargain in these words: "God, if You let me live and see my loved ones and family again, I will never hurt them, or any other human being. And I will become a good Jew and do all the things expected of a good Jew."

These bargains with God, despite the admonition of the Mishnah not to "serve the Master for the sake of reward,"[17] were psychologically life-preserving and pragmatically this-worldly, survival-oriented thinking. They are, moreover, attitudes well within the Jewish value system. Judaism is based upon the concept of a covenantal agreement (brit) entered into by the people Israel and their God in which both parties are expected to abide by certain expressed and implied stipulations as recorded in the Torah-contract. The appropriateness of a Jew's negotiation with his Maker arises from such a covenantal relationship.

THREE

The Faith of Holocaust Survivors

THE HOLOCAUST WAS NOT one single fierce apocalyptic blaze, a sudden leaping, gutting storm of thermal annihilation. It was rather a prolonged, smoldering, day-after-day conflagration consigning six million to charred oblivion and tens of thousands of near-victims, snatched from the flames of the inferno, to a seething internal devastation, a combustion of the psyche.

What went on in the mind and heart of the Jew through the length and depth of his drawn-out desolation? Did men of faith lose their faith? Did men of no faith hear the voice of God out of the Holocaust?

Questions touching upon faith and belief in the Holocaust years are answerable in ways similar questions about religious practices are not. It is true that an indeterminate number of survivors were able to keep certain religious observances throughout the Holocaust years. One survivor interviewed claims never to have missed putting on tephillin in the various labor concentration camps in which he was confined. Many another recited daily and holiday prayers throughout the duration of the Nazi carnage. Some never neglected a day of prayer, even to their last moments in the death camps. Still others observed the seder and the festivals in some surreptitious and innovative manner wherever circumstances found them. A Hasid now living in B'nai Brak worked as a painter of the crematoria at Auschwitz for nearly thirteen months and "witnessed virtually every day the destruction of upwards of 12,000 Jews—men, women, and children. In all that time I never once went without wearing my prayer shawl. It was always with me, on my person. In Birkenau, at Auschwitz the death camp, I always hoped that

God would save me from the cannibals. I remained optimistic throughout and believed that I'd be freed."

For the overwhelming majority there was little or no opportunity
for the performance of mitzvot during the Holocaust years. And our
survey was intentionally designed to inquire of the survivors' Jewish
religious behavior "prior to the Holocaust," "subsequent to the Holocaust," and "today"—disregarding the Holocaust years themselves except insofar as the survivor was able to assert or deny that his or her
subsequent religious changes were attributable to the Holocaust. Survivors were not asked to record the observances kept during the genocide
period.

Unlike religious observances, the expressions of faith and belief are
inward; they are not dependent upon tangible, hence conspicuous, concrete action. Belief as well as disbelief were equally credible and feasible
espousals within the camps, the forests, the haylofts, and other hiding
places. It is always possible and reasonable to "remain a believing Jew in
one's heart" regardless of circumstances. It was not necessary, therefore,
to refrain from inquiries regarding religious ideas held during the Holocaust years, or to inquire how these ideas were influenced by the survivors' Holocaust experience. And survivors at given moments recall
with remarkable accuracy and vividness what went on in their minds
and hearts during their ordeal.

The words "belief" and "faith" are almost always used interchange-
ably in this study. At certain times, however, it is clear from the context
that there are important distinctions between them. In those few instances the term "faith" refers to opinions concerning God's very existence. "I have faith in God" means "it is my view that God exists."
"Belief" refers to God's nature, whether He is conceived as a Person, as
in Martin Buber's Eternal Thou, or as an impersonal Force in the universe. Among the better-known contemporary belief conceptions are
Paul Tillich's Ground of Being and Mordechai Kaplan's Power which
makes for salvation. The Principle of Concretion, Emergent Energy,
Process, Central Monad or Spirit, Substance, the Ideal Fulfillment of
the Moral Enterprise, Cosmic Consciousness, and Maimonides's Un-
moved Mover, Active Intellect are all formulations and definitions of a
God who is an impersonal Force to whom man does not relate in the
same way as to a Person. These usages and definitions constitute beliefs
in God's nature and essence. Faith refers to existence; belief to essence.

In this chapter dealing with faith and belief, in addition to the time
periods or stages "before the Holocaust," "after the Holocaust," and
"today," which record the survivor's progression in the practice of

	SHORTLY BEFORE THE HOLOCAUST	DURING THE HOLOCAUST	SHORTLY AFTER THE HOLOCAUST	TODAY	NEVER
The belief in God who is involved in your daily life					
An impersonal God					
Tragedies like the Holocaust are the will of God *					
The belief in the coming of the Messiah *					
That the Jews are the chosen people *					
That the torah is the word of God *					
That Judaism is a true religion *					
That Judaism is the only true religion *					

* Discussed in Chapter 4, "The Meaning of the Holocaust," and Table 10, p. 127.

religious observances, the time period "during the Holocaust" was introduced to register changes in religious creed and religious ideas during this period. Survivors were asked to record in the accompanying table whether they subscribed at any or all times during these four stages to eight Jewish religious beliefs.

Religious Change During the Holocaust

One of the primary objectives of this work is to determine the effect of the Holocaust upon the faith and beliefs of its Jewish victims during the very time they were undergoing the suffering at the hands of the Nazis three decades ago. The intention is to focus upon religious change as it was being experienced.

One may or may not be conscious of undergoing religious change at the given point of time in which it is occurring, but reconstructions and efforts at recollection subsequent to the fact of the transformation have their own advantages: greater detachment, objectivity, and perspective as well as insight into its long-range impact. Moreover, those traumatic years to most survivors appear still in their psyches as but yesterday, hardly decades ago, as William Niederland has shown.

Should religious change ever be expected in response to suffering? Is suffering discounted by the devout before it occurs? Or does religion itself provide overarching meaning to it—as Max Weber's "Theology of Suffering" suggests—transforming the experience of suffering into a vehicle of redemption rather than a justification for revolution. Does this view perhaps explain to some extent the relative quiescence of a certain number of believing Jews heading for the ovens?

Our study does not provide easy answers to these complexities. Even our most pointed question concerning the number of survivors who claim to have been changed religiously during the time of the Holocaust is complicated by those who, while admitting to a change in their beliefs due to the Holocaust, refuse to pinpoint a specific time or place as the occasion for change. These Holocaust survivors maintain that their beliefs underwent a process of change which began sometime during the actual years of the Holocaust and continued through the following years and beyond. And they find it difficult and perhaps pointless to differentiate between the stages "during the Holocaust" and "after the Holocaust." Most others, however, encounter no such difficulty in designating the approximate time their religious change took place.

The phrase "during the Holocaust" refers to the stage or period covering all or part of the war years, often referred to in this work as the genocide period. It does not necessarily imply that the modifications in religious faith came about "because of the concentration camp experience" or "due to the Holocaust." Farther on in this chapter we will turn our attention to the study of the survivors who specifically and consciously attribute the changes in their religious faith and beliefs to the Holocaust or to the concentration camp experience exclusively.

Nevertheless it is noteworthy that our survey statistically substantiates the intuitive reasoning that *the most pronounced changes in religious belief occurred "during the Holocaust" as compared with "immediately after the Holocaust" or even during the stage we have referred to as "today,"* which covers the effects of nearly a quarter of a century of living in the land of Israel.

When Belief in God Changed

Of all survivors, 21 percent recorded changes in their religious faith in the period "during the Holocaust" by either ceasing to believe or by beginning to believe in God, however defined; or by belief changes between a personal and an impersonal conception of God. Another 8 percent recorded these changes for the period "immediately after the Holocaust." In all, then, and without attributing to the Holocaust itself sole accountability for the development, 29 percent of all survivors reported changes in their fundamental beliefs relative to God at some point from the beginning through the termination of the war years. Another 11 percent, the overwhelming majority of whom were then as now living in Israel, claimed to have changed their beliefs about God sometime after the war through the present as reflected in the period we have termed "today." All told, 40 percent of all survivors modified their faith since before the Holocaust years.

It is noteworthy how many Holocaust survivors changed their religious beliefs over the years from Europe through the period of the Holocaust up to the present in Israel. Later on we shall consider the number of survivors who lost as against those who gained faith because of the Holocaust. But here our attention is drawn to the fact that *of all survivors whose beliefs concerning God were modified over the years, 70 percent locate the point of reference within the Holocaust period* (53 percent "during the Holocaust"; 17 percent "immediately after the Holocaust").

One of many survivors understanding the complexities inherent in questions of faith described himself, in a comment, as follows:

> It is extremely difficult for me to answer the questions as to my belief in God during the many times I faced death. It is even difficult for me to understand my faith before the Holocaust, but the most accurate thing I can say is that I did not believe in a personal God. I believed instead in a God who had no relationship with me or with mankind. We kept our distance. But I did believe in a kind of God idea before the Holocaust. That is how I filled in my answer.
>
> During the Holocaust, on the other hand, there were many times I strongly believed in a personal, even caring and concerned God who was conscious of my anguish and my whereabouts. And I tried to get through to Him, calling out to Him to help me. At other times I was a devout atheist. . . .
>
> But since in the camps I more frequently believed than disbelieved, I chose for my answer that I believed.
>
> In contrast to previous times, today the question is not as difficult for me to answer. It is not as though the dilemma has been thoroughly resolved. But for the sake of the truth and accuracy of this poll, I simply have to say that today I am an atheist and that is

how I answered the question. But you must understand that for me, throughout my entire life, the question of my belief in God has never been easy to answer.

Questions pertaining to religious faith are by their very nature more difficult to answer than questions relating to practice. This is true particularly in connection with sustained traumas like the period of the Holocaust. It is rather clear, for example, that during the Holocaust years a considerable number of survivors at various times believed emphatically in a personal God, and at other times, perhaps the very next moment, disbelieved quite as emphatically. One's mind often reflects the upheaval of one's surroundings. The very same individual may have simultaneously harbored belief and disbelief in equal measure or may have "at times not believed."

Moreover, even in normal circumstances two different individuals may profess similar beliefs regarding the nature of God, and one may consider himself a nonbeliever, the other a believer. Conversely, two individuals may refer to themselves as believers or nonbelievers and yet hold entirely disparate ideas relative to God's nature and existence, and each may disagree with the other's self-appraisal. Faith, by its very subjective character, is extremely complex and proves to be a difficult proposition to survey. Nevertheless, despite its complexities, only 5 percent of all Holocaust survivors surveyed chose not to respond to the questions concerning their beliefs about God.

Belief in God Before the Holocaust

Before the Holocaust period began, 55 percent of all survivors believed in "a personal God who is involved in man's daily life"; 14 percent more believed in God as a distant, impersonal God not directly concerned with man's activities. For these survivors, God was a power or a natural Force in the universe (koach elyon), removed and remote from man. In all, then, *69 percent of the survivors surveyed claimed to have believed in God before the Holocaust.*

Even should our reasoning of a previous chapter be correct in holding that the entire European Jewish community before the Holocaust, and the six million victims, were each collectives "more religious" than the survivor community, the finding that only slightly more than two-thirds believed in God is not nearly in conformity with the higher figure one might have expected from predominantly East European–raised Jews. Conceivably 75 percent, or even 80 percent and higher, might have more likely been anticipated. Still, our 14 percent differential between believing Jews and observant Jews is not unreasonable or unexpected.

Accordingly, from our findings here and from our findings of the previous chapter, European Jewry before the Holocaust may be regarded as a religiously observant (55 percent keeping at least six religious practices) but not an especially or intensely God-believing collective.

Twenty-six percent of the survivors surveyed classified themselves as nonbelievers before the Holocaust. These were predominantly individuals who referred to themselves as atheists; apparently, agnostics also classified themselves as not believing in God. This may provide a partial explanation for the nearly 3 percent of survivors who were observant before the Holocaust and registered as nonbelievers. But inasmuch as this latter group includes European Jews who were observant for family reasons (e.g., for the sake of the children, for the stability of a marriage with an observant spouse) and others who practiced Judaism for cultural reasons before the Holocaust, 3 percent may properly be regarded as an extremely small percentage of observant survivors claiming not to have believed in God prior to the Holocaust.

One would, of course, have expected to find a far larger percentage of survivors who believed in God among nonpracticing Jews than nonbelievers among observant Jews. Many Jews can readily reconcile their faith in God with their lack of Jewish observances, but it requires a considerable effort at explanation and justification for a practicing Jew to deny belief in God.

In all, 82 percent of the survivors who were observant before the Holocaust expressed belief in a personal God who is involved in the life of man. And 13 percent affirmed belief in an impersonal God. The same burden of justification obtains for the latter: to justify or at least to provide explanation for their religious practices in view of their religious beliefs.

The Jewish survivor who believes in God generally offers one of two explanations for not keeping Jewish observances. The first is that he admits simply and freely to not being a good Jew. He ought to be keeping Jewish observances according to his own internal logic but is simply unable to do so. He often adds that perhaps someday in the future he will be able to. The second reason is that while he believes in God, he does not necessarily believe that He is the source of the regimen of practices that other Jews feel bidden to observe and therefore does not assume the same obligations other Jews have for keeping them.

These last explanations are the ones most often offered by the non-practicing survivors who profess belief in a personal God, a group which constituted 27 percent of all survivors who were nonobservant before the Holocaust. An additional 13 percent of these nonobservant survivors professed belief in an impersonal God. Seven percent did not choose to answer the questions. And fifty-three percent, consistent with their nonobservant behavior, classified themselves as nonbelievers.

Belief in God During and After the Holocaust

A popular maxim that has gained more than limited currency even as a social theory suggests that "there are no atheists in foxholes." [1] That is, in times of great crisis and danger one turns to religion. Our survey among Jews victimized by Nazism does not lend credence to this widespread notion. Holocaust survivors, as a collective, rather than gaining faith in God during the Holocaust were losing faith in God by a full 17 percent: 38 percent of all survivors reported that they believed in God during the Holocaust; a decrease from 55 percent before the Holocaust. And the category of nonbelievers absorbed the full 17 percent, rising correspondingly from 26 percent to 43 percent.

The trend continues immediately after the Holocaust, but with the introduction of a shift in emphasis. The category of nonbelievers remained the same when the war years were over. But the category of believers in a personal God was further diminished to the low point of 36 percent with a corresponding rise in the category of believers in an impersonal God.

Belief in God Today

During the following twenty-five years spent in the land of Israel the slight transition toward the profession of belief in an impersonal God became, if not a growing surge, then certainly a moderate trend at the expense of the category of nonbelievers. The percentage of believers in a personal God rose slightly during this period or, perhaps more correctly, reclaimed some of its earlier pre-Holocaust adherents. Significantly, Holocaust survivors living in the land of Israel for more than quarter of a century discontinued, by 12 percent, from the high of 43 percent recorded for the time of the Holocaust, their profession of nonbelief in God. Only 31 percent of all Holocaust survivors currently claim to be nonbelievers.

What do these survivors profess today, now that they disclaim atheism or agnosticism? Nearly one in every four Holocaust survivors (24 percent, a rise from 14 percent during the Holocaust and from 16 percent immediately after the Holocaust) today claims to believe in an impersonal God—a Force or Power in the universe (a koach elyon).

One survivor spoke for many others in offering the following reasons for his belief in an impersonal God:

I've thought about it a great deal. And I've reached these conclusions: There were two strong beliefs held by many of us after the Holocaust. These two beliefs were especially held by the intelligent and educated ones among us whom one talked to and with whom one discussed such matters. It seemed there weren't too many of us at the time at all interested in such intellectual "games" or discussions. But for a few of us discussions and thinking of this sort did go on to a great extent during those years.

To many of us it seemed clear there was no God as we had previously understood Him to be. Or, put differently, if there was a God at all we had never properly understood Him or what He really is.

So we spoke of a limited God, an imperfect God, a not-all-powerful God or even a devil as God. Most of us rejected these concepts for one reason or another. Or at the very least we modified these kinds of God concepts quite unsystematically. Or if we accepted them we did so only partially. These are not impersonal God ideas of course, but rather than say we believe with certainty in God who participates beneficially in the affairs of man, a personal God, which we can't accept, we can at least, with less hypocrisy and greater ease of mind, subscribe to an idea of a more distant God like Nature, a koach elyon.

And so over the years this is what some of us came around to. For many it must have been a sudden thing. For many like myself it was rather a slow, long-drawn-out decision—like a process—how to believe, in what to believe. And it's not over yet.

The second thing is that you must remember that we are Jews. And we care about being Jews. And Jews believe in God—of some form or other. So if not the full, complete God or Father we'd like to have fulfilling our fantasies, one we can talk to and pray to, we can still be a far lesser hypocrite when we join other Jews in worship at the synagogue if we can at least claim a "sophisticated" God is our God, an impersonal God.

The Pre-Holocaust Observant

It is revealing to focus, as in the previous chapter, upon the community which was observant before the Holocaust and to trace their changes in faith through the Holocaust to the present. Earlier we reported that, as one would expect of a religiously observant collective, before the night of oppression began, the overwhelming number of these survivors, 82 percent, professed belief in a personal God who "is involved in the affairs of man." Another 13 percent professed belief in God as an "impersonal Force." And only 3 percent registered as nonbelievers in God. During the Holocaust, however, a radical transformation of faith took place. These observant survivors who had previously believed in a personal God were reduced to 61 percent, a significant loss of more than 20 percent. They were still further reduced, to 56 percent, immediately after the Holocaust, where the figure has remained until today. That is, *more than one of every four of these apparently religiously disposed survivors lost their faith in a personal God*. The many years living in the land of Israel since the Holocaust failed to restore their original faith.

During the Holocaust these survivors became nonbelievers. Even the group professing belief in an impersonal God suffered a slight 2 percent loss at this stage. Significantly, believers in a personal God did not, during the time of the Holocaust, begin to turn to a belief in an impersonal God as they did in subsequent stages. Rather, the category of nonbelievers rose dramatically from 3 percent to 26 percent during the Holocaust and up to the high point of 28 percent by the time the Holocaust was over.

Survivors began to turn toward a belief in an impersonal God in small numbers immediately after the Holocaust, when the category rose to 14 percent. From that time on, during the years these survivors lived in Israel, they increasingly turned to the profession of a belief in an impersonal God. This category, having reached 20 percent, nearly equals the category of nonbelievers, which today has been reduced to 22 percent.

In summary, then, *survivors who were observant before the Holocaust and whose faith underwent changes through the years were predominantly losing belief in a personal God during the Holocaust; and in the time since the Holocaust these survivors have become believers in an impersonal God.*

The Effect of the Holocaust upon Faith

Perhaps the foremost subject of this study concerns the survivor's own appraisal of the effect of the Holocaust upon his or her faith. After it was first established in the interview whether the survivor was a believer in a personal God, an impersonal God, or no God at all before the Holocaust and at the three subsequent stages, he was then asked whether and how the Holocaust itself (or, for most, the concentration camp experience) affected his belief concerning God. Depending upon his answer to the first series of questions, the next relevant questions were taken from the following:

> In your opinion did the Holocaust or your concentration camp experience:
> Cause you to believe in God
> Strengthen your belief in God
> Weaken your belief in God
> Destroy completely your belief in God
> Confirm your atheism
> Weaken your atheism
> Cause you to believe in an impersonal God
> Strengthen your belief in an impersonal God
> Other

As one might expect from so large and varied a population as Holocaust survivors, each one of the religious postures enumerated above claims a sizable following. A statistical breakdown of these several survivor subgroups will be offered here along with a running commentary and an interpretation of the remarks made by a number of survivors. We will turn our attention first to representative spokespeople of the survivor population maintaining that their Holocaust experience has had no effect upon their religious faith. These included believers in God as well as atheists. *In all, 47 percent averred that the Holocaust had no influence on their beliefs about God. That is, nearly half of the entire survivor population were unaffected.* Concentrating on this group alone, our study discloses that *54 percent did not waver in their belief in a personal God; 18 percent remained steadfast in their affirmation of an impersonal God; and 28 percent were consistent in their atheism.*

The Atheist Survivor

For the survivor who has always been an atheist the Holocaust's lack of effect is understandable and his or her explanation all but commonplace and predictable. Before the Holocaust he did not believe in God; the Holocaust brought no justification for him to re-evaluate his denial of God's existence.

An atheist survivor who was seized in the forests surrounding Riga and deported to Buchenwald offered the following typical remarks:

> I can't imagine how anyone can believe in God after what has happened, particularly the Jewish victims but even the rest of mankind, regardless of not being involved personally. How can you believe in a God who can permit that atrocity on such a grand enormous scale?
>
> I never believed in God. Not before the Holocaust, not during my stay in the camps and not afterwards. I didn't need the Holocaust as proof of God's nonexistence. I was never in doubt that He didn't exist. What upset and astonished me was to see other Jews went on believing, behaving, and praying and keeping the commandments while they were going through the worst ungodlike hell imaginable. And I saw many of these Jews and was stupefied, even angered at times, by their persistent belief in a God who obviously didn't exist or He would have done something.
>
> Of course it occurred to me then, as it does now, that it might have had psychological benefits to believe in God and put one's complete trust in Him and that's the explanation why more Jews did not forsake their God in the death camps. It *was* better to believe than not believe. Maybe believing in God even helped some to survive. But in the camp it struck me as ridiculous that Jews could really and sincerely believe in God. For me the Holocaust had no religious effect whatsoever because I already was an atheist. But how come it didn't change others to atheism? I often wonder about that.

The Believing Survivor

More complex indeed is the analysis of believing survivors whose faith in God did not waver during their ordeal.

This population requires far more attention than the atheist survivors, not only because there are nearly twice as many but, irrespective of numbers, for the theological implications raised by their steadfast belief:

Where was God? Why do good men suffer? How can good men who suffer remain good men? Why do good men who suffer not follow the advice offered Job to "curse God and die"?

This population interests us also for the number of survivors who evidently are emotionally unable to come to grips with the challenge to their faith raised by the Holocaust. We shall examine this group first.

Three decades have elapsed since the Holocaust was consumed, but to this day the passive and inaudible presence of God, sought vainly in the whirlwind, continues to bewilder survivors as much as ever. For believing Jews a persistent and frequent response to the problem of God's whereabouts during those dark days is, "I do not permit myself to think about it." However, one candid survivor, himself a devout Jew, is persuaded that this declaration, when it is not merely the conventional abdication of the responsibility for serious thinking, is a convenient if platitudinous ruse for avoiding frank and open reflection on the subject. For these survivors God's whereabouts amounts to nothing less than the single most recurring enigma even as the problem, which reaches far beyond the strict symmetries of theological speculation, is being wholly and vehemently denied. Nevertheless, it is indisputable that numerous believing survivors would simply choose not to be brought consciously to the scrutinization of God's withdrawn presence:

"I never think about God any more," insists an attorney and university professor who experienced the ultimate agony of being forced by the Germans to choose between wife and mother, which should live, which should die. "I don't let myself. I work, work, work, work, from the moment I get up in the morning till late in the evening, although I am above the age and beyond the need. I intentionally carry a full teaching load at the university and at the same time maintain an intensive legal practice. I never slow down lest I start thinking. All this that I would not ask myself about God. I am an observant Jew. How can anyone be anything but, after what has happened? And yet in all honesty it is true I 'davan' but I no longer pray. I can no longer speak to God as formerly; I speak at Him. Yet, I find that the synagogue and the mitzvot are as important in my life today as before— and as consoling. How could I go on without them? But as for God Himself—can you believe this?—I just continue to recite prayers. I never let myself think about Him."

Moreover, for pious Jews there exists a ready religious attitude or prescription, which is psychologically supportive against the threat represented by the outsider and his questions, and behind which they may pause to regroup and find escape when subsurface rumbling doubts assail: the prohibition against thinking alien thoughts that may conduce to irreligious behavior or provoke "appikurish" (philosophically anti-Jewish) ideas. Virtually anything at all may, at various times, be so classified; and from the inquiring stranger just about everything is alien until such time as he is less strange—and more trustworthy.

The believing Jew is generally "not allowed" to ask himself or reflect upon questions that may, because he has not acquired the wisdom of the sage, give way to skepticism.

A significant number of believing survivors would rather not be compelled to consider God's role in the Holocaust. But, in fairness, there are others who also claim their faith was not affected, that is, neither strengthened nor weakened. They deliberately follow the antithetical route of theological speculation and religious inquiry. And they welcome the inescapable challenge and the travail it engenders:

> It is *all* I think about. . . . My life is a running, nagging dialogue with God . . . He is always on my mind. Why? Why? I sometimes find I have been walking the lonely, crowded streets of Tel Aviv, wandering aimlessly, conducting a question and answer session with Him—with no satisfactory answers forthcoming. I believe in Him with the same certainty as ever. The Holocaust couldn't change that. But I find I want very much to keep after Him and try to the best of my ability to overcome the obscurity of His ways and I can't escape Him, however much He may have wished to escape us. I will do this to my last breath. I know it. More than this, I believe this is precisely what a Jew must do, to keep after Him for answers. And it brings me a measure of repose and comfort to conduct these conferences, to be God's interlocutor, to keep after Him by creating and inventing, like the traditional Jew of the past in history, new arguments *against* Him, and new justifications *for* Him. For me it is the entire Torah, the Etz Chayyim [Tree of Life]. Although I have no choice to the contrary, I am happy to hold fast to it.

The greatest number of these believing Holocaust survivors who to this day besiege God in head-on religious encounter do so involuntarily and unwillingly. For them it is not a cathartic, untrammeled exercise in the search for religious truth, but rather submission to an irresistible psychological imperative:

> I'd rather be free of it all; but it possesses me. I'd rather just live . . . not think of my daughter, my wife, my mother, all of

whom perished . . . rather not think of my aged father who has been living a kind of death for thirty years and only now has, thank God, been freed by his senility from his unbearable burden. I often wish I could join him in his blessed senility; but I'd sooner, if I had my way, not even live as long as he. That way I'd be free of my burdens toward God and He'd be free of all He owes me. We'd be quits. Man was not intended to think about things beyond him. God's silence during the camps is one of these things. If I could I'd stop asking God The Questions altogether, but I can't.

Atheists, Believers, and Emotional Health

From these passages it would appear that the God-fearing, believing Jewish survivor is troubled and discontent with his belief, and less tranquil and secure than the atheist, who has no Presence to confront with ultimate questions. It is reasonably safe to assume that believing Jews feel themselves constrained to challenge God in ways which obviously find no parallel burden for the confirmed atheist. One must not conclude, however, that the atheists are emotionally healthier or happier, less troubled or tortured in their convictions than the believing Jews. The paucity of such testimony of torment merely reflects the fact that the atheist does not have the same opportunity to release and express similarly felt hostility and anguish. There is no evidence that atheists are less neurotic, as is believed in some antireligious quarters, particularly among Jewish communists and socialists.

When, during the course of an in-depth interview, a belief in God is professed, the ensuing questions unfold of their own momentum: Where, in your opinion, was God during those blackest hours? Why did God let it happen? And how can one believe in God after Auschwitz? These questions, however much one would wish it otherwise, compel self-introspection, and invoke thoughtful, revealing testimonies, whereas similar occasions were not often provided the confirmed atheist who did not feel the need to explain or justify or brood over parallel, unanswerable, ultimate questions. The atheist has other matters to understand and explain, of course, but not "Where was God when . . .?"

It also became evident that a number of Holocaust survivors in the course of the intensive interview may very well have sensed that the questions to follow would concern God's failure to respond, and to circumvent the entanglement at once they chose to identify themselves as "atheists," thus parrying the dilemma and forestalling the subsequent,

far more difficult, questions before they were posed. That this occurred
on occasion during interviews was demonstrated further on in the interview when parallel, corroborating questions were raised concerning the
nature of God and His ways. In these instances a belief in God was often
professed indirectly and by circumlocution, suggesting that *some Holocaust survivors registered as atheists because they would sooner deny
God than attempt to justify His ways.*

The complexity of the paradox of believing Jews "denying God" but
remaining essentially, or at least statistically, unchanged is further enlarged by the following insights provided by a survivor who worked on
the clearance detail of the gas chamber, washing down the corpses with
a water hose:

> As far as religious belief in God is concerned, it seems to me in the
> camps there were two kinds of believing Jews. If we ignore the
> genuine atheist and think of the believers only, there were two kinds
> of reactions, two extremes and several stages in between too, but
> essentially two contradictory responses to God for the horror of life
> in camp. They are, either complete submission to God, capitulation
> to his enormous incomprehensible inscrutable will; or blaspheming
> Him, cursing Him, not really denying Him but detesting Him, des-
> pising Him, menacing Him; threatening Him, threatening to with-
> hold faith in Him: "God, if you don't do something I'm going to
> stop believing in you . . ." As though you can try to convince God
> that you can turn belief on or off like water from the tap. . . .
>
> You've got to be very close to God, you have to know Him very
> well to blaspheme Him. Only a deeply religious person can despise
> God, shake his fist at God and abuse Him. A blaspheming Jew is a
> believing Jew. And the camps were composed of these Jews in great
> numbers. There were Jews who always tried to keep their heads
> covered when they ate, even if they only had the palm of their hand
> to serve as skull cap. And they never took a gulp or bite without
> mumbling a prayer over the bread, regardless of how hungry they
> were. Moments earlier these same Jews were threatening God with
> denying His existence.
>
> Being an atheist in the camp was no easy thing.

As the numerous interviews of Holocaust survivors progressed, it
became evident that many professing atheism were in reality unconsciously seeking to punish God by shouting his nonexistence to His face—
hardly genuine atheists. One survivor reflecting on his own atheism compared it to a deserted lover crying in his hurt, "I don't love you any-

more: for me you no longer exist." Thus *for many "atheist" survivors, God's nonexistence was often declaimed when it was radical abandonment being experienced.* Labeling oneself an atheist is not necessarily a theological posture. It is as often an expression or manifestation of a psychological need, an emotional device to "get back at God," to "hurt" Him, "punishing" God for hiding His face at a time when His presence was desperately sought.

The next quotations are set forth to refute the idea that believing survivors are unable to come to grips rationally and thoughtfully with the theological problems of God's comportment during the Holocaust. On the contrary, many survivors who remained steadfast believers in a personal God throughout the Holocaust years and until the present had in fact worked out their thinking quite sensibly and judiciously, even in a somewhat sophisticated way, and without resorting to extremes. And with little reluctance they offered their considered thoughts and ideas on the subject of God during an interview.

The Steadfast Believer

Approximately one of every four survivors remained believers in a personal God through the Holocaust to the present. The first two comments below are typical of these Jews who survived the Holocaust with their belief in God intact and unaffected. The third testimony of a steadfast believer is hardly typical. It is from a former prisoner whose duty was to carry corpses to the crematoria. The fourth brief quotation is from a survivor whose professed belief in an impersonal God also remained intact and unaffected.

Perhaps for a very young person the Holocaust could have been expected to cause a significant change in his beliefs. A young person in his teens or twenties may not have arrived at a mature, clear idea of God yet, and so the Holocaust would appear as an important, critical event influencing and determining his faith. And it is conceivable to me that a young person could altogether lose his faith in God at the time he was undergoing some of the terrible things we all endured in the camps.

But I was neither young nor without other terrible experiences in my life such as the loss of a parent and the death of a child. I was already nearly middle-aged when I was shipped by train to a Nazi camp. I suppose I had already discounted in my religious thinking and belief all blame against God for these personal tragedies. I had already gone through it earlier and still emerged a believer. So the Holocaust had no further effect on my faith: not positive nor negative. But for a young person, that's another matter entirely, and I could understand what it could do to the immature mind.

———◆———

The years that I endured the Nazi concentration camps had no connection whatever with my belief in God. The camps had nothing to do with God; and God, while not "on vacation" or absent from them, cannot be blamed for them.

It never occurred to me to question God's doings or lack of doings while I was an inmate of Auschwitz, although of course, I understand others did. I said kaddish for the dead and arranged for kaddish to be said for me, if I should die, by a friend I met in the camps who had also survived the camps but who has since died. But I was no less or no more religious because of what the Nazis did to us; and I believe my faith in God was not undermined in the least. It just never occurred to me to associate the calamity we were experiencing with God, to blame Him, or to believe in Him less or to cease believing in Him at all because He didn't come to our aid.

God doesn't owe us that. Or anything. We owe our lives to Him. If someone believes God is responsible for the death of six million because He didn't somehow do something to save them, he's got his thinking reversed. We owe God our lives for the few or many years we live, and we have the duty to worship Him and do all that He commands us. That's what we're here on this earth for, to be in God's service, to do God's bidding, to be God's people, His holy people. Sometimes it means suffering, but it's not because God wants us to suffer. It's because other people hate us for being God's chosen and for never having hurt others as they hate and hurt others.

Our religion is proven true because it works. Our religion never permitted us to commit the crimes that their religion permitted them to commit against us.

This was clear in the camps and that is why I was a believer before and a believer since and a believer within the camps.

———◆———

I know what kept me from going altogether mad while in Sobibor. What kept me from going under was my powerful and continuous faith in the nearness of God and in the existence of the hereafter.

It was my belief in God and the fact that there was a belief in God held by others that helped me retain my equilibrium and my sanity and some common sense as well. My faith also kept my physi-

cal being from falling apart and, in fact, kept me from killing myself at once.

To me God is more than an idea. He is more than something that
exists only in my head or my heart but not out there in reality. He
must be physical and be able to hear. But how can I not believe in
the God that kept me and others from going insane? I simply chose
at one point that I would believe in Him, no matter what. And that
was that. I don't really know if that is a true faith because of the
way I went about it: I refused then and continue to refuse now to
challenge my faith and to summon God to a disputation. If I went
ahead and challenged God and my challenge was victorious then I
would be all alone. I would have been utterly alone in the camps, and
I could not have survived. And I couldn't survive today.

Confined within the barbed wire of Auschwitz I understood to
separate the wicked deeds of men from the workings of the entire
universe. The system of the world and the idea behind its function-
ing is God. I have always believed that. I never believed God to be a
kindly old man with a beard watching out for the welfare of each
and every person.

And within the workings of the world man can commit atrocities
and murder or refrain from atrocities and murder. He is free to
choose. But the universe goes on regardless. God is not a puppeteer
pulling the strings and making man dance . . . God doesn't act to
stop murder and He doesn't, on the other hand, encourage murder.
The Holocaust can't be blamed on the idea behind the Forces of
nature. It has nothing to do with God who is in no way like a man
anyway.

Survivors Affected by the Holocaust

Our survey discloses that *53 percent of all survivors—more than half the
survivor community—consciously and specifically asserted that the Hol-
caust affected or, to a certain extent, modified their faith in God.*
Of these, 72 percent can be said to have been turned away from
faith in God. That is, for nearly three of every four survivors affected
by the Holocaust, either a complete loss or an attenuation of religious
faith resulted. Included among these are survivors who claimed their
religious faith had been weakened by the Holocaust; others who lost
their faith entirely; and those for whom belief in a personal God had
been displaced by belief in an impersonal God idea. Also included in this

grouping are survivors whose atheism became strongly reinforced by the Holocaust and even survivors whose pre-Holocaust belief in an impersonal God was weakened or entirely undermined by the Holocaust.

The remaining 28 percent of the survivors, that is, more than one of every four survivors who had been influenced religiously by the Holocaust, were brought "nearer to God." And since it has always been considered less plausible for an irreligious individual to become religious— for whatever reasons—than a religious person to lose his or her faith, *the Holocaust must be considered as having influenced a rather sizable population of survivors to become (more) religious*. These include pre-Holocaust atheists who became believers as well as survivors whose belief in God, personal or impersonal, was strongly reinforced by the Holocaust. On balance, however, it can be said that the Holocaust served more to undermine than to buttress the faith of survivors.

Particularly among survivors whose religious beliefs were changed, as opposed to "merely" affected, by the Holocaust, is this the case. There were 10 percent fewer survivors changed than affected (45 percent as against 55 percent), but of these fully 87 percent were changed in the direction *against* faith in God, and only 13 percent were turned *toward* religious faith. The proportions are more evenly balanced among Jews "affected" but unchanged by the Holocaust. Because believing Jews were likely to see the hand of God in the Holocaust, reinforcing their belief, a full 40 percent of the affected but unchanged survivors claimed to have been brought closer to God. But even among those "merely" affected, the greater majority, 60 percent, were turned away from religious faith by the Holocaust.

It is highly instructive to set forth the distribution of survivor subgroups affected by the Holocaust and to listen to their own words on the influence of the Holocaust upon their religious beliefs. Specifically, 11 percent of all survivors claimed that the Holocaust strengthened or reinforced their belief in a personal God who is involved in the affairs of man. They had been believers before the Holocaust and became the more so because of the catastrophe.

Belief Reinforced

These believing Jews should occasion little surprise. It might have been expected that a certain number of survivors would be predisposed from the outset to see the hand of God through the darkness, sustaining and buttressing their already vigorously robust faith. It is also plausible to reason that the category of unaffected believing Jews, particularly those who defiantly insist that the Holocaust has had no influence whatsoever on their religious faith, is linked in continuum with this subgroup of affected survivors for whom the Holocaust reinforced faith. The survivor's piety which affirms that "the Holocaust did not destroy my faith" or "the concentration camp did not affect my beliefs" may be considered very similar, if not virtually identical, to attitudes such as "the Holocaust brought me even closer to God" or "being in a concentration camp caused me more than ever to believe in God."

And these convictions were expressed repeatedly by believing survivors. But the reasons behind the Holocaust's having strengthened the faith of these survivors were not readily forthcoming. There appeared to be considerable reluctance among the members of this subgroup, far more than among others, to articulate and explain their avowals. The most frequently heard remarks from these survivors were concerned with the enormity of the tragedy as evidence of the presence of God.

Nevertheless, a number of these survivors expressed rather unconventional convictions concerning the Holocaust's reinforcement of their faith in God. For some, the presence of God was seen and confirmed in the Holocaust in the same way as His presence was manifest to them in the pages of the Bible. For example, Lamentations, the elegy on a previous calamity that befell the Jewish people, may be interpreted as teaching that now as then God plainly works in the affairs of man, particularly as He chastises and punishes His own people. It may be true that the human mind cannot begin to grasp the purposes and mysteries of God's ways—although perhaps the future may reveal these. But that God orders all things according to His design is indisputable, so irrefutably self-evident to these survivors that theological expositions on His existence in the face of obvious proofs like the Holocaust are unnecessary for the open-minded, futile for the purblind, and redundant for the faithful.

For some the very fact of their survival reinforced faith. Their own piety was recompensed by the gift of their life; the piety of others was proved suspect by the fact of their death. According to this reasoning, God metes out strict justice and each person is repaid according to his merits. One survivor put it this way:

> I lived through the Holocaust as did many others because we deserved to live. Had we not deserved to live, we would have been cut off like all the other sinners. God watched over me and answered my prayer. It's not sufficient to be a practicing Jew, keeping all the mitzvot; it's what goes on in your heart that also counts. And if someone is observant and does all the things God commanded, but he

does them because he is seeking rewards from his Master God, then his acts are worse than worthless. They had the wrong motivations to begin with and that is why many lost their lives. Like Cain, God refused their offering and they forfeited their lives.

Another survivor who was left for dead in a heap of bodies of his murdered family felt "that God had some higher purpose to have seen to it that I survived. And that reason surely included my being a good Jew—believing in God and keeping His Commandments."

Most unaffected believing survivors viewed the Holocaust as an inexplicable mystery. The Holocaust was somewhat more comprehensible for these believing survivors whose faith was reinforced or strengthened. According to many of them, God is continuously challenging man's faith. And the Holocaust is but one, however enormous, of many challenges. Their faith met the challenge and emerged triumphant.

This view, moreover, was not infrequently an extension of the idea that Jews have throughout history always been victimized by other nations because of their special status as God's people. Each calamity as it followed upon the heels of the previous one is seen as further proof of God's continuous presence and special relationship with the Jewish people. Since God is always testing and challenging His people, the Jew must always try to be equal to the challenge, although it may not always be clear to him that he is being challenged or why he is being challenged. One survivor who by her own testimony was kept alive because her beauty appealed to one high-ranking German officer remarked:

> Hitler was merely the instrument of God. I don't know why, and man can never get to know why because then he would know the mind of God and in effect be God. But because we don't know why God does something doesn't mean we can't know that God is there and that He uses certain historical figures for His purposes. Maybe His reason was to begin to redeem us, bringing us to this land. Perhaps He had to make Jews want to uproot themselves from their homes in Europe and want to leave for Israel to build a homeland. Whatever His reasons, one thing seems clear, that He uses the nations [the goyim] to accomplish His goals.

Faith Weakened

Those who claimed that the Holocaust weakened—but did not altogether shatter—their faith in God constituted 14 percent of all survivors.

These are survivors who believed in God before the Holocaust and continue to believe after the Holocaust. But doubt, more for some than for others, assails their faith. Notwithstanding the fact that they remained believers, they admit to a diminution of their faith. For some there will always be an unresolved dilemma, and while they haven't adequately worked through these conflicts, they have given thought enough to have, on balance, remained believers. One survivor said:

> There were times during the Holocaust and since that I was pretty close to abandoning my convictions—many, many times in fact. But always I found myself praying and turning to God in other ways. When I'd think about it [God's existence] objectively, I often would tell my wife, "You know, I don't think I believe in God any more." And she'd chide me and say, "You do too." And of course she'd be right. It's not something so easy to give up. But at the same time I certainly do not believe with the same strength and the same fervor and the same certainty as once I did.

Another survivor, a powerfully built ritual slaughterer now living in Jerusalem, whose faith was weakened, said:

> Before the Holocaust God was part of my everyday routine. I would not permit myself to go anywhere without taking the time of day into account and where I would be and I would plan to be where there was a quorum of Jews to pray to God.
>
> My whole life revolved around God and synagogue worship, every day morning prayers, afternoon prayers and evening prayers. And aside from the regular prayers I spoke to God almost like one would speak to a friend. But everything changed with the Holocaust. Now if I go to the synagogue a couple of times a year I would consider it a lot for me. I still believe in God, but it is not the same. He is no longer so close to me; and I simply don't believe so emphatically in Him any longer.

Atheism Reinforced

Those survivors whose faith in God was strengthened by the Holocaust have their counterpart among the 3 percent of all survivors whose atheism was reinforced by the Holocaust. The following comment is representative of the Jews in this group:

I was in my late teens when my family and I were taken away, half starved, half dead with thirst, crammed into a windowless, dirty cattle car. I had come from a religious home, but I already, before the German murderers brought us to their annihilation camp, no longer believed in God—although, then, I couldn't tell you why exactly. It was simply intellectual reasoning and study and school and discussions with friends that made me a hesitant, uncertain atheist at that time. But five minutes of seeing dead bodies scattered along the road; corpses dangling in grotesque formations from the electrically charged barbed wire fence; living skeletons appearing more like ghosts than humans staggering around and dying at our feet; heaps of the dead and dying, by the hundreds. Five minutes and I knew I could never believe in a God who'd not prevent this. I was positive I'd be an atheist all the rest of my life.

In the camps people prayed for a miracle to deliver them from death. I knew I'd never expect one and could not pray for one because now I knew for certain what I'd vaguely felt before, that there is no God at all.

An Impersonal God

Another 3 percent of all survivors maintain the Holocaust caused them to replace their belief in a personal God who was involved in the affairs of man with a belief in an impersonal God idea who does not take an active role in man's activities. These survivors may also be viewed as an extension of the category of survivors for whom the Holocaust weakened faith in God. Not all Jews who believe in an impersonal God would agree that their belief is somehow "less than other beliefs." A number would suggest that theirs is not so much a belief different in degree or intensity but rather in kind or in class. However, most will admit that it *is* "less" than faith in a personal God. And many consider themselves to be maintaining religious views more closely associated with agnosticism (and even atheism) than with belief. "I could no longer believe in God," one survivor said, "the way I had believed in my youth [before the Holocaust began] and I admit there is more I do not understand; I'm not a Maimonides or a great philosopher. But in spite of the chaos and barbarity and inhumanity I experienced and witnessed in Treblinka, I can see order and design in the universe. I believe that. So I believe in a God like that, a God who is the idea behind the order, like gravity, and not in a God I can talk to or who has so much free time He can pay attention to me. There's no other way I can explain it."

An insignificant 1 percent of all survivors lost the belief they had held in an impersonal God because of the Holocaust. And the remaining fraction, less than 1 percent (four survivors in all), found that their atheism became less certain because of the Holocaust. For these latter, the Holocaust weakened their disbelief. They are still atheists. But because of their interpretation of the Holocaust they are not as convinced as they once were. The former subgroup saw in the Holocaust proof that "there is nothing out there in the universe, not even a mind or an idea governing it, just chance." And the latter, although retaining their atheism, "saw something in it all [the Holocaust] to justify the further consideration of the possibility that there might be a God after all. The Holocaust was too much a 'peak event' in the history of civilization not to admit the possibility of a Hand behind it."

These two final minute groupings round out the population of survivors whose religious faith was affected but not changed by the Holocaust. We must now turn to the study of the population of survivors whose religious faith was radically changed because of the Holocaust: those who lost faith and those who became believers.

Faith Lost

The most publicized survivors are surely those who lost their faith in God, those who became atheists because of the Holocaust and their concentration camp experience. Our study reveals that they indeed constitute the largest subgroup of survivors who were affected religiously by the Holocaust: 16 percent of all survivors ceased to believe in God because of the Holocaust.

Four representative, although not necessarily typical, statements by such survivors follow. These generally were the most loquacious survivors, and the group most anxious to discuss their religious views and to disclose their reasons for abandoning their faith.

Why do you have to do research? What's it all about? It serves no purpose whatever. There's nothing so complicated that it requires this scholarship. We who went through the different camps no longer believe in God. It's as simple as that. We, because of our experience and what we witnessed, know there is no God. God is a myth.

This is what I think: We were sent forth by humanity, by mankind, although it was not even aware it was doing so, to find out once and for all if there's a God. That's the meaning of the camps. It was meant to bring Him out into the open if He existed at all. Nothing else or less significant could have brought Him out into the open, to respond and to act and to show His face. It was a stupendous test; unconscious and unintentional but a test nevertheless. And God failed the test and proved His own nonexistence. And I, as part of the experiment, stopped believing in Him altogether. Just as certain laboratory experiments are conclusive and incontrovertible, so was this.

If He wouldn't come out then, during those times, when?

Now when man writes his history he can say there was a vast laboratory experiment conducted by man during the 1940s to see if there is a God or not. The conclusion was no God exists. There were guinea pigs in the test and other kinds of experimental animals, but mainly guinea pigs—Jews of course. I know. I was one of them.

———◆———

I began to understand what happened to my faith and my belief after liberation. This was the summer of 1945. It was at Buchenwald and Sabbath services were being conducted. Before, I would have automatically and unthinkingly attended, with little or no reflection. And I would have joined in the prayers with pleasure.

In fact had it been previous times I, having been away from prayers for a long period of time, would have returned and raced to services to sing the songs and chant the prayers with much pleasure and much enthusiasm.

This time I stood like a Golem and couldn't budge an inch toward the dining hall used for the services where the Sabbath was being welcomed. Everyone was dressed in their best new clothing and singing together familiar melodies, holding the small United States Army prayer books and swaying to the melody. I felt as though they were from a different period in the distant past, before the Ice Ages or maybe from a different planet altogether.

My eyes filled with tears but my lips wouldn't quiver with prayer. It was as if I had lockjaw or a paralysis of the mouth. My mind began racing toward past times of joy in the synagogue with my father and my grandfather and the other Jews of our town; happier times and happier places.

How could they conduct services, resuming their prayers as if nothing had happened. I certainly couldn't. Too much pain. Too many recollections of the distant past. It felt like centuries ago, not just six years . . . all those holidays and tunes leading me deeper into the past, recalling an atmosphere of holiness and beauty now utterly destroyed. I couldn't even hum along with the congregation. It was impossible for me to set foot in that place. Impossible to pick up the prayer books again although part of me wanted to. Impossible for me to pray to God again. Impossible to be what I was once and am no longer. It was dead for me like everything else. Now Palestine meant everything. The past meant nothing. And I virtually never set foot in a synagogue again.

◆

I'll tell you why I lost my faith in God in the Holocaust. Because if God exists then He's a monster. And Hitler was God's deputy on earth. Do you want me to believe that? I'd rather be an atheist.

Maybe man's existence without God is meaningless, but I'd rather have a meaningless life than a God who allows pogroms and the slaughter of the innocent. And I refuse to believe God is a horrible sadist. There are no other choices at all. God either does not exist or He is the Devil. I'd simply prefer to believe in no God at all.

◆

I can understand when one single person, even a very good person, called out to God but God does not answer. Perhaps what that good person believes to be good for him really is not. And it can be said that God knows the future and in His wisdom denies the petition and the prayer goes unanswered. It is even easier to understand, of course, when a totally evil person called out to God for help with something evil and God turns away in disgust. And I can understand, too, when an evil person who asks God for something quite good for a change and still God refuses to heed him because of all his past evil deeds. God should shut His ears to such a person. That is his punishment. And it is also quite comprehensible when an entire people, an evil people like the Germans, prayed for evil such as victory for themselves in a war they started, a war to conquer the world and subject the peoples of the world to themselves and to expand their dominion over the surrounding territories and God eventually thwarts their evil designs. These are all quite understandable to me. Some of these are absolutely essential for the world to endure with order and without chaos, and we know of many such examples throughout history.

But the reason I no longer believe in God is different from these things. When an entire people, a good people who never were evil, prayed for a good purpose: their deliverance from destruction by an evil people, and for whatever reason God turned away and refused to answer their sincere and genuine prayers, when good people, good prayers for good purposes go unanswered, the only conclusion I can arrive at is that God does not exist.

Guilt and the Denial of God

It is no small irony that those Holocaust survivors who became non-believers appear to feel the urgent need to explain and justify their non-belief to a far greater extent than believers seem to feel the need to justify *their* belief.

For atheist survivors the need for self-justification appears to be linked with a sense of guilt which exceeds the contrition and remorse experienced and occasionally expressed by other survivors for having outlasted the devastation. There prevails the added shame, consciously admitted and articulated by a number of survivors, of betraying the martyrdom by which six million others—including townfolk, parents, children, siblings, and spouses—perished. They felt they were not true to them for failing to carry on as the observant, God-fearing Jews the dead were believed to have been, particularly in the Polish community. It is difficult to judge whether many other survivors would agree with the several themes of the following confession, but it is an important statement nevertheless:

> It is disloyal, I know, for me to be the goy I am today when I should be behaving and believing like the good Jews they were. I feel terrible about it; but I don't *do* anything about it—except occasionally urging my kids to go to the synagogue on the holidays as though that would make up for it. Now, today, I am an atheist, and intellectually I don't want the State of Israel governed along religious, halachic lines. But for the sake of the Six Million and especially the deeply religious among them who were destroyed, I feel otherwise emotionally. Perhaps, I often wonder, if we'd be forced by the government to comply with many religious restrictions, I'd feel less guilty just being alive.

Richard L. Rubenstein in *After Auschwitz* has correctly discerned one of the theologically sophisticated responses meant to relieve the guilt feelings ensuing from renouncing the belief in God:

> After the death camps, life in and of itself, lived and enjoyed on its own terms without any superordinate values or special theological

relationships, becomes important for Jews. One cannot go through the experience of having life called so devastatingly and radically into question without experiencing a heightened sense of its value, unrelated to any special categories of meaning which transcend its actual experience.[2]

Or as one survivor expressed a similar thought conversationally:

> . . . the only thing I believe in, after I tasted a full measure from the cup of death, is life itself. When I say I'm an atheist, I mean that not only do I deny God's existence, but I refuse to seek a source for values in the universe beyond those which I and my fellow man devise and improvise on the spot as we live from day to day.
>
> That is quite sufficient: the life I see and experience. I don't need philosophy. And I certainly don't need God.

It is important not to overlook the distinction between guilt feelings for having survived the Holocaust when loved ones did not, and guilt feelings connected with, in the words of one of them, "the failure to behave and believe as good Jews should after the Holocaust."

> I don't feel badly at all that I lived. I of course feel dreadfully—physical pain and mental suffering—that so few others lived. But I don't feel guilty about it, just terribly sad and at the same time thankful that I am alive and can tell about what happened and can recall the family I lost and all my townspeople too and the terrible sights I witnessed as well. I am obliged and compelled to remember all of these, but there is no guilt attached to my survival. However, I do feel guilty for my failure to behave and believe as good Jews should after the Holocaust. This bothers me very much, but I can't help it.

Des Pres points out that "with very few exceptions, the testimony of survivors does not concern itself with guilt of any sort."[3] Further on Des Pres writes, "survivors do not bear witness to guilt, neither theirs nor ours, but to objective conditions of evil."[4] There are, indeed, few expressions of guilt for having withstood the extinction, although they most certainly exist.

More prevalent among survivors, however, is the disappointment in themselves for the shortcomings in their own religious lives and the inadequate transmission of the Jewish heritage to their offspring in Israel and doubtless elsewhere as well. In this connection guilt is experienced by many survivors to this day.

There is also no denying the feelings of guilt experienced by con-temporary Jews in other parts of the world, non-European Jews, who were not personally touched by the Holocaust: guilt for not having been there, guilt for not having done enough then, and for being among those who "let it happen," guilt for putting it out of mind, for pur-chasing German products, and similar forms of guilt.

Although there is more guilt concerning religious inadequacies than for the fact of survival, most survivors do not express feelings of guilt over either of these. And those who in the course of an interview speak of having forsaken religious beliefs or religious practices hastily point out that they do not feel guilty about these because, as many have said, "while I may have become less religious, I have nevertheless become a better Jew in my heart." Their commitment to the Jewish people, their feelings of identity with other Jews, the pride they take in being a Jew—and a survivor—as well as their loyalty and commitment to the survival of the State of Israel, compensate for and offset whatever guilt feelings may obtain in connection with deficiencies of their religious lives:

> I lost my faith and stopped believing in God when I saw the Nazis take pious, innocent, bearded religious Jews out to the courtyard and butcher and slaughter them for sport, having competition and playing games with these Jews as they murdered them for their amusement—like huntsmen sporting with animals—and leaving others, less pious than they, unharmed. How can you believe any-thing after you've seen something like that? But I will see to it that not another Jew has a single hair of his head harmed again, not without a fight. Because of it I am more intensely Jewish than I ever was before, and Israel is all we have left to defend and to look for-ward to in the future.

How many Jews who became irreligious see themselves nevertheless as better Jews? It is impossible to tell. In the first draft of the question-naire for this research it was intended to look into this fully. However, whereas in America and elsewhere in the diaspora such a question may have some validity, in Israel it cannot. In Israel, survivors may see themselves as Jews who are less religious than they had been in Europe. But they do not see themselves as indifferent or inadequate as Jews. And in Israel there is virtually no guilt attached to their being alive, and not very much guilt at the kind of Jews they are religiously—so much have so many sacrificed in lives and anguish—since arriving in their home-land.

Atheism Justified; Atheism Shaken

In most cases, the atheist survivor, when asked to justify his own disbelief, feels convinced that in the face of the death camp experience he has the right, more than any other man alive, to declare God nonexistent and deny that the omnipotent God of Israel can ever again be affirmed, "for how can one possibly believe in Him after what has happened?" The feeling is that as a survivor his experience alone renders his theology incontrovertible and irrefutable, "until the theologian has walked before the 'selection' himself." And even then, "whoever has survived is disqualified."

Immediately after the war, considerable defiance was manifested and proudly expressed in disbelief and in atheism. The posture said: Now we assuredly know we must rely on ourselves alone, not on God, and I prove it by denying Him. This attitude was intertwined with the idea of immigration to Israel and the popular assumption that the denial of God was a form of self-reliance grounded within the *halutziut* (pioneering) spirit. It was often framed as "God abandoned us, now we've abandoned Him."

After the immediate shock of the Holocaust subsided however, and the immigrant survivors began to adjust to the realities of their absorption in Israel, so apparently did the need for belligerent posturing diminish. And although many survivors clung to and even reinforced their particular degree of belief or nonbelief—whichever was the case, whether atheistic, agnostic or theistic—they nevertheless attenuated the intensity of their antagonism toward their religion and the God who was felt to have abandoned them at the darkest hour of their most urgent need.

Another factor, in addition to passage of time, contributed to the diminution of the survivor community's antagonism toward religion. The war of June 1967 and the recovery of the old city with its temple site proved for many to be the religious antidote to the Holocaust. Numerous survivors who had previously attributed their loss of faith to God's abandonment at Auschwitz attested to the rekindling of their faith as a consequence of what was seen as the miraculous character of the Six Day War.

It also emerged that a number of Holocaust survivors who regard themselves as atheists because of the Holocaust appear never to have been hostile or aggressive in their atheism. Or else, with the passage of time, they appear to have abandoned hostility and aggression. Unlike many other atheist Holocaust survivors, they feel no need to seek converts. They have generally thought through their atheism and their

Jewishness thoroughly, deeply, and privately. And they approach their
Holocaust experiences with considered theological detachment and seri-
ousness. One such survivor, who has earned several advanced academic
degrees in the humanities after gaining his freedom from Plaszow, Gross
Rosen, and Buchenwald labor and concentration camps, spoke these
words quietly and with considerable restraint into a tape recorder:

I am a Jewish atheist and a very religious man, and I know there
are others like me. My own personal progression was from strongly
held belief before the war to angry defiant I'll-change-the-world
atheism afterwards, to the views I have held now for the last fifteen
to twenty years which I describe as atheism combined with a positively committed Jewish cultural identification. I am an active
member of my neighborhood Beth Knesseth. The prayers help me
affirm my Jewishness. By means of the traditional prayers, I identify
with Jews vertically throughout history—particularly with the Six
Million—and horizontally with all other Jews the world over today,
everywhere today. Soviet Jews, American Jews, Syrian Jews, they
are all my brothers. I observe the Shabbat after my fashion by driv-
ing my family to the park, to the seashore, to some public place like
a museum or if possible a cultural event. You generally have to buy
tickets in advance. We return to a big special Shabbat meal. We nap
and may afterwards read something aloud as a family from Jewish
literature: Shalom Aleichem for example in Yiddish for my children
to hear and learn the language of the Six Million; Bialik and Ahad
Haam and even Agnon for his piety and the piety of the generation
of the camps. Friends come by. And heavy, thought-provoking
Shabbat discussions are inevitable. We chant Havdaleh to conclude
the day and inaugurate the week, whenever we remember or are so
inclined.

   I've thought about it at considerable length and I do not believe
in God, a personal God. Nor can I believe in a force for good in
the universe, either that "it" exists or is "God." Not after all that
I've experienced. I reject the idea that God is an Active Intellect or
at least am not convinced by Rambam or any other Jewish thinkers
and philosophers I have studied. I just don't believe. And so sadly,
even regrettably, for me there is no God. Nevertheless I can see
myself dying Al Kiddush Hashem—if that means for the sanctification of my people's heritage and my Jewish identity. I don't mind
so much being an atheist because I don't believe I'm less a Jew or not
as good a Jew because of it.

It has already been suggested that for some survivors there are unmistakable guilt feelings associated with the need to justify their non-belief. Apparently, these sensibilities derive not so much from having endured while loved ones perished but from the felt betrayal of those of the Six Million, often family and townsfolk, who were themselves observant, "for we have abandoned them, our brethren, and have become like our own adversaries, pagans like our murderers." However, for the atheist survivor who has taken his stand not in defiant atheism but in his people's legacy, in its destiny, and in the land of Israel, the guilt is vitiated if it exists at all. And his atheism is most convincing.

Survivors whose atheism was shaken because of the Holocaust were too few to surface statistically. One, noticeably scarred by the swagger stick of an overseer, spoke these words:

> My entire crowd in Frankfurt was composed of atheists, myself included. I still am an unbeliever and so are a number of friends who survived from my circle having departed Germany before the war— I wish I had been among them. But as far as my beliefs are concerned, I used to be a confirmed atheist, now I am not so sure. The camps shook everything up in my mind as well as in my body. I am no longer so sure about anything. Before the war, I used to have faith in mankind's essential goodness, if not in God's existence. I know that faith in man's goodness is gone. And I have doubts about doubting God too, at times. Very little is left of what had been my philosophy of life.

Intellectual and Emotional Atheism

The genuine atheist who has arrived at his theological position through personal experience and serious philosophical reflection may at the same time harbor within him intense, piercing psychological feelings relative to God's abandonment. Feelings and ratiocination should not be confused; neither should they be dismissed as invalid when contradictory. For whenever a near-victim speaks of God's absence in moments of desperate need he may quite justifiably at other times, if not simultaneously, consider himself a genuine atheist on intellectual grounds. These are two distinct, although clearly overlapping, levels of reasoning and experience.

Furthermore, the full sense of abandonment experienced emotionally by many survivors may, before too long, strike an intellectual chord conducing to the total rejection of God and leading to intellectual atheism as well. We cannot know for whom, and to what extent, this process applies. But our findings disclose that today, some three decades after the reign of terror ended, 31 percent of the survivor population look upon themselves as nonbelievers. And 16 percent, that is, *half of all these nonbelievers, maintain that they arrived at their atheism because the Holocaust was irrefutable evidence that there is no Providence in the universe.*

As to the crucial distinction between experiencing God's radical abandonment and intellectually concluding that He is nonexistent, one must not assume that it was invariably overlooked by the survivors themselves. A sensitive poet speaking on behalf of a small but articulate section of the Holocaust community conveyed his awareness of the distinction in these terms:

> I call myself an atheist although I know deep in my heart that God exists. It is just that I refuse to give Him the satisfaction of acknowledging it.
>
> I and others of the Saved Remnant are among the few of this world who understand what the death of God really means. We Jews of the Polish Jewish community lived with God as with an ever-available, always nearby Father who guided and sustained us and upheld our faltering steps. Suddenly He was there no longer; we were utterly alone.
>
> I shared a bunk in camp with a brilliant and sarcastic man who until his own death recited the kaddish nightly—for God! He often laughed at himself bitterly, sardonically: here I am chanting the prayer for the dead to the very One whose death I've pronounced. Does my dead God hear the prayers I'm reciting over His grave?
>
> Some pitiful professional theologians have spent years at their comfortable desks working out the details, like at a game, of the theology of God's death and in the process have established a name for themselves and no small measure of success. Do you understand what it is to make the steep progression in the course of a few anguished hours—and from terrible personal experience—in a Nazi death camp? With the meaning of one's life going up in black smoke from tall chimneys?

Faith Gained

This section, examining survivors whose religious beliefs were changed by the Holocaust, is concluded with the study of those who became believers in God. In the wake of the Holocaust it was to be expected that every variety of religious change would find survivor representation. But what would the proportions be?

It had been assumed that atheist survivors would nearly unanimously find in their Holocaust experience justification for their atheism. The reasoning has been presented previously that it is not as likely for an irreligious person to become religious as it is for a religious person to relinquish his faith as a consequence of a cataclysmic tragedy. Granted that it is an understandable phenomenon for a religious person to lose faith in God in the face of tragedy. Granted further that it may be rather unconventional and uncommon for a man or woman without faith to find God in personal tragedy—so many other options and contingencies are available. But what is "normal" apportionment translated into statistics? Can one expect the ratio of believers losing faith against atheists gaining faith to be 20 to 1, 5 to 1, 2 to 1? If 16 percent is the proportion of all Holocaust survivors who relinquished their faith in God due to the Holocaust, what percentage of survivors should we expect to have become believers?

Our survey discloses that in the matter of religious faith as in the matter of religious observances it may be reasonably argued that a striking number of survivors were in fact inspired *toward* religion by the Holocaust: 5 percent of all survivors were transformed into believers—seemingly an insignificant figure. However, when one examines the ratio of survivors who were changed religiously directly by the Holocaust, quite another perspective is revealed: *Of all survivors changed religiously by the Holocaust, 76 percent became atheists and 24 percent became believers. That is, three of every four survivors whose beliefs were radically altered by the Holocaust lost faith. And, unpredictably, nearly one of every four religiously transformed survivors began to believe in God because of the Holocaust.* Moreover, if 16 percent of all survivors specifically attributed to the Holocaust their loss of faith and 5 percent gained faith in God then, overall, *the net loss of faith among all survivors came to 11 percent.*

The final cluster of quotations represents the survivor population which found God in the midst of their near immolation.

I'm writing a book about how I became "converted" to Judaism in Buchenwald. It's not an entirely unfamiliar story. I was nothing before being sent to the camps, an atheist, a nonbeliever, a cynic, and skeptical about religion. But it didn't take long before I found myself strongly believing in God and convinced of His presence. And very soon I was moved to praying to God to deliver me from the hell I was in.

It all started with a religious experience when I heard the doomed men and women heading to their fiery end singing Hatikvah, the Jewish national anthem, which means hope! Can you imagine that? Then they began chanting shma yisrael adonai elohainu adonai echad, which means, in spite of my own personal doom I believe in one God who is eternal and incomparable. In just a short while they were no more, only ashes. And I knew my own turn was next and I was afraid. But it took me just that brief moment of time to begin, in tears of fear and despair, to believe in God and to pray, really pray to Him. And every night I prayed for my brothers and sisters and parents that they survive. God listened and heard and even answered my prayers even though they did not all survive . . . but I and my younger brother lived because God watched over us. I also prayed that God would one day utterly destroy all the Nazi murderers. And God's anger rose against all the Jewish enemies in Europe and here in the Middle East as well, in answer to our prayers.

From the time I arrived in the camps and became religious I was able to be less and less afraid of the oncoming death even though death peered at me constantly around every corner. My newly found faith supported me. And it still does to this day.

———————◆———————

It's no secret among those who know me, friends and relatives and others who ask about it, that I became religious because of the camps.

I think it started way back when our family business was confiscated by the Nazis along with all our wealth and property and personal belongings. And we had nowhere to go. It freed me to think for the first time in my life about spiritual things and the meaning and purpose of life. My first reaction, when the pogroms against the Jews started, was that all this senseless misfortune was just proof of my disbelief—in God, in the chosen people, in the validity of the commandments. And it was therefore strange and contradictory for me to be compelled to wear the Star of David bearing the word Jew on my clothing, and along with other Jewish boys to have to use the name Israel. I felt nothing, hardly a Jew at all in the religious sense. . . .

How stupid and immature I was then. I now understand that proofs of God's presence are not on the surface and obvious and revealed to everybody. Certainly never to the unthinking or simpleminded. When I finally arrived in Dachau I began to admire men of of God daily in many miracles and later in the final destruction of the Nazi empire and in the triumph of Jews in Israel.

Man must be accountable in his actions to Someone who metes out justice, that is, to God who is in control. And in the camps I saw divine control within the terrible immorality. Afterwards I witnessed divine justice.

———◆———

There are a number of reasons and no one reason alone for becoming a religious Jew. But perhaps the main reason is that the Six Million are too holy and pure to be used as an excuse for disbelief.

When I hear of other survivors who say they became atheists because of the death of the Six Million I become very excited and angry and I always let them know that it is precisely because of the Six Million that I became a religious Jew, keeping the commandments and developing in myself a deep faith in God.

The Six Million sacrificed so much, their very lives and our memories of them as individuals, how can you betray them again after they've gone by using their death as a justification for becoming a goy. . .?

Steadfastness of Pre-Holocaust Convictions

Another area of inquiry remains to be examined, one which puts aside the question of the Holocaust's impact upon the religious faith of survivors and concentrates instead upon the steadfastness of pre-Holocaust convictions.

In this category, 39 percent of all survivors, some of whom were affected religiously by the Holocaust, some who were not, consistently maintained their belief in a personal God who is involved in the lives of people.

Another 21 percent of all survivors were atheists before the advent of the Holocaust and are atheists today. For some the Holocaust reinforced, for others the Holocaust provided challenge to, the certainty of their disbelief.

Still another 8 percent were survivors whose belief in an impersonal God idea did not waver throughout the years, although for some the Holocaust may have strengthened and for others it may have weakened their convictions.

These figures complement our previous calculations. Since, as was disclosed earlier in this chapter, 55 percent of the total community were believers in a personal God before the Holocaust and here we find that 39 percent remained believers throughout the subsequent years, then 16 percent of the original believing community lost their faith. And, similarly, since 26 percent of the entire community were atheists before the Holocaust and here we see that 21 percent retained that persuasion, 5 percent abandoned their atheism and became believers. The ratio of 16 percent to 5 percent corresponds precisely with the figures evaluated previously of survivors who altered their pre-Holocaust convictions.

We should not conclude this section without the observation that despite the trauma of the Holocaust experiences a total of 68 percent of all survivors retained unwaveringly the religious or irreligious convictions of their childhood and youth. These results are incompatible with prevailing concepts concerning survivors, particularly those which hold that survivors would overwhelmingly and with near unanimity be changed religiously by the Holocaust most especially by losing their faith in God. Our findings instead support the theory of the staying power of one's early theological training and conditioning as far more potent factors in determining one's religious disposition.

After the war, many Holocaust survivors were conscious of their need "to make a decision about religion and about God," even among those for whom there was no radical reversal in the substance of their belief. But clearly some survivors were more conscious of it than others. For a number of these Jews, after the camps and before immigration to Israel, there seemed to exist only two opposing extreme options: all or nothing at all. Absolute piety or total renunciation. Or as one rabbi, ordained before the war in a Lithuanian Yeshiva, put it: "We thought then that the options were, join the Naturei Karta and become religious fanatics or give it all up for complete assimilation and the abandonment of Judaism. What we went through was far too charged for anything between, for anything but an extreme response about God. A choice, falling short of the extreme, appeared grossly inadequate and unworthy of what we experienced."

The desire to resume a normal life after the camps was felt far more deeply than the abstract theory of the either/or. Most survivors resumed their lives without recourse to either fanaticism or assimilation, to either atheism or blind faith. Where emotionally capable and except for intermittently recurring moments, most survivors simply preferred to put the matter out of mind. Living life was far more compelling.

Religious Conversion and Survival

Our study discloses that the traumas and dislocations of the concentration, labor and death camps and of the hiding places were more likely to be conducive to the abandonment of faith than a turning toward faith. And yet many of the diaries and memoirs of survivors as well as the various oral testimonies recorded in this study and elsewhere suggest quite the reverse was true.

Leon W. Wells in the *Death Brigade* writes that "among the religious groups who prayed daily were inmates who, before the war, were not religious at all. Many of us underwent a complete transformation here." [5]

Practicing Judaism in such lethal surroundings often increased the already highly charged dangers the Jews faced in the camps. Does our study document a far greater loss than gain in faith for the reason that many more of the religious converts failed to survive? Can it be that these Jews went to their deaths in greater numbers than other Jewish victims and are not of a sufficient count today to testify adequately to their Holocaust-acquired convictions?

One of the several unwelcome implications of this theory—should it be acceptable at all—is that for a Jew (and not necessarily for members of other faiths) religious commitment and piety are not life-oriented in a death context. If this is true, has it always been the case throughout Jewish history?

There is obviously no way of gathering statistical evidence to support or disprove so radical a hypothesis as this, but if the survivors who "underwent a complete religious transformation" were more likely to have been destroyed than Jews who forsook their faith and the others who remained as they had been, is it because they and other religious Jews were oppressed by antireligious groups and took greater risks than those who were nonreligious?

Wells may be implying as much in his description of the social order prevailing in the *Death Brigade:*

> Some of us were religious; others didn't care one way or another.
> Still others were antireligious, not from conviction but to be "smart."
> Most of the "leaders" and "tough guys" were of the antireligious
> groups, and they had different ways of oppressing the ones observant
> of their religion. For instance, instead of giving the religious ones
> their cigarette ration on Friday, the leaders doled it out on Saturday,
> when it is forbidden by religious law to smoke. But the religious
> ones kept to their way of life despite all difficulties.
>
> It was forbidden to take anything into the prison yard without
> permission from the Untersturmfuhrer. Even if, inside the barbed-
> wire compound, one were found with a piece of wrapping paper

for use in the toilet one would be tortured and then sentenced to death.

The religious ones didn't pay much attention to this law, and when they found a Jewish prayer book in the clothing of the people that were shot, they would smuggle it out and bring it into the tent. This was much more dangerous to possess than money or gold. Money or gold once smuggled into the camp could be hidden. The prayer books or tefilin [phylacteries] were used daily, and the people prayed morning and evening.

On the eve of Yom Kippur in the Death Brigade one could sense the approach of the holy day. When we returned from work, nearly all of us washed up very quickly, ate, and changed our clothes. A few minutes later, in one of our tents, we began, in whispers, but also in a holy and dignified manner, to pray. As collective praying could get us into bad trouble with the Germans, the "antireligious" group kept guard outside the tents, watching for Schupos or SD's who might approach, and also taking care to see that we did not become so loud that we could be heard outside the tent. Many of the nonreligious ones took part in the prayers, and many fasted the whole of the next day.

In our condition fasting was by no means an easy matter. We had to work as hard as on any other day, and because of the terrible thirst caused by the stench and the smoke some of us had to break the fast.

Among us were some who would usually refuse to eat meat, because, here, of course, it was not kosher. They ate the soup only because they had to eat something to keep alive, and to die of one's own volition is forbidden by the Jewish religion. As I mentioned before, cigarettes were a rarity, and among the religious people there were some who not only did not smoke on the Sabbath but who wouldn't even take a cigarette to save for smoking later.[6]

Perhaps, rather than the fact of the greater vulnerability of religious as against nonreligious Jews, the survivor lists themselves contain a built-in misrepresentation of the proportions of the two subgroups. However, the pious—including even the strictest Hasidim—as well as the nonreligious, enrolled in the survivor organizations or enlisted in Holocaust research centers which provided the population for the study. It is improbable that those who became religious because of or during the Holocaust withheld their names from survivor rosters to a greater extent than those who were changed the other way.

Regardless of whether these or other speculations hold true in explanation of the phenomena, the finding of this study is that most of those religiously turned or transmuted by the darkest, most hellish setting on earth had seen, not the face of God at Auschwitz, as some surmised, nor the extravagant abandonment of His people, as others maintained, but rather God as delusion, His Presence as preposterous—and, as can be seen throughout this study, their identity as Jews more valid and precious than ever. Perhaps even those Jewish prisoners who became religious in the camps, that is, those who underwent a conversion in their practice of Judaism, were consciously or unconsciously affirming that identity in defiance, frequently at their own peril, as the single form of resistance remaining for them, and as a refutation of Nazism.

It is worth observing in this connection that no antonym exists in English or Hebrew for religious conversion which conveys nonpejoratively a turning from a belief in God to another set of beliefs without Him, which were just as valid for them. There is therefore no straightforward and sympathetic designation for those of our study who "went the other way" by relinquishing faith in God while keeping all, most, or some of their Jewish practices intact, or taking on certain Jewish observances as a renewal or reinforcement of their commitment to their Jewish identity.

FOUR

The Meaning of the Holocaust

WHAT WAS THE MEANING OF THE HOLOCAUST for survivors of the Holocaust? That the Holocaust would be seen as invested with meaning by a certain large number of survivors could have been anticipated well in advance of conducting the study. Was the nature of the Holocaust's meaning for this group of people to be viewed as secular, religious, political, or metaphysical in character? How many and which survivors beheld meaning and even purpose in the suffering, anguish, and death the Holocaust brought, and what do survivors say in the aftermath of the Holocaust concerning the nature of God? These were questions deemed worthy of precise scientific inquiry of the survivors themselves.

Catastrophes and God's Will

Whether major catastrophes of mass death and destruction such as the Nazi campaign of extermination are to be ascribed in some way to God's will was the first in a series of questions on articles of personal faith posed to survivors. In the interviews, survivors were asked whether they held to this belief at four different stages or time periods: before, during, after the Holocaust, and today (see p. 87). In this section of the questionnaire no distinction was made between human acts of destruction, such as wars, pogroms, homicide or genocide, and acts of natural devastation, such as floods, earthquakes, or cyclones. The intention here, rather, was to elicit the changes, if any, in attitude and

126

TABLE 10. Beliefs of Holocaust Survivors Through Four Stages

	BEFORE HOLOCAUST	DURING HOLOCAUST	AFTER HOLOCAUST	TODAY	NEVER
Catastrophes (like the Holocaust are the will of God	26%	29%	24%	24%	67%
Coming of messiah	35	28	26	28	65
Chosen people	49	36	36	41	43
Torah is word of God	54	39	36	41	41
Judaism is a true religion	64	47	49	61	22
Judaism is only true religion	41	33	32	36	53

religious belief over the course of time, especially as it may be attributable to the Holocaust (see Table 10).

Today, some three decades after its conclusion, 26 percent of all survivors responding to the question recall that before the Holocaust erupted in flame, they held to a belief that there is indeed a correlation between massive human calamities and the will of God. The Holocaust may or may not have been thought of later as singular or unique. But these survivors, one of every four, claimed that prior to the Holocaust they believed in a cause-and-effect relationship between the wrath of God and the enormous devastations that perennially befell mankind generally or their fellow Jews particularly.

During the Holocaust the percentage increased, but only to 29 percent, surprising not that there would be an increase at the time of the stress period but that the rise was not far greater. One Treblinka survivor among the incremental 3 percent declared:

> I expect a great many people like myself felt at the time of their
> suffering that God was doing it to them. When we suffer pain
> we're all ego and self-centered. When it's happening to you, you
> think God must be right there and He is responsible. Before
> the war I would never believe that God had anything to do with
> such terrible suffering and inhumanity, but during the war I
> thought there is no other explanation because it was almost
> supernatural and far, far too massive and too terrible, the suffering

we endured, not to be connected in some direct way to God's active presence, perhaps His displeasure with us.

And yet, for nearly every survivor whose opinion changed this way, another changed in the other direction. One of the latter, a Polish-born Auschwitz survivor who after the war worked for the Haganah guiding displaced Jewish persons toward the Mediterranean coast in the direction of Palestine, reflected that "before the Nazi campaign I may have felt at times that God was responsible for those obscene atrocities the world has known, but once I and my family and friends became victims of it, once we were involved personally and we knew we didn't deserve it, I never again felt that way."

Every other religious doctrine surveyed (belief in the coming of the messiah, the Jews as chosen people, the Torah as the word of God, Judaism as a true religion, and Judaism as the only true religion) all without exception sustained a decline of faith during the Holocaust years. Not only in the general survivor community but also within the smaller subgroup of the devout, those who throughout the years retained their faith in God, was there an attenuation in the various religious beliefs at the time (the one exception was the doctrine of the messiah, which remained constant during and sustained its attrition immediately after the Holocaust).

The only article of faith to gain adherents during the genocide period was that the Holocaust and similar devastations are the will of God. It would seem that for many individuals the imminence or the remoteness in time and space of a religious doctrine determines to a large extent its currency and adoption. There has been ample documentation in many books by survivors revealing that while the devastation of the Holocaust was being experienced it moved its victims urgently to affirm life. This affirmation was invariably expressed in practical terms by concrete, if extraordinary, acts calculated to enhance survival, simply to endure. These were acts that they could never have previously conceived of themselves as performing, but which the grotesquely unfamiliar conditions of the camps demanded. According to our findings, these extreme circumstances called as well for theological interpretations and religious responses relevant to their predicament. Indeed, many survivors turned to the ideological resources of their religious heritage to make sense out of the senselessness of it all. Apparently, however, the reverse is also true: The Jewish principles of faith regarded as irrelevant to the exigencies of their circumstances, despite the time-honored reverence in which they had been held, were more likely to be disregarded and disesteemed if not disreputed and denied.

After the Holocaust, 5 percent fewer of the survivor community continued to believe in the correlation between God's will and such calamities (for several of the reasons discussed immediately below), and that group, 24 percent, remains constant to this day. It may appear from this, then, that no really significant fluctuation occurred through the years and that the Holocaust did not appreciably increase or decrease the correlation in the minds of the survivors. And clearly there was no stampede of faith in the general survivor community. Nevertheless, within the constricted subgroup of survivors associating the Holocaust with God while enduring it, 18 percent changed their minds subsequently. And this attrition must be seen as hardly inconsequential. From these figures the Holocaust, at least temporarily and as it was being experienced, brought a small number of survivors to see God's presence behind it and a slightly larger number to denying that faith after it was over.

Despite the fact that it was the only religious principle of those examined by this study to gain rather than lose proponents during the genocide period, the belief that the Holocaust was the will of God remained the principle least embraced. This development is understandable, since affirming that belief is tantamount to blaming God for their predicament—a theology thoroughly unacceptable to most Holocaust survivors.

Significantly, two-thirds of the entire survivor population never related the Holocaust and other events of destruction with God's will, whereas one of every four survivors did so at one time or another during the thirty years this study spans. It will be shown further on that even for this latter group, when other choices are offered such as "it is inappropriate to blame God for the acts of man," "it is not for us to judge the ways of God," "God was unable to prevent the destruction," and "nothing could excuse God for not having saved them"—options that do not all necessarily contradict the correlation—fewer than 10 percent stay with that selection. Except, as in this question, when there are no alternatives, many survivors apparently would rather not connect the Holocaust with God or to be thought of as among those who "judge" or "blame" God for the destruction even as they may hold to the view that by and large great tragedies are indeed a consequence of God's will.

Atheists and Other Irreligionists

For those survivors who remained atheists throughout the years, catastrophes like the Holocaust could have no connection whatever to a nonexistent diety. Survivors who defined their God as an impersonal Force in the universe overwhelmingly (88 percent) dismissed any relationship between It and devastations such as the Holocaust. For most of these survivors God is to be thought of as synonymous with vast, impersonal, Nature "taking the death of men in its stride." Accordingly, as one such survivor remarked: "God is too remote to be concerned with or to care about the evil of man."

A Bergen-Belsen survivor teaching in a Tel-Aviv secondary school explained his philosophical views in these written words:

> I know my ideas are not traditionally Jewish. They are in fact
> somewhat heretical, but I believe the Holocaust was not the will
> of God because only that which contributes to the betterment
> of man is the will of God. Perhaps the Holocaust was the work of
> the evil influences of the world, personalized as the Devil,
> Satan, or some malevolent Power in the universe, maybe even more
> powerful than God who is the Force for good in the universe.
> Or perhaps it's more correct to say God is not the all-powerful
> Power we've always thought Him to be, just the personalization of
> one of the many, various Powers, including the evil Powers.
> And man can help enthrone the evil or the good by his own actions.
> He is free to enthrone God or the Devil. When it's the good it's
> God; when otherwise it's not—but the Holocaust was not God's
> doings, not if you understand God as koach elyon, the Force for
> good, as I do. And God is the One but not necessarily the only One.

For a portion of the remaining 12 percent the Holocaust can *only* be explained with reference to an impersonal God. For, as one of these survivors, a scholar of considerable reputation, put it,

> Everything is the will of such a God, even the Holocaust. God
> is not good or bad, but the good and the bad are part of God. And
> perhaps it is all but pointless to pray to God for He is the
> totality of the energies, human and non-human, comprising the
> entire universe, simultaneously the direction of the movement
> towards the end of time and its objective, seen only by the mind
> of God. History itself and all the events, good or evil in it,
> are part of the design of the world. One event of history unfolds
> into the next: the diaspora, the Holocaust, the rebirth of Israel,
> the response of Arab terrorism and whatever the future may bring.
> All these can best be explained only by an idea of God as an

impersonal Force (koach elyon) and as an aspect of the dimension of God Himself. And still I pray to God. And it helps; because talking to oneself does help. It also helps to move me in the way I want and should be moved. Accordingly, I pray to God by praying to that aspect of God which is my self, my own humanity. When I influence myself by my prayer I've also succeeded in influencing God. And my prayers are efficacious.

Neither of these two subgroups whose theology defined God in highly sophisticated and impersonal terms was affected by the Holocaust or statistically changed in their views during the four stages.

Devout Survivors

Of the survivors who remained believers in a personal God throughout the four stages, 37 percent claimed never to have believed that catastrophes such as the Holocaust are the will of God. Nearly two-thirds believed at least at some point during the years that the Holocaust came about because God willed it. In fact, among devout survivors, the peak of this belief occurred during the Holocaust itself, when fully 63 percent connected the horror they were undergoing with God's purposes. Before the Holocaust, 12 percent fewer, only 51 percent of all believing survivors, made the direct connection between God and the catastrophes which befall man.

It is hardly astonishing that believing Jews would see evidence for the hand of God, particularly during the time of their own peril. After the Holocaust, however, 10 percent, remaining firm in their faith in a personal God, ceased to believe He was the author of it. And that percentage remained unchanged to the present. *The fact is that few believing survivors retained the view arrived at during the war years that catastrophes like the Holocaust are attributable to God.*

One survivor from Holland who spent the major part of the war in hiding as well as two months in the internment camp Westerbork among others in the East explained that

. . . when the war began I became even more religious than I was before, and the worse it got for me in the camps I was sent to the more I believed that God was testing us or perhaps giving us a second chance to pass His test of faith. The Holocaust could only have been God's doings, I thought then. Before the Holocaust

I never would have associated the brutality of men with the
will of God but during my stay in the camps it seemed to me
that man had no control over his actions and his behavior appeared
as though determined for him—perhaps by God.

I don't mean the Nazis weren't responsible for their acts,
just that their killing was by rote, mechanical, seemingly in
accordance with a vast predetermined plan as we were systematically
sent to death. We'd live just so long until we could no longer
work, until we lost strength, and then we would go to our end in
the gas chamber. Some would even volunteer for it. Most accepted
it passively. It made no difference whether we died or lived,
whether our end came sooner or later.

After liberation I understood that the Nazis and their
collaborators were simply evil men and that God did not plan for
His chosen people, His children Israel, to die. It was not God's
will at all.

In each of the final two stages—immediately after the Holocaust and
today—over half (53 percent) of all believing survivors who answered
the question maintained that catastrophes like the Holocaust are God's
will. Just under half denied it. That the evenly balanced disagreement
among devout survivors may be indicative of uncertainty rather than
a polarization of belief is suggested by the failure of more survivors to
answer this question, whether the Holocaust was the will of God, than
any of the other questions of the series including belief in the coming
of the messiah, that Jews are the chosen people, or whether the Torah
is the word of God. It appears that, although more than three decades
have passed, the issue of God's role in the Holocaust has not been resolved satisfactorily in the minds of many believing survivors.

For many others, however, regardless of which position is taken,
their very faith in God buttresses the certainty of their convictions concerning God's will and the Holocaust. And both sides of the dispute
quote the Bible and other Jewish sources extensively in support of their
views.

Maimonides, in his *Guide for the Perplexed,* found it necessary,
when discussing God's attributes, to speak in negative terms, as to what
God is not, rather than to claim knowledge of what God is. Apparently
modern survivors who believe the Holocaust was not the will of God, instinctively perhaps, followed this line: "The Master of the universe is not
a stage director ordering human beings like actors to do His will. He
certainly doesn't command men to murder men." "God doesn't move

men around like they were puppets." "We are not machines nor automatons and God is not a master engineer pushing evil buttons. Do they who say the Holocaust was God's will think God is Frankenstein and man His monster or that man was created as God's Golem to murder and pillage and commit barbaric deeds? Is that what they think God is like?"

To many of these devout survivors God has a special relationship with Israel. Nevertheless, there is little expectation that God will ever intercede or should have interceded in protection of His people when evil men arose against them. The Jew may beseech God to avert impending disaster. Perhaps God's failure to act in direct response may be because man is essentially free, having been granted by God a will of his own to do good or evil. Several survivors cited Scripture, especially the verses seen by Jewish tradition as the classic proof text for freedom of the will: "See, I set before you this day life and prosperity, death and adversity. For I command you this day, to love the Lord your God, to walk in His ways, and to keep His commandments, His laws, and His norms. . . . I call heaven and earth to witness against you this day: I have put before you life and death, blessing and curse. Choose life— if you and your offspring would live—by loving the Lord your God, heeding His commands, and holding fast to Him." [1]

Among other Jewish sources, Maimonides was also cited by several respondents in their case for freedom of the will: "Every man is granted free will. If he wishes to do good and be virtuous, he has the ability to do so. If he wishes to do wickedness and be evil he may do that. Since good or evil are in our own hands, and since all the evil which we have committed came about in complete consciousness we ought to repent and desist of our evil—since our ability to do so rests in our own hands. This is a most important principle; no it is the very foundation of the Torah and of the commandments."

Believing survivors who refuse to attribute the Holocaust to God most frequently stress man's role and man's ability to control his fate. For them, man is accused and God is exonerated. But devout survivors who do see God's workings in the Holocaust are not as consistent in their argument or as single-minded in their views. They offer various possible reasons for the Holocaust or none at all, for "Who can know the workings of the Almighty?" And, quoting Psalms, " 'His thoughts are very deep' . . . but, assuredly, the Lord of the world 'had his reasons.' "

Since nothing on earth of such magnitude can happen which is not in accordance with God's will, the Holocaust must have had purpose and justification in the mind of God. The devout survivors expressing this view in the main pointed less to the villain than to the victim. They also "blamed man" for calling down God's wrath and cited verses from the Bible and Prayer Book. But for them it was not the free will of the Germans but, frequently, the wickedness of the Jew himself that precipitated the death of the Six Million:

> But if you do not obey Me and do not observe all these
> commandments, if you reject My laws and spurn My norms, so
> that you do not observe all My commandments and you break
> My covenant, I in turn will do this to you: I will wreak misery
> upon you—consumption and fever, which cause the eyes to pine and
> the body to languish; you shall sow your seed to no purpose,
> for your enemies shall eat it. I will set My face against you: you
> shall be routed by your enemies, and your foes shall dominate
> you. And if you remain hostile toward Me and refuse to obey Me,
> I will go on smiting you sevenfold for your sins. I will loose
> wild beasts against you, and they shall bereave you of your children
> and wipe out your cattle. They shall decimate you, and your
> roads shall be deserted. And if these things fail to discipline you
> for Me, and you remain hostile to Me, I too will remain hostile
> to you: I in turn will smite you sevenfold for your sins. I will
> bring a sword against you to wreak vengeance for the covenant;
> and if you withdraw into your cities, I will send pestilence
> among you, and you shall be delivered into enemy hands. And
> you I will scatter among the nations; and I will unsheath the sword
> against you. You shall not be able to stand your ground before
> your enemies, but shall perish among the nations; and the land
> of your enemies shall consume you. Those of you who survive
> shall be heartsick over their iniquity in the land of your enemies;
> more, they shall be heartsick over the iniquities of their fathers;
> and they shall confess their iniquity and the iniquity of their
> fathers, in that they trespassed against Me, yea, were hostile to me.[2]

Half of all the devout survivors, then, dissociate God from the Holocaust. Most of these, stressing freedom of the will, point to man's—that is, Germany's—role in the Holocaust. The other half stress God's role in the catastrophe as it emerges from His special relationship with Israel. Most of these viewed the Germans and others primarily as instruments of God's purpose, although many hasten to add that they as mortal men are not wise enough to understand the reasons for God's actions. They add also that the German people and local criminals are nevertheless to be held responsible. (In Chapter 5 we shall study in greater detail the theological views and opinions of the various survivor groupings relative to God's role in the Holocaust.)

Two Survivor Subgroups Compared

In connection with God's will and the Holocaust it is particularly revealing to compare survivors who retained their faith with survivors who lost their faith. From the outset, even before the war, the two groupings of survivors may have harbored contradictory instincts, attitudes, and predispositions toward God despite the fact that both were originally believers. For example, before the Holocaust half (51 percent) the survivors who retained their faith believed that catastrophes such as the Holocaust were the will of God, but among survivors who lost their faith only 28 percent, a little more than a quarter, believed that.

One would have thought that survivors who refused to see a connection between human violence and God's comportment would have been more likely to retain their faith when such violence is committed since in their view God is not responsible. Instead, the very reverse is true, and by a considerable margin. The number of survivors affirming God's role in the Holocaust among those who continued to believe in God throughout the four stages rose by 10 percent during the Holocaust but fell by 18 percent for survivors who lost their faith.

The explanation, however, is self-evident: The doctrine that the Holocaust is God's will cannot be maintained when faith in God Himself is lost. Perhaps, simply, an individual who does not often see God's workings in the affairs of man is more likely to lose faith in Him altogether than the individual who finds God virtually everywhere and who may even attribute to God the "responsibility" for mass tragedy.

Quite instructive is the fact that survivors who lost their faith were, before the Holocaust, nearly twice as likely to have seen no role for God in catastrophes than survivors who believed in God throughout. And during the genocide period, while fully 63 percent of the latter group saw the hand of God in their immediate suffering, only 10 percent of the former group believed God was playing a part in their tragedy. Sometime after the Holocaust even these 10 percent were to lose their faith in God entirely. It is noteworthy further to contrast the survivors who lost their faith with survivors who retained their faith. Unlike the uncertainty of the latter group, virtually none of the former failed to respond to the question of whether catastrophes like the Holocaust are the will of God.

Former Atheists

Although their total number is admittedly small, two-thirds of all former atheists who acquired faith in God believe that catastrophes like the Holocaust are attributable to His will. For many of these survivors the belief in God and the belief that He was the "Author of Auschwitz" came to them simultaneously during the time of their desolation. And all retained these convictions to this day: Radically transforming convictions arrived at during the nadir of one's desolation are not easily dislodged. The remaining third of former atheists never believed that catastrophes like the Holocaust are the will of God. Many of these may have gained faith during the depths of, but they never attributed to God responsibility or accountability for, their peril.

A considerable number of the first group of survivors turned to and found God in their extremity, and some even saw the Holocaust as evidence of punishment for their past sins of disbelief and their failure to be good practicing Jews. One survivor of Ravensbrueck camp for women falling into this category said:

> It may seem childish now, although it didn't seem so at the time, but I made a bargain with God. I'd believe in Him and after it's all over and the Germans smashed then I'd go back home and be a good Jew. I'd repeat this over and over as I'd march near death with hunger and cold alongside the other unfortunates to the Lager at night and back to work in the morning. And the more I said it the more I believed in it and in Him and the more certain I was that I'd survive and live to see my enemies shattered and to see my relatives alive again.
>
> Of course, I never returned home again and never saw my family again. And there were many moments even when I believed in God that I thought I couldn't live on and I should let myself die. But my strength prevailed—both my physical strength and the spiritual strength I acquired from my newly purchased faith.
>
> I thought then that God was exacting vengeance on us for our rejection of Him and His ways and so if I promised I'd change God would also change His plans for me and I'd live . . .

I kept this thought to myself until now—and more than its truth it helped me survive.

Belief in the Messiah

> I believe with a perfect faith
> In the coming of the messiah
> In the coming of the messiah
> Do I believe
> And although he may tarry
> Yet do I believe.

Thus sang survivors on their death-trek toward the crematorium. Was this a theological statement being made? That is, did they genuinely believe in a coming of the messiah—as articulated in their song based on Maimonides's twelfth Principle of Faith—or rather was it for them a chant of high courage, a refrain of defiance and an expression of Jewish solidarity in the moment of their mortality? Or was it perhaps a composite of all of these elements?

Was there a belief on the part of European Jews in a messiah before the Holocaust, during and after it; and do survivors have faith in the coming of the messiah today, some three decades after the liberation of the camps? Our interest focuses primarily upon the possible changes regarding this article of faith which the Holocaust may have brought about.

The messiah, according to Jewish thought and especially in hundreds of references in the Talmud, was an "annointed one," yet to come, deputed by God to inaugurate an era of peace and national glory, particularly by the freeing of Israel from its oppressors. Perhaps some small segments of the popular Jewish mind thought otherwise, but the rabbis understood him to be a flesh-and-blood creature, a human being, divinely appointed to fulfill his mission, and not a superhuman Redeemer. The predominant view was that he would be a charismatically endowed descendant of King David who was, as were all Jewish heroes, simply a mortal man. Rav Saadia Gaon (C.E. 882–947), the medieval philosopher and author of *Emunot v'deot* (beliefs and opinions) affirms that the messiah will deliver Jerusalem from her enemy and then settle there with his people. And Maimonides provides an entirely rational description of the days of the messiah as an era when Israel will be an independent nation in its land free from the yoke of foreign oppression:

"The sages and prophets did not long for the days of the messiah that they may exercise dominion over the world, or rule the nations, or be glorified by them nor to eat, drink and be merry. Their steadfast desire was that Israel should be free to dedicate itself to Torah and its wisdom." [3]

In times of extreme national calamity the hope for his coming naturally became most ardent and provided great solace for the people. Was there an increase in messianic speculation and expectation during the intolerable years of the Hitlerian oppression as well?

As a corollary to the doctrine of the coming of the messiah, the rabbis postulated that there will first be "the travail of the messiah." Adopting the popular imagery of a mother suffering the pangs of birth, the rabbis dilated upon the severe pain and hardships that first must be experienced before his arrival could be brought about. Mankind must first either become absolutely perfect or, more likely, sink into a nadir of immorality and depravity, and only then may the light of the messianic presence shine forth: "Houses of study will be converted into brothels, the learning of the scribes will waste away and pious, saintly, sin-fearing men will be condemned." [4]

Moreover, the rabbis stressed the political and secular nature of the circumstances surrounding his coming which seemed to resemble and anticipate a twentieth-century world war: "If you see the kingdoms in conflict, look for the footsteps of the messiah. Be assured of it because that is what happened in the days of Abraham. When the kingdoms fought with each other Abraham was redeemed." [5] And frequently the rabbis employed the metaphor of the "Wars of Gog and Magog" to symbolize the world's political condition made ripe for the coming of the messiah.

In the midst of the suffering, immorality, and the bitter clash of nations during the Second World War, was the belief in the messiah spread, and were hopes raised for the time of the advent of the messianic era on the part of its victims? To answer the question it was first necessary to determine whether they believed in the doctrine of the messiah before the Holocaust began.

Our findings disclose that not only before the genocide period but afterward as well, the coming of the messiah proved to be, for survivors, the least admissible principle, after belief that the Holocaust was the will of God, when lined up against the doctrines of chosenness, the Torah as the word of God, Judaism as a true religion, and Judaism as the only true religion. Nevertheless, it is far more widely accepted than belief in resurrection and life after death, as will be shown later on.

The Holocaust and Messianism

Before the Holocaust, a full 35 percent of the entire survivor community believed in the coming of the messiah. None of course believed that he had already come, although one, speaking darkly and without amplification, suggested that "the Holocaust itself was the messiah. He has come and gone. And everything in the world is different."

There appear to be two predominant reasons for what modernists might assess as a strikingly large group of survivors expressing belief in the coming of the messiah, a concept often thought of in contemporary nondevout circles as an ancient and outgrown dogma. For most, particularly the very devout represented by the next lengthy quotation cited, the coming of the messiah is simply a traditional article of faith which requires no justification or reflection and elicits nearly automatic assent such as the belief in God or chosenness; and it is hardly a primitive or outdated doctrine. But for many others it is the very ambiguity of the concept that invites assent. And, in our survey, virtually every possible interpretation was in fact expressed as to the meaning of the messiah. Some take it to mean literally a man sent of God who will come to change the order of things, "bringing," as one former Dachau inmate suggested, "the prominent down and the downtrodden to prominence." And on the other end of the spectrum, simply put by a French-born survivor: "When war will finally be no more, then the messiah will have come."

One devout and ultra observant Hungarian-born survivor aligned himself with the view that the coming of the messiah was no more and no less than a traditional article of Jewish faith which by definition commands assent:

I'm too unlearned to know the specific details of the coming of
the messiah but our sages from the earliest time taught that he
would be sent by God when He decides to send him, that is when
we Jews deserve him and merit his coming. Maybe when he finally
comes, a long time from now, all of us who have died before—
the average man and all the holy martyrs who gave their lives for
the sanctification of God's name and all who were observant
and believed in God and did right in their lives and all who will pass
away in the future, myself among them I hope, will be reborn in
some manner or form and join the righteous who will gain the
privilege of eternal life with the company of the messiah. I don't
of course know what it will be like exactly but I have faith in

it anyway as do all true Jews. Jews have always believed in
this and I see no reason not to.

One former labor camp inmate's words are noteworthy for the remarkable statement on his own "resurrection" as well as with regard to
the ambiguity of the idea of the messiah, which contrasts in the extreme
with the previous view:

> It's crazy, I know, but I believe in the coming of the messiah
> although I do not know what that means exactly. And I do not
> believe in the resurrection of the dead although I myself have
> actually been resurrected from the dead. You see, I died once.
> Sunk deep into death. Not into mere unconsciousness, mind you,
> but into death. There is quite a difference, you can be sure. I know
> because I have experienced them both. Death was sweet and
> pleasant, a very good feeling contrary to the accepted view. But
> I was pulled out. Quite against my will, entirely unwillingly,
> I should add, and brought back to the land of the living by a
> fellow inmate who later succumbed himself in the camp, a man
> who yanked me back from the dead. I was dead and I was
> resurrected. And yet despite this experience I believe only in the
> coming of the messiah because that could mean anything at all
> and I happen to accept one particular understanding of what
> that means to me and reject others. But I do not accept the popular
> idea of the resurrection of the dead, especially if you have been
> dead a long time, not like I who died for a short time. Then there
> is no coming back at all. And when someone jokes about being
> just a little bit dead and everyone else around laughs at how
> ridiculous is that notion, like being a little bit pregnant, I don't
> laugh at all. I know better, having been dead just a little bit
> myself once.

During the Holocaust, 7 percent of our survivors discontinued
their belief in the coming of the messiah. Still, more than one in four
(28 percent) continued in that belief. In fact, the 7 percent attrition
during the Holocaust was the smallest rate sustained by any of the six
articles of faith surveyed. Again, perhaps the singular ambiguity of
the doctrine may have continued to uphold it even though the other
doctrines are clearly not without their own considerable ambiguity.
Additionally, during the genocide period, even though our research
failed to reveal one survivor who cited the Holocaust as a source for his

belief in the messiah, some, as the next former Treblinka concentration camp inmate explains, seized upon the belief in a messiah for the sake of their sanity and self-preservation. And indeed, for devout Jews in particular, no other religious doctrine is a more appropriate reaction to their condition than that a messiah might be imminent to extricate them from, and bring meaning to, their experience of intense suffering:

> The Torah tells us that the messiah will come and so he will.
> When God decides to send him. During the Holocaust, I thought
> that he'd come just as I prayed and expected a miracle to save
> us when death was all around us in each of the camps I was
> sent to. It didn't happen, of course, but that doesn't mean God
> has abandoned us. It certainly does not mean that the messiah will
> never come. My faith in God and my faith in the Torah and in
> Paradise [literally, the Garden of Eden] meant a great deal to me.
> My prayers and beliefs kept me alive. That is another way of
> saying, God looked after me.

Nearly all the survivors who foresook their belief in the coming of the messiah during the genocide period thought that he should have come to save Israel at that time and that no other time could have been more suitable for "a great deliverance" to be effected. The following survivor, who had celebrated his Bar-Mitzvah a month before he was evacuated to Bergen-Belsen and whose sense of irony and sarcasm was as droll and good-natured as it was bitter, is representative:

> I went from camp to camp, some were better, some were worse
> than the others. But it was more advantageous to stay put in
> one and learn the best survival methods of that camp in order to
> endure the war. Although I was very lucky and I survived in
> spite of the many camps, I lost my faith in almost everything,
> particularly the coming of the messiah, and I most clearly remember
> it happening to me. I said if he doesn't come now he'll never come.
> I said, if not now, when? I said this is the worst ever, he's sure to
> come. I waited and waited and the only one to come was the angel
> of death. He came often. His visit was frequently very welcome.
> There was no one busier than the angel of death. And don't
> think we didn't look for him. But the messiah never showed. And
> don't think we didn't look for him too. But after a while I
> just stopped believing he would come. I knew then it was merely
> wishful thinking.

Immediately after the Holocaust, an additional 2 percent ceased to believe in the coming of the messiah, for much the same reason as cited above. As one reflected, "when I thought about it after the war was over, I realized that if he hadn't come then, the only conclusion has to be—there is no messiah." But today, a slight 2 percent increase returned the belief in the messiah to its mid-Holocaust level of 28 percent—undoubtedly a consequence of the generally favorable climate for belief and observances in the Jewish homeland, which won adherents for nearly every article of faith.

One Lithuanian-born ghetto and death camp survivor, who is classified as having returned to a belief in the messiah among other traditional beliefs, spoke these words:

> I believe in the messiah but he will come only when we have
> paved his way to come. When the world will be made an almost
> perfect ideal place by man himself, then he will come and bring
> about the completed perfection. Man's actions must precede the
> messiah's. During the war, even though I and others may have,
> at various times, expected he'd come, then mankind was at its worst
> behavior and not deserving of the days of the messiah. So why
> should we have expected him? He couldn't come in the midst of
> war and murder and the killing of the blameless and innocent.
> When man prepares the way for him to enter the world, then, and
> only then, can we hope for his arrival.

Fully 65 percent of all survivors never believed in the coming of the messiah, because, as one of them classified as moderately observant sarcastically and rather harshly put it:

> I can't think of anything more ridiculous and absurd than the
> belief that a messiah is going to come. No doubt riding on
> some white ass like out of the biblical epics in the movies. Can you
> just visualize that—in the atomic age of jet planes and rockets?
> And what will he do when he comes? His purpose is to lead us all,
> all the Jews of the world, marching and singing and dancing
> behind his slow-moving ass, towards the Holy Land. Through the
> now suddenly-made-peaceful Arab lands, no doubt. Well, he
> must have come already in spite of the fact that no one has seen
> him, because we are in our own land, ruling it just like the
> fulfillment of the messianic promise. Only an imbecile could
> believe in a messiah.

Nontraditional Survivors and Messianism

In the nineteenth century, Reform Judaism began to reinterpret the doctrine of the coming of the messiah by replacing the traditional belief in a personal messiah with a belief in a messianic age, which means a world perfected by, in the words of the 1937 Conference of Reform Rabbis in Columbus, Ohio, "the establishment of the Kingdom of God, of universal brotherhood, justice, truth and peace on earth. This is our messianic goal."

It is noteworthy that while atheist survivors, without exception through the years, rejected belief in a messiah whether traditionally conceived or reinterpreted, those survivors who understood God in impersonal terms as a Power, or Force, in the universe, were also inclined to reinterpret the concept of the messiah and almost invariably did so in line with the ideas of Reform Judaism.

In fact, it is surprising that no more than 22 percent of these survivors at the high point before the Holocaust were disposed to reinterpret the messiah idea as they had the God idea. That the reinterpretation of the God concept was already suggested by the questionnaire itself while a reinterpretation of the messiah idea required a certain degree of original thinking and initiative is one obvious explanation. Additionally, in the mind of the Jew, discarding the messiah idea does not constitute withdrawal from the mainstream of Judaism quite in the same way as does the total rejection of the God idea. As one articulate Belzec survivor observed:

> I am a very modern person and I often do not believe in anything. But the definition of a God who is not a person but is a power, is not hard for me to accept. And since there are two conflicting attitudes residing in my mind simultaneously, the one atheistic and the other of not wishing to be thought of as a non-Jew, the problem is to a great extent resolved by the acceptance of a modern idea like this about what God is. But as to a messiah, that is not important for being a Jew anyway, and I have no inner conflict about it.

During the Holocaust half of the survivors conceiving of God as an impersonal Force discontinued, from 22 to 11 percent, to espouse belief in an idea of the messiah; and that percentage remained constant until the present. These were generally survivors who reinterpreted the coming of the messiah as an anticipation of perfectionist utopianism and the ushering in of the millennium.

To espouse a conviction in the perfectability of mankind in the midst of its genocidal refutation is a severe challenge even for the most confirmed optimist of this subgroup and accounts for the loss of half their number. One such survivor said that he had been "terribly naive thinking that the world was getting to be a better place, which is what I thought was the meaning of the coming of the messiah. But now we can all see that mankind is evolving into a worse creature, not a better one. My own experience is perfect proof."

To continue, 78 percent of all survivors expressing belief in God as an impersonal Power in the universe at no time affirmed a reinterpreted idea of the messiah; 34 percent of all survivors who lost faith in God believed in the coming of the messiah before the Holocaust and all, without exception, discarded that belief, as well as most others, during the Holocaust years.

Their counterparts, survivors who gained faith in God, did not believe in the messiah before the genocide period. During—but not necessarily because of—the Holocaust, however, 33 percent of these survivors began to believe not only in the existence of God but in the coming of His messianic deputy as well; and after the Holocaust that number rose still further to 50 percent and changed no further thereafter.

Generally, members of this small subgroup began to believe in a rather traditional idea of the messiah just as their newly acquired faith was essentially the conventional idea of a personal God. Especially noteworthy is the complete absence of evidence that any of these—or other —survivors claim that the Holocaust itself inspired belief in the coming of the messiah. (This finding will be discussed further in the next section on the chosenness of the Jewish people).

Devout Survivors and Messianism

Of the survivors who remained believers in a personal God throughout the four stages, one-third claimed never to have had faith in the coming of the messiah. Except for the belief that the Holocaust was the will of God, no other article of faith was rejected as frequently by devout survivors. Nevertheless, overall, devout survivors held firmly and unwaveringly to this faith throughout the years: Before and during the Holocaust two-thirds of all devout survivors answering the question—and only 4 percent refrained from doing so—claimed to have believed in the coming of the messiah. Immediately after the Holocaust, perhaps because, as several survivors indicated, "Upon reflection, with the experience still so close, the feeling was if he hadn't come then, when we Jews were being destroyed wholesale, I can no longer be sure he'd ever come," 6 percent relinquished that faith—but the figure returned to two thirds (66 percent) for the period we designate "today."

Two of every three devout survivors expressed belief not in the messiah as a poetic metaphor or symbol for the mechanical, inexorable if nonlineal progression of civilization in the direction of an ideal human state, but in the traditional conception of messianism as a direct, divine intervention in the affairs of man. A rather typical articulation by a north Tel-Aviv secondary school teacher is recorded first, and an atypical opinion by a Kibbutz Lohamai Haghettaot member follows:

> There's nothing embarrassing about believing in the coming of
> the messiah. It doesn't mean we should expect him any moment or
> he should come when we want him to. Jews never believed he
> was awaiting our summons. But Jews always believed he would one
> day be sent by God and by his coming civilization would turn
> around and become the kind of world we haven't been able to
> achieve on our own.
>
> But we will not be misled by false messiahs as we have been
> on numerous occasions in the past: Shabbatai Zvi and Jacob Frank
> and others who deceived us because all Jews wanted so badly
> to believe the time was right.
>
> A totally new age has been ushered in with the Holocaust, the
> time preceding the age of the messiah. The Holocaust should
> change the calendar. We should no longer see ourselves, according
> to the regular, ordinary calendar, as being in the 5730s, because
> there is nothing regular or ordinary or even normal about our
> times. We should be now in the year Holocaust plus 31 or 32 or
> whatever, with perhaps Kristallnacht [night of the broken glass]
> as the starting point of the new era, the era before the messianic age.
> Just like 1970 is a thousand nine hundred and seventy years after
> Jesus, so we should calculate B.H. as before the Holocaust and A.H.
> as after the Holocaust. We are now in the time of A.H., after
> the Holocaust and before the coming of the messiah. He will come.
> Our extraordinary postgenocide epoch warrants it.

Jewish and Christian Messianism

Consideration by survivors of messianic faith and theory occasioned a number of passing references to Jesus and Christianity. Prior to ad-

ministering the questionnaire, little thought was given to eliciting survivor reaction toward Christianity except in connection with the history
of anti-Semitism and the comportment of Christians toward Jews during the genocide period. In other contexts within the questionnaire
survivors spoke of the Christian religion's responsibilities for, and failures during, the catastrophe. Here ample, if unplanned, opportunity
was provided for respondents to volunteer their understanding of
various fundamentals of Christian theology—and Jewish theology as
well.

Without exception, and regardless of their religious dispositions,
survivors inclined to reflect on the messiahship of Jesus were hostile, even
pugnacious, toward him. One observant survivor, after affirming his
own belief in a personal messiah, tendered the first view, which follows.
The second and third comments were offered by moderately observant
and nonobservant survivors, respectively:

> You don't have to believe in a miracle-man to accept the coming
> of the messiah. If you do, be careful you're not being brainwashed
> by all the Christian religion's absurd and nonsensical teachings
> that have accumulated over the years, teachings which describe
> the Christian messiah but not the real messiah yet to come, the
> Jewish messiah.
>
> The Christian messiah walks on water and performs other
> cheap tricks like Pharaoh's magicians. He is also a saint type,
> austere and meek—although also nasty at times when, for example,
> he curses out trees for not bearing fruit out of season and so
> forth, one who turns the other cheek and gives away his cloak
> after his coat has been taken away by force. For him, the Christian
> messiah, the end of the world is at hand anyway, so what does it
> all matter what you have or what you do? The Jewish messiah
> is masculine not feminine, strong not weak, a powerful fighter,
> like Samson and Bar Kochba, and I believe in that.

◆

> Some messiah the Christians have. He was such an absolute
> failure the first time, he's got to come back again. Couldn't he get
> the job done right when he was here? So now you have to
> believe in a second coming. Sure, because after all, what is better
> about the world since his first coming? Nothing. In fact it's
> all gotten worse: religious wars fought over him and in his name,
> inquisitions, crusades, and pogroms and assorted other horrors
> and suffering in his wake. My idea of a messiah is one who is not a

failure. He is to bring about a better world of peace and love and goodness, all quite the opposite of what this Jesus, the Christian messiah brought about. Practically a third of the world accepts him, this Jewish man, as a messiah; let them. They appropriated our Bible and pretended it's theirs. They say they are the new Israel and the new chosen people and they worship a Jewish man of 2,000 years ago as their God and messiah. Let them.

———◆———

Christians can't make up their minds whether Jesus was a God or a messiah or what. So they try to mix up the two together to make everyone happy. If he was a God how could he be put to death? Gods don't die or they are not Gods. If he was a messiah, how is it that the people he was supposedly sent to redeem knew better and never accepted him or recognized him to be a messiah? Because they, the Jews, never accepted him it is their fault, not his, so they must be wicked, so very wicked they are even deserving of death. And so the mass murder of Jews is quite permissible to the Christian theology which teaches that Jesus was the messiah. There's the best explanation of the cause of the Holocaust yet.

The final comment comparing Jewish and Christian thought was offered by a nonobservant Vilna-born survivor who reinterprets the coming of the messiah

> . . . as a time in the distant future when the world will be at peace. If you take away from Christians Jesus the messiah who was supposed to be the Son of God, born miraculously of a virgin, crucified and resurrected and a host of other miracles, if you take all these miracles away from Christians you have nothing left because there is nothing left. Nothing that isn't Jewish. Take the miracles away and he ceases to be a Christian. He becomes nothing. No Jesus the messiah, the Christ, no Christianity. But if you take away the miracles in Judaism—those that appear in the Bible, for example—like the sun standing still or the plagues or the parting of the Red Sea, you lose nothing at all. They are not the foundation of Judaism. There is nothing essential about them. And that is why, for Jews, the messiah never comes— because we don't need miracles to be Jews. Only for Christians has their messiah come. When they say their God is dead, they're right. He is.

The Chosen People

In earliest biblical times the religious doctrines providing maximum firepower for theological controversy were the belief in one God or many, that is, monotheism as against polytheism in its various conformations and the related question whether the God of Israel is a national God, the deity of Israel exclusively, as against His serving as world deity. These disputes were ultimately resolved by positing God's universality, Israel's particularity and chosenness.

Persistently, in many of the various eras of Jewish history, past and present, among the theological issues of greatest discordance and factionalism for Jews was and is the election of Israel.

In the biblical formulation of the tenet, God has, through an historical act, selected Israel to be His peculiar people. "He has chosen thee from all the nations on the face of the earth to be a people peculiarly His own. It was not because thou art the largest of all nations that the Lord set His love upon thee and chose thee, for thou art really the smallest of all nations." [6]

In the daily morning service, the second benediction declares: "Thou hast chosen us from all peoples and tongues, and hast brought us near unto Thy great name forever in faithfulness that we in love give thanks unto Thee and proclaim Thy unity." The kiddush for Sabbath and Holy days, the Havdalah and blessings immediately preceding the Shema and recited over the Torah reading all express this belief.

According to its fundamental expressions in Jewish thought, Israel had been chosen by God to be "a kingdom of priests and a holy nation," [7] His people, His messenger, His witnesses, and His light to the peoples of the earth. God covenanted with and revealed His Torah to Israel that His people may live by its commandments and teach them to the nations. Therefore, the Jewish people were chosen not so much for special prerogatives, concessions, or glorification as for service and as a blessing to all mankind in its mission of bringing redemption to the entire human race. As such, to be so selected may be regarded as a privilege, but it imposed a heavy burden as well. In the Midrash, Simeon ben Yohai felt it necessary to reconcile the doctrine of God's universality with the election of Israel by having God say to Israel: "I am the God of all mankind nevertheless I have joined My name only with yours. I am not called 'the God of worshippers of stars and planets' but only 'the God of Israel.' " [8]

In more recent years Mordecai M. Kaplan's Reconstructionist Movement, as one of its cornerstone principles, uprooted the doctrine altogether from its liturgy as Kaplan had expelled it from his philosophy. And Reform Judaism felt constrained to modify it slightly by removing "from all the nations" from the kiddush and by freely rendering, in the Union Prayer Book, all passages containing the words "Thou hast chosen us" with "Thou hast ennobled us" and "Thou hast called us" to signify the idea of election as vocation for a mission and to neutralize charges of Jewish claims of superiority over other peoples. Despite these disclaimers and other disavowals, the doctrine of chosenness retains its primary and paramount place of importance in contemporary Jewish thought.

The purpose of administering the questionnaire was obviously not to test survivors' knowledge and appreciation of the historical development and theological nuances in the concept of chosenness. And yet interviews quickly established that there dwelt in the minds of survivors fewer uncertainties and perplexities concerning their understanding of the meaning of chosenness than, for example, the meaning of messianism —two frequently paired teachings. Generally, survivors deliberated and contemplated far longer answering questions in connection with other tenets of faith than with chosenness. This despite its own manifest ambiguity. They may have differed with each other in their interpretations, but survivors had largely made up their minds previously: "You either believe the Jews are special in some way or you don't. In what precise way may not be so important. But that they are, is," explained one of the many similar-minded survivors.

That there prevailed not only greater decisiveness but greater conviction and acceptance as well can be seen distinctly in the antithetically rival categories of survivors losing faith and those who were gaining faith as a consequence of the Holocaust.

All survivors who lost faith in God discontinued belief in the coming of the messiah as well, but 10 percent of these retained faith in the concept of chosenness. And of all survivors who gained faith in God because of the Holocaust, none had believed in messianism or in chosenness before the Holocaust. However, whereas only half eventually became believers in the coming of the messiah, a full 83 percent today consider the Jews the chosen people. And survivors who remained atheistic throughout the years believed in neither doctrine before the catastrophe, while today 18 percent see the Jews as chosen (obviously in ways other than by God) and none, still, accept the teaching of the coming of the messiah. Even among consistent believers, 14 percent more today accept chosenness over messianism.

In fact, our findings reveal that for the total survivor community before the Holocaust began, only the teachings that the Torah is the word of God and that Judaism is a true religion proved more prevalent than the idea of chosenness. In later years the degree of belief in chosenness came to equal the belief in the Torah as the word of God, (41 percent) leaving only the idea that Judaism is a true religion in higher approbation, by some 20 percent.

The Tolerance Principle

It is no longer true that Holocaust survivors cannot be moved to speak much about the meaning of their experiences. They now have a good deal to say about themselves, about each other, about each other's sayings about their shared experiences, and about the nature and function of such talk. As this study demonstrates, they also speak both individually and collectively of the religious ideas affected by their experiences.

Under critical scrutiny religious ideas often spawn innumerable interpretations. In the domain of the interpretive critic, whether survivor or theologian, we cannot judge the remarks they make as simply true or false, accurate or inaccurate, right or wrong, but only as plausible, reasonable, acceptable, sensible, and the like. The interpretation of a religious idea can also be judged radical or traditional, heretical or historical, un-Jewish or as adumbrating aspects of the heritage.

We do not wish to imply that in all cases of ambiguity no particular interpretation can be established over its rivals. Jewish tradition has its mainstream and its rivulets. But whether for theology or, as John Hospers observes, for literature, what has been characterized as the tolerance principle obtains:

> A frustrating and at the same time fascinating aspect of complex works . . . is their resistance to a single interpretation, in that many propositions seem to be implied, some of them contradicting others. . . . Nor need any of the conflicting interpretations be wrong; both of two contradictory propositions may really be suggested [and] they may both really be implied.[9]

Religious thinkers themselves readily admit that a particular theological thesis may support alternative and even incompatible interpretations. There is no cause for astonishment therefore when survivors, or the many sectors of any population for that matter, express divergent interpretations of the same religious doctrine. The very fact of their differing backgrounds and personalities help generate alternative and often contrary hypotheses.

The idea of the election of Israel is particularly subject to and tolerant of plural readings and propositions even if it is perhaps less ambiguous than the idea of messianism, for example, which as one survivor suggested "connotes to me the supernatural while chosenness is entirely reasonable and this worldly."

As in the case of messianism, nearly all possible expositions of chosenness were espoused. But although the central core of the concept is the metaphysical uniqueness of the Jew, the predominant denotation of chosenness for survivors was that of singularity in history, of the people Israel being sui generis. One survivor expressed the preponderant opinion: "How can anyone, Jew or non-Jew, who looks at the experiences and contributions of the Jewish people, unless he be blind or prejudiced or, if Jewish, full of self-hate, fail to see the extraordinarily profound uniqueness of the Jewish people?"

Nonbelieving survivors especially often sought to evade the various implications of the tenet, such as how chosen or chosen by whom—elementary matters for believers, of course—and for what purpose or role, until pressed to do so in the interview. Yet when survivors were bidden to reflect upon these and other ancillary and related issues their views, as often as not, whether consciously or unconsciously, reflected traditional Jewish theology.

Sacred and Secular

There are basically two approaches for affirming the doctrine of chosenness: one sacred, the other secular. The first is most often expressed in terms of the traditional article of faith which asserts simply and straightforwardly that the Jews were divinely chosen. In the words of the Bible: "Thou art a people holy to the Lord Thy God, who hast chosen thee from all the nations on the face of the earth to be His own possession." [10] As such, particularly for the devout, it requires no justification or reflection and elicits nearly automatic assent. One ultra observant survivor's remarks were typically representative:

> There is no explanation for it. It just is. God is God and He
> has the right to choose whomever He pleases. It's God choice to
> choose the Jews if He likes. And it was His choice to make us
> an eternal people. We are mortals and we do not question God. And
> we never ask Him why. All we know is that God chose the
> Jewish people to be His own as a man picks his bride for his own
> and that's that.

A devout Treblinka survivor said, "I believe it but I know I can't prove it even if others think it can be proven by some logical arguments." Another devout survivor, however, with an atypical perspective in his espousal of chosenness, rebutted by proclaiming:

Whatever people God might have chosen would by that act have become different and special and uncommon and there would have been a need for some way to refer to it, some name to signify it to itself and to others. Call the people, if you will, X, or call them Jewish. Makes no difference. And call its religion Y, if you will, or Judaism. It is impossible logically for X and Y or Jews and Judaism not to exist if God exists and acts in history. So the nation that God took to Himself as special became known as the Jewish people and we, quite by accident and good fortune, are its component parts, the individuals of the people. And that accident implies that there are obligations, the duties of the Torah which is the price and reward of membership.

At the other extreme are survivors who see the Jews as chosen but refuse to propound it as a religious category. Among these are respondents who claim, "The Jews are chosen by history and by circumstance, not by God." "Other peoples have chosen to single out the Jews for good or ill, mostly ill. And that has made the Jews unique." "Anti-Semitism has made the Jews chosen; Hitler, Stalin, Torquemada, Chimelnitzki and others have chosen us." "We were by fate and destiny chosen to be an eccentric, abnormal, freak of a people, always under the glare of the spotlight—in Europe, in Soviet Russia, in America, here is Israel, everywhere." And, "The fate of the Jew is inextricably linked to the fate of the world."

As a secular proposition chosenness becomes essentially an expression of pride in the extraordinary career and the noble achievements of the people. For example, one survivor commented: "No other people has contributed so much to the benefit of civilization and so little to its detriment."

One particularly gifted spokesman for this view composed the following brief treatise, excusing himself for a moment from the give and take of the interview and seating himself at a desk in an adjoining room after giving instructions not to be disturbed:

Wherever, in whatever parts of the world mankind was making advances, always, throughout history, there was the Jew.

History is entirely unthinkable without him. He was either leading the advances and making the breakthroughs himself like Freud, Einstein and Marx, or supporting and upholding, like a tiny, intellectual and creative avant-garde army, the forward movements of society. Spain, Poland, Germany, America—wherever the wave of civilization created and hit its peak, there, bobbing on the top of the wave was the Jew. He was knowledgeable, educated, talented, industrious and reliable. He brought much to the task and gave his all.

Only the Jew continually as a people prepared the way for man's ascent. All others receded and faded and were gone. The Jew alone had been chosen, due to his own exceptional traits plus the needs of the rest of mankind for him, chosen to be history's bright beacon throwing light upon the road ahead leading toward the messianic future.

And a number of similar-minded survivors were able to add, in the words of one, "although not all peoples were chosen, and some are perhaps more chosen than others much as some individuals are more gifted than others, there were obviously, as history shows, other nations which were also chosen to play their parts on the stage of history in leading roles as opposed to bit parts. The Greeks, for example, and the Romans, and now perhaps the Americans—but always the starring role is left for the Jews."

And another survivor added pithily that "everyone is chosen except that some do what they were chosen for and others do not." And yet another said, "if all peoples would feel themselves chosen as we do—and they should!—then wars would be no longer, poverty and unrighteousness would vanish from the world and peoples would place the enterprise of study and education above all the rest."

The same idea of multi-chosenness can become translated into religious terms. It states, in alignment with the previous citations, that various peoples besides the Jews are in some way chosen. For these survivors, however, it was a choice divinely ordained. One who worked in the clean-up detail at Auschwitz, sorting the baggage of the newly arrived prisoners, suggested:

Certainly Israel is chosen. All peoples and all individuals are chosen and special and unique; none duplicated by any other. God chooses many peoples and individuals like Moses and Jesus and

Akiba and Freud and Einstein. Most of those He chooses for reasons He alone understands are Jews like all of these I mentioned. But there are others too. Darwin, for example, and Dag Hammarskjöld and others. God chooses in unknown ways to grant genius and talents to some and not to others. And we are told in the Bible that God led the Jews out of Egyptian bondage but He also led the Philistines out of Caphtor and the Cushites out of Cush.

There were many devout survivors, of course, who stressed primarily the sacred, doctrinal justification for the chosenness of Israel but secondarily recognized historical confirmation as well, as the next quotation illustrates, whereas, conversely, other devout survivors, represented by the second quotation, posited the survival of the Jew in history as confirmation of the doctrinal thesis.

I believe in the chosenness of the Jewish people because the Torah says so, which is really quite enough for me, and also others ought to acknowledge it simply because the history of the Jewish people proves it. We alone were chosen to receive the Torah on Mount Sinai. We alone were commanded to live by its laws and to act as teachers of God's truth to the world. And this is the reason we Jews have been oppressed and murdered periodically throughout the centuries.

———◆———

The survival of the Jewish people is proof positive of its chosenness. The incredible story of our survival from our biblical enemies, from Egyptian bondage and Assyrian mass murder, from Roman savagery and Christian Crusaders and Inquisitions and ruthless Cossack pogroms and the Nazis committing genocide upon us and then Arab terrorism—and still the Jewish people lives! The survival of the Jew in the face of overwhelming and impossible odds is the greatest miracle the world has ever known and it proves beyond a shadow of doubt that the Jews are chosen and proves too that God exists and is protecting and guarding them and seeing to it that the Jews will always remain alive in this world forever, regardless of our enemies.

And not to be overlooked are the uncharacteristic remarks of a heterodoxical Sobibor survivor who conceptualized chosenness in an amalgam of secular and sacred:

It is not that God chose the Jews. It is rather that the Jews chose God and chose to live differently and distinctly, that is, morally—without murdering others; and separately too, as a community apart. God didn't create man; rather man, also the Jew, created God in his own image. And once we Jews invented for ourselves a God of Justice we had no choice but to try to live ourselves with the aim of being just. When we chose we took upon ourselves certain responsibilities and commitments of how to live. And we represented these values throughout history as well as in our own time. And it continues to be our responsibility because that is what we chose for our role in history. And history shows we pretty well succeeded: Very few other peoples can match our record of justice and of decent behavior toward peoples who are different than ourselves. Even the Torah reminds us to be decent to those who are strangers because we were strangers ourselves once when we were in Egypt. We behaved well *in* history primarily because we learned so well *from* history.

Chosenness and Superiority

One must not assume that survivors of a particular category—the devout, for example—were more likely to couple chosenness with superiority. There were traditional-minded survivors who affirmed it ("If God chose us then if we hadn't merited it by our willingness to keep the Torah and by our character before, then by the choice itself did we become elevated over other peoples, because how could any show of preference by God Himself not make the object of His choice supreme, the world's elite?"); others denied it emphatically. And a number of survivors who understood chosenness in nonreligious terms nevertheless added the element of Jewish superiority to the secular construction. One such survivor spoke in these words:

Simply bear in mind the experiences of the Jewish people and then try to insist that the Jews are *not* exceptional. And think of the treatment the Jews have had to absorb in the wrath of jealousy from other peoples throughout history and from other faiths. Just think of these and you have to understand at once and believe at once in the superiority of the Jews morally and ethically and every other way as well—which is both the glory and the tragedy of being a Jew.

And another nonobservant survivor said:

> Sometimes there is a unique confluence of wind and rain and earth
> and sun which produces the perfect vineyard, yielding the
> most exceptionally choice wine. And sometimes there is the unique
> merging and interfusing of geography, historical experience
> and national character which brings forth the choicest people—
> Israel.

What may be especially significant, however, is that not one survivor claimed, with Judah Halevi, the medieval Jewish poet and philosopher, that chosenness implies racial or inherent biological superiority.
Some, of course, may have thought it, but none volunteered it. Indeed,
from all segments of the survivor community came forceful denials of
such claims. The same survivor who spoke of Jews as "elevated over
other peoples" also pointed out what is surely the most telling argument
against racial or genetic superiority that "any man or woman can become Jewish and part of the elect of Israel. Although it is difficult in
the extreme to be a Jew, the whole of mankind is eligible if they willingly forsake idolatry, convert according to the Torah, and become
part of the people and keep the commandments. . . . No one, regardless of his origins, is automatically excluded or prevented from entering
the covenant and becoming part of the Jewish people."

Others said: "Chosenness means different, not better." "We Jews
are just pioneers; first, but not best." "We've got obligations, not
privileges." "We're a separate folk but not an elite one." "Chosenness
means not ordinary but it doesn't mean superior." And, constantly,
"Anybody can become Jewish."

In recent times, Ernest Van den Haag, C. P. Snow, Nathaniel Wyle,
and other social scientists have argued for the view that the Jews are
intellectually superior genetically. For those survivors who did define
chosenness as better, it was most infrequently in terms of an intellectual
elite but rather conceived most often in these terms:

> My wife is the best wife in the world; my parents were, God
> bless their souls, consecrated and holy. There was no man more
> gentle than my father, no woman as kind and giving as my
> mother. I also sincerely believe that my children are, each one of
> them, extraordinary and unusually gifted kids. I also know that
> my neighbor feels exactly that way about members of his own
> family. And you know what? I find no fault with that at all. My

neighbor's wife is the best wife possible for him. I hope he believes that. I also feel my people are the finest and I can give you many reasons and give examples, too, as to why they are the best. And I expect and hope that others feel the same way about their family and their people and their city and their country and their houses of worship and everything that is theirs. Men and women should feel that the people of their lives nearest to them are best. All I ask is that "feeling best" not be taken to mean others are inferior, *untermenschen* deserving of discrimination or even destruction.

But a considerable number of other survivors, less generous perhaps, rendered the concept in accordance with the following view:

If a father has many children he can't but have a favorite. God too is the God of many peoples but He clearly prefers Israel, His first born, the love of youth. All the other children may say they are their father's favorite but deep down they know they are not and they know who really is. And God separated the one from the others, "the holy from the profane, the light from the dark, Israel from the nations." The beloved child, Israel, is separated from the goyim and the goyim know it deep in their hearts.

Chosenness and the Holocaust

Before the Holocaust began, half (49 percent) of all survivors believed in the concept of chosenness. That percentage dropped to 36 for the time periods designated as during the Holocaust and immediately thereafter. Its acceptance recovered by 5 percent during the years survivors lived in Israel until it reaches 41 percent today—for a net loss of 8 percent.

Survivors who believed in chosenness throughout the years invariably saw no justification for relinquishing the concept. Indeed, as the following ultra observant survivor's words testify, the Holocaust most often reinforced the conviction:

The Jews are certainly the chosen people of God, a special people. When God gave us the Torah and made a covenant with us, from that time on we were His own people—forever. The other

peoples of the world have a purpose. They exist to be used by God
to keep Israel always conscious of her special status and to
remind her and teach her to keep the commandments of the Torah.
The proof is that God often has punished His people for their
sins by having the different nations cause the Jews to suffer
in one way or another, by exiling His people or by Holocausts like
the one we all went through. In the camps I understood this very
well. But He also lifts their burdens and rewards His people
when they have suffered enough and punishes her enemies like
Pharaoh and the Nazis. When we stop sinning God will stop
punishing us and we may enjoy the rewards and benefits of being
His chosen people. That will be the days of the messiah. May
it come soon and in our day. Amen.

And another, entirely nonobservant survivor, devout in his beliefs,
who affirms chosenness, maintains that "God chose the Jews to defeat
Hitler. If Hitler wasn't entirely and compulsively set upon killing us
and expending valuable energy and manpower on this bloody job when
he should have used his resources for the war, the Nazis would have
won the war. But, like in the Five Books, God hardened his heart as
He hardened Pharaoh's heart and we Jews became martyrs again and
saved the world from Hitler."

Survivors who forsook the concept during the Holocaust and immediately thereafter were not necessarily of one mind in their reasoning, but they most frequently cited the destruction as justification for
their abandonment of the doctrine:

How crude and presumptuous to say you're chosen and preferred
over others. And how demeaning to all of them. And all
religions or nations that make such claims are arrogant—like the
Nazis who saw themselves as superior *Herrenvolk* and *Ubermenschen*. Before the Holocaust, before I saw firsthand at my
own peril where such thinking can lead, I too thought we Jews
were superior to all others, chosen by God although I never thought
of myself as special. My close friendship with a wonderful
non-Jew in the camps also helped change my mind. And
remember the Nazis, who also thought they were chosen, killed
millions arising out of such a belief, which is nothing but vanity
and haughtiness and conceit. And so I refuse to have beliefs
such as they and I don't wish to become as they, and I know
where all this kind of imperious, lordly thinking can lead.

An underground fighter and Monowitz slave labor camp "graduate" made these remarks:

> I do not believe we are chosen. Besides, you have to understand about the true self-image and self-evaluation of anyone who keeps saying that he is special or chosen. It's probable he's covering up the very opposite feelings of inferiority and inadequacy and he really doesn't think much of himself, so he goes around like a cock flaunting himself and posturing and pretending and trying to fool others and himself. The Nazis were like this. Now we Jews don't have to do that, we're too accomplished and talented and gifted and creative and our accomplishments speak for themselves. There is no need to boast or call attention to ourselves by what we say. Better to call attention to ourselves by what we do.

And another survivor said simply, "I now believe the Jews are different, yes, we are different; chosen, no." And others said, "During the Holocaust I realized that the idea of the Jews or anyone being chosen is nonsense; just boastfulness and snobbery." "When I looked around at our degradation I knew we were hardly chosen." And, finally, "Chosen? For what? To be butchered? I don't believe that any more."

The State of Israel restored that Holocaust-lost faith for some ("I began again to believe we Jews are very, very special, very, very different, chosen; that the resurrection of the state is a miracle which can only be understood as God's keeping His promise to His people. Although I gave up much then, including this, now I see things more clearly"); and undermined it for others ("If you have anti-Semitism against the Jews then the Jews compensate by saying the opposite—we're better and chosen. But Israel, the state, counteracts anti-Semitism by our very existence, our presence on the map—and we no longer need to see ourselves as chosen. At long last we are normal"). It has already been shown that the former group far outnumbered the latter, perhaps in part because of the generally favorable climate for belief and observances in the Jewish homeland.

It has been suggested previously that there may be more than one conceptual thrust to each theological issue. This does not imply, however, that there must of necessity exist an interpretation for every idea to suit, and be appropriated by, every survivor. With regard to chosenness, 43 percent of the entire survivor community throughout the four stages rejected all interpretations of the idea known to them, quite incidentally rendering it the least fluctuating and most evenly contested article of faith. The beliefs that Judaism is a true religion (22 percent) and that the Torah is the word of God (41 percent) had fewer rejections. And the beliefs that Judaism is the only true religion (53 percent), that the messiah will arrive someday (65 percent), and that the Holocaust is the will of God (67 percent) all were disdained by more survivors.

The rather impressive 22 percent rejection of messianism over chosenness may reflect the consensus that the latter concept is more immediate to one's present life and more central to Judaism. And indeed, chosenness is unquestionably a biblical proposition, whereas messianism is decidedly a later accretion, disputably biblical, primarily Talmudic. Chosenness, a concept that arrived earlier in Jewish life and thought than messianism, appears to have greater longevity potential. Messianism, while hardly obsolete, does not seem to have seized hold of the modern post-Holocaust consciousness. To survivors, and perhaps to others as well, the Holocaust may be seen as evidence of the election of Israel, insofar as the Jew was "chosen" then to play a more than ordinary role in human events. At the same time the Holocaust may have shown messianism to have been merely wishful thinking.

One survivor who consistently rejected the idea of chosenness uttered the following remarks:

> Not before, not now. I never believed the Jews are chosen because
> that means God prefers one people over another and I don't
> believe in a God who discriminates amongst His own creatures.
> And we're certainly not better than other people, all of whom
> have their own glorious chapters of history and their own
> creation stories and their own marvelous redemptions from
> slavery—like the blacks. And many have their own sufferings and
> Holocausts like the gypsies and the Armenians, and again the
> blacks. And their own heroes and their own national revolutions
> and their own myths and history and calendar. Everything that
> has happened to the Jews has also happened to many other
> peoples and races too. Does anyone anywhere really believe as
> Christians say that the messiah has already come? And can anyone
> really believe, apart from the very narrow-minded among us,
> that the Jews are the chosen people?

And another said succinctly, "Just because the Nazis claimed we were inferior doesn't mean we should claim to be superior."

A most appealing testament was made by one of the 8 percent of all survivors who abstained from deciding on the question of chosenness. The war had interrupted his rabbinical studies a short time before his ordination. But he is today classified as a moderately observant Jew who conceives of God as impersonal and who maintains that "the catastrophe shattered the piety of my youth":

That's a very difficult question. Sometimes I think we most
certainly are chosen in some manner or other and there's proof
all around. And other times I cannot accept such arrogance
and conceit and I'm embarrassed by such claims because surely
we're no different or better than other peoples. And I would
deny their claims of singularity and chosenness. And so I can't
make up my mind. But I'm in good company since, it seems to
me, the prophets too were confused and uncertain about it. Read
Amos, for example. Sometimes he says that God says that He
only knows Israel among all the families of the earth and will
therefore punish her for her sins. At other times He says all the
nations are alike in that He brought them all out of their various
exiles just as He delivered Israel out of hers in Egypt. Israel,
then, is just one of many on a long list of God's because He's
the God of all mankind, according to this view, and the list
even includes the enemies of Israel like Amon and Edom and Moab,
all of whom are chosen. But then again, we're the only ones to
survive till today. Is it just chance? Sometimes I'm positive that
that's all it is, but who's to really know what to believe?

And another abstainer, who worked in the laundry room at Treblinka, expressed the opinion of many others by suggesting, "We Jews are special, even a blessing to the world. That much I can agree to. But chosen? That I cannot say."

It must be recognized at once that many survivors sharing these insights—and they may well constitute the large majority—conceived of chosenness in its strictest sense: metaphysical uniqueness, that is, chosen by God. And they had difficulty with it. Had the questionnaire intimated or had they allowed themselves the latitude of construing chosenness in nonmetaphysical, secular terms, that is, without God, a far greater number would unquestionably have endorsed the concept. But so inexact and untidy an interpretation may well have appeared as a distortion to them, blurring its contours, its authenticity, and its true meaning and rendering it entirely unacceptable.

There is something rather ironic—a break with history perhaps—in that thirty years after the genocide period survivors would record with confidence recollections of the inception of their belief in chosenness but not in messianism. In previous periods of extreme national desolation and calamity, messianic speculation and expectation increased dramatically among Jews. Not, apparently, during the years of the Hitlerian oppression—judging from the response of survivors. Chosenness may have lost more adherents than messianism overall (7 percent as against 13 percent) during the Holocaust years. And yet, according to the evidence of this research, no single survivor can be identified as having begun to believe in messianism because of the catastrophe and no such statement has been forthcoming. On the other hand, quite a few survivors identify themselves as having been convinced of chosenness as a consequence of the Holocaust. During the Holocaust years, none of the six articles of faith appears to have attracted any sizable following among survivors. As has already been noted, the only belief not to have lost support was that the Holocaust was the will of God, which gained a slight 3 percent during the Holocaust and declined by 5 percent in its aftermath. As a general rule, faith declined as a consequence of the devastation, and during it as well.

In the midst of the genocide period and their own victimization, more than the seven percent indicated by our findings relinquished belief in the election of Israel. But what must be understood is that an unknown but not inconsiderable number of others at the same time began to adopt the thesis, making it a part of their lives and balancing out the larger number forsaking that belief.

A number of these latter survivors contributed the following thoughts:

"God chose the Jews to be the world's victims."

"Auschwitz made the Jews different and separated them from all others—this is how we are chosen."

"The Jews were chosen by others to blame everything on them."

"Once I was too stupid to realize the Torah proved Israel's chosenness; now I'm not so stupid to miss the lesson of the Auschwitz crematoria."

And another speaking to the same theme wrote:

If before the Holocaust the idea that Jews were in some way
chosen was merely myth or legend created by the Jews themselves
then I would say the Nazi program of genocide transformed
that fiction into a reality. If we weren't chosen before, we are most

certainly now. . . . It is no longer in the imagination, the
Jewish imagination. It is now a down to earth concrete fact for all
future time. We Jews are forevermore chosen. The Nazis saw
to that.

A Dutch survivor of several labor camps and of Bergen-Belsen said, "I
learned this: Even if we say we're not chosen the goyim won't believe
us and will insist we are. Our friends as well as our foes believe the
Jews to be chosen and different and peculiar—so I guess we are."

One final comment by a survivor whose mind was opened to the
concept of chosenness during his experiences as an inmate of Dachau
is an appropriate conclusion to this section: "Jews chose to be chosen
people by acting properly toward their fellow man. Others refused to
choose to become chosen—but still could. It is always open to them to
join us. We make it difficult, not impossible. But first they have to
learn morality."

Nontraditional Survivors

The subgroup of atheists is instructive for an appreciation of attitudes
toward chosenness which the Holocaust affected. Survivors who reject
the existence of God were obviously not expected to accredit articles of
faith connecting Him with the Holocaust or the Torah. Some might—
and did—accept the opinion that Judaism, even without God, is a true
religion (12 percent) and a few (3 percent) even that Judaism is the
only true religion. While consistently rejecting messianism throughout
the four stages, regardless of its tolerance of various reinterpretations
and however defined, 3 percent indicated that after the Holocaust they
had begun to accept the notion of Jewish chosenness. And today, after
years of living in Israel and internalizing the meaning of their Holocaust
experiences, nearly one of every five (18 percent) atheist survivors
professes the conviction that the Jews are in some manner a chosen
people.

Finally, the subgroup of survivors who lost faith in God remains
to be canvassed regarding their attitudes toward the concept of chosenness. It has already been suggested elsewhere that these survivors who
classified themselves as believers in God before the Holocaust were
even then quite different in religious attitudes from the consistently
devout. Both groups believed in God before the Holocaust. But they
differed from each other in their attitudes toward the various parallel
articles of faith. Survivors who retained their faith had been more

solidly confirmed in these other beliefs—among them chosenness—than survivors who lost faith in God during the genocide period.

They may in truth have lost faith in God partly because they had fewer other convictions to hold on to. Conversely, survivors who remained believers may have been inculcated with a greater number of supplementary religious tenets surrounding as well as buttressing their faith in God.

The affirmation of chosenness among survivors who ceased to believe in God fell from 73 percent to 20 percent during the Holocaust and still further to 10 percent afterward. Nevertheless, testifying to the strength of the concept among Jews of every sector is the fact that only the conviction that Judaism is a true religion—a far less specific and more easily affirmed tenet—commanded greater acceptance among these survivors than the election of Israel.

For traditionalists messianism predominantly means deliverance. For modernists inclined to reinterpret messianism, it may mean society's ultimate perfectability—a vision far more unlikely to preserve its partisans or win new proselytes in the depths of absolute depravity than that of deliverance.

And our research shows that traditionally devout survivors held fast to their pre-Holocaust messianic faith during the genocide period, though, for survivors reinterpreting the meaning of God, the concept lost favor by half. For this modernist subgroup, chosenness means singularity; quite reasonable, even justifiable in the midst of the singularity of Auschwitz, which itself can achieve a certain deplorable and egregious logic if Jews are thought of as exceptional, chosen, for good or for ill. In this view the world of the concentration camps was set apart from the rest of the world precisely because the Jew was set apart from the rest of humanity. And indeed our research reveals that only 6 percent of these modernists relinquished chosenness during the Holocaust (28 percent before the Holocaust; 22 percent during, after, and today). This is not to suggest that survivors inclined to the reinterpretation of religious ideas were enthusiastically disposed to doing so for the concept of chosenness. We are merely seeking to understand why chosenness had somewhat greater staying power than messianism for these survivors.

Devout Survivors

Before the Holocaust, survivors who later acquired faith "in the face of death" believed in neither messianism nor chosenness—nor in God, for that matter. During the Holocaust, twice as many began to believe in the election of Israel as in messianism (67 percent to 33 percent). For these, as for the consistently devout, messianism meant the *Mashiach*, God's "anointed one" and not mankind's perfection. And chosenness meant God's election of Israel and not the unique Jewish contribution to civilization.

After the Holocaust the adherents of chosenness among these survivors increased to a full 83 percent. The progression may be best explained by one such survivor, who had been assigned to duty in a dispensary until liberation, as follows:

> When I started to believe in the Master of the universe, when
> I realized how foolishly mistaken I had been all those years not to
> see what was before my eyes and what the camps opened my
> eyes to, that did not mean that all at once I accepted everything
> else in the Torah. I hardly knew what was in the Torah. I
> had to first study and learn. Then at last I understood what "Thou
> hast chosen us" means and what is meant by "the Torah speaks
> in the language of man." I gradually came to everything of the
> commandments I now keep, and to the faith I now have. In the
> future I may be able to keep even more and believe in more,
> God willing.

A comparison of these survivors whose religious faith was Holocaust-born with those who had always believed in God reveals that in certain respects they had become even more punctilious in matters of faith than the veteran devout. Before the Holocaust, 82 percent of the veteran subgroup affirmed chosenness. During the Holocaust it declined to its nadir, 73 percent, a loss of 9 percent for these devout survivors. But it recovered immediately after the Holocaust to 76 percent and rose again to 80 percent, nearly a full reattainment of its pre-Holocaust status.

Significantly, at the same time that this article of faith was dropping to its low point, the same period during which some of these life-long devout survivors were challenging the concept of chosenness, the recently devout were beginning vigorously to appropriate it for themselves. For them it rose from nil to 67 percent. And indeed it rose still further for these survivors to 83 percent after the Holocaust, a full 7 percent more, and a level higher, than it *ever* reaches for their veteran counterparts. And since to this day it remains higher for them, perhaps chosenness has had a hidden agenda for the acquisition of faith among certain survivors. In fact, chosenness and the belief that the Holocaust was the will of God were two articles of faith with larger representation among these survivors than for all other subgroups, including the veteran believers. The explanation may perhaps be that the horror of the Holocaust experience—which for them could only be explained by God's existence and His deliberate design emerging from His special relationship with Israel—brought them to an appreciation of their Jewish religious identities and an acceptance of what for them must be one of its several implications: chosenness.

Torah

For survivors the Holocaust was the consummate ordeal of faith, with regard not only to God's existence and comportment but to most parallel convictions as well. As our study reveals, however, the ordeal was less severe for certain doctrines than for others. The relative paucity of survivor discourses and testimonies evoked by the doctrines of the Torah's divine origin and Judaism's truth suggests that they may not have conveyed the same decisive significance for survivors as messianism, chosenness, and God's will. Although these latter may be characterized as no less abstract or remote, they, despite their decline in favor, apparently touched more responsive and relevant chords in times of extremity. And survivors report they did give these issues more than fleeting attention. While the Holocaust of our time appears to have been the exception, the evidence of history suggests that messianic speculation has always tended to increase during times of oppression, as did consideration of the election or special nature of the people. Above all was the mind directed toward contemplating the divine will.

The subjective impression arising from interviews is consistent with the thesis that Torah and Judaism's truth were simply not pivotal issues for Jews in time of crises. That these articles of faith forfeited more survivor support during the Holocaust years than did messianism, chosenness, and God's will should not be taken to mean that these were agonized over more than the others and finally found wanting. Rather they had been the more popular doctrines to begin with and therefore had greater decline potential.

A comparison of the declines and recoveries of these doctrines reveals the following: In the total survivor community the belief that the Torah is the word of God fell a full 15 percent from its pre-Holocaust high of 54 percent. The belief that Judaism is true religion lost even greater survivor backing (17 percent). But the latter eventually recovered most of its support, reclaiming more than any other article of faith (14 percent), to just short of its pre-Holocaust level. The belief that the Torah is the word of God lost nearly as much but recovered least (2 percent) of all Jewish convictions of this series. The following testimony may provide an explanation for this phenomenon.

A Bergen-Belsen survivor was asked why, of all the beliefs lost during the Holocaust, the conviction that the Torah is the word of God remained the only one still discarded by him some thirty years later, all others having been reclaimed by him over the years. He said:

> It was relatively easy for me to give up the religious practices I had kept all my life, and most beliefs as well, not so much at that time out of a loss of faith but rather because I simply stopped. Other things were far more pressing and urgent. But once having given them all up it was far more difficult getting back into the swing of it again. It just became unnatural for me. Then once I got married and I settled in to more normal living and I acquired my schooling and my degrees at the university and I began my profession, I slowly returned to many of my former religious habits and to many beliefs. Several neighbors who became friends should be given a good deal of credit for encouraging me in the resumption of my religious life. But although I have been able to reinterpret satisfactorily for myself most of the ancient religious dogmas, the fact is that man and not God wrote the Torah. Anyone who has ever studied the subject outside a Yeshiva knows this.

Those unfamiliar with the mentality and temperament of concentration camp inmates might consider it altogether astonishing that given the nature of their duress there was any reflection whatsoever on such abstract and nonsurvival matters as, for example, the divine origin of the Torah. But the truth is, a great deal of theological reflection and speculation took place in many of the camps, at the various frightfully degenerating stages—to a large extent motivated by that very unspeakable duress. For many "it was precisely that which kept us going— these discussions on God and Torah and religion and philosophy and politics—these and the desire to survive and tell the world what happened to us, and of course dreams of revenge."

In extremity some Jews turned to Kabbala, Jewish mystical inquiry, to make sense of their estate. Others, in smaller numbers, supplemented their piety with sorcery, invoking spirits by way of ouija boards and

seances conducted in utmost secrecy. A Holocaust survivor of the
Stuchin Ghetto who now writes fiction in Yiddish and operates a
bicycle shop in Netanya describes the regular gathering of a group of
men around a small wooden table deliberately built entirely without
nails for the purpose of communicating with spirits. These were men
of various religious persuasions, mostly pious Jews with covered heads,
and some nonbelievers. They would formulate several questions, which
were to be answered through the movements of the table.

> Mostly the "magic table" was kept secret because no one wished
> to harm the religious beliefs of other Jews of the ghetto. And
> they felt others would not understand, would mistakenly think
> it was black magic or witchcraft being performed. Actually
> these were mostly pious, believing Jews, reliable men who could be
> depended upon not to intentionally move the table, men who were
> searching in every direction for a sign from beyond themselves,
> for understanding, for finding a way out and for answers. Everyone
> in the ghetto had become more religious than previously, myself
> included. Although I was just a little boy at the time. This
> group of some twenty or thirty men would meet regularly to make
> inquiries of the table. They'd ask only questions which could be
> answered by yes or no or by numbers. For example, the question
> which comes immediately to mind concerns a particularly cruel
> contingent of German army officers. These soldiers would rotate
> periodically and we wanted to know of the table when this group
> would be relieved since they were extremely brutal. In fact,
> they had a little Sabbath game of entering the homes used for
> synagogues and taking out a number of Jews to shoot for sport.
> I saw my own grandfather killed this way. And when the
> German soldiers saw me watching in horror from a little distance
> away, they began to shoot at me as I ran away. Fortunately
> they missed but I'll always remember how they laughed while they
> fired at me as I ran. Anyway, that's the kind of questions they'd
> ask. The Jews of the ghetto also began to believe that the words
> of the Torah if understood correctly had special secrets to
> reveal to us about our own present circumstances if one knew how
> to study and read the words properly. We reached for everything
> in the ghetto, anything which might tell us something about
> our survival or which could be interpreted as a good sign,
> anything which might provide hope.

Deliberating on whether the Torah is the word of God was obviously not among their foremost preoccupations. And yet, apparently, at various times during their internment certain survivors gave it more than passing thought. And one spoke for others by recollecting:

> I didn't think about that in any special way or with great
> frequency then, but I did think about it from time to time and
> believed in the Torah most emphatically. I'd go over and over
> in my mind the verses I had committed to memory as a child. And
> surprisingly, many verses I never realized I knew, verses from
> the Torah which seemed to have special meaning for where I was
> and our circumstances, would suddenly cross my mind and
> make me think and would cause me to see things from the
> perspective of the Torah. Verses from the Torah helped many of
> us. As is said in truth, everything is in the Torah.

According to Jewish tradition, the entire Torah was submitted by God to mankind simultaneously in all ("seventy") languages and at the desert mountainous no-man's-land of Sinai, thus signifying the Torah's universality so that all men may lay claim to it. However, since Israel alone willingly accepted it, she became God's people and to whom and through whom the divine will is revealed (devar adonai). And God's word par excellence is the Torah.

In its broadest sense, Torah—from the Hebrew root meaning "teaching"—designates the entire corpus of Jewish traditional law and literature from Genesis to the most recent rabbinic and scholarly writings. Narrowly interpreted, Torah refers to the five books of Moses, the Pentateuch alone. That the Torah is "from heaven," that is, that the Torah in its entirety constitutes the revealed, eternal word of God including His commandments, is a pivotal, fundamental axiom of Judaism. It remained virtually unchallenged or modified until the advent of Higher Criticism, the rise of the Science of Judaism (*Wissenschaft des Judentums*) and the spread of the Reform movement in the nineteenth century (although even earlier Baruch Spinoza had broken radically with rabbinic tradition by denying its divine nature and Mosaic authorship). These groups subjected the Torah to historical–critical investigation and concluded essentially that it was written by various authors, compiled, edited, and redacted over a relatively lengthy period of time.

The Mishna teaches that after the exodus Moses received the Torah "from Sinai" and commenced the process of transmission, which extends to current times. It also powerfully supports the conception that every word of the Torah is God's own with a passage which claims that any Israelite who denies that it is God-given forfeits his portion in the world to come.[11] And whoever acknowledges that the Torah is the word of God but maintains that even one detail was inserted by Moses on his own initiative is to be regarded as one who abhors God's word.[12] For the most part, modern Orthodox Judaism continues to uphold these teachings despite the various scholars from perhaps as early as Talmudic days who have felt obliged to maintain that there are parts of the Torah which literally cannot be of divine origin.[13]

Contemporary non-Orthodox Jewish thinkers have attempted a synthesis of the classical formulation with the historical–critical approach. The new teaching maintains that while the Torah is indeed a product of Jewish history, as Higher Criticism suggests, it nevertheless is divine in that it was generated or revealed in the encounter between God and man.

Survivors have not been schooled in theological subtleties, but their singular experience justifies a close scrutiny of their religious views especially as they are affected by that experience. What have they believed through the years at the various stages concerning the divine authorship of the Torah? Before the deportations more than half, 54 percent, of the entire survivor community believed that the Torah is the word of God. In fact, of all the other articles of faith, only the thesis that Judaism is a true religion had more supporters, 64 percent.

For many, Torah means the Holy Scriptures in their entirety; for others, the Pentateuch, or even more restrictedly, the Ten Commandments alone; for others still, it refers to both the Written (Bible) and Oral (Talmud) Laws. For nearly all, the contours of these definitions are imprecise and inconsistent as they indeed are within the tradition itself. Regardless of its precise identification, the most prevalent survivor attitude toward Torah—one which also upholds its divine origin—appears to be that of profound wonder and awe:

"It's too great to have been man-made."

"The Bible couldn't have been written by man."

"God had to have handed it down; no one—surely not us, mortal man—could have written it."

"The greatest thing the world has; of course it came from God."

"Just read a few verses from the Torah and you know immediately and instinctively and intellectually that the Torah and nothing else in this world is of divine origin."

With respect to the precise meaning of Torah it is necessary to take note of the survivors, predominantly Orthodox, for whom an exact definition is a matter of great importance. For example, a learned ultra observant survivor of six different camps interjected these remarks in the course of an interview:

> The Torah is the word of God but it has to be enlarged and
> broadened by the Oral Law or it has no meaning for the Jew.
> Whoever says the Word of God is the Torah and means only the
> Bible and not the Talmud and the rest is a Karaite and worse,
> more like a Christian Fundamentalist than a Jew. The Jew doesn't
> read the Bible literally and without sacred interpretations.
> He reads it with the explanatory help of the tradition.

As has been shown, the concepts of chosenness and messianism may be affirmed as either secular or sacred propositions. That the Torah is the word of God is by definition exclusively religious and admits of no secular categorization. Nevertheless, numerous nonreligious or quasi-religious nuances that reject the idea of its divine origin, but at the same time uphold the Torah's extraordinary and awesome nature, have been articulated by survivors:

> The Torah is very great. Whoever wrote it was a great genius and
> geniuses are God's special children to whom God speaks and
> whom He inspires.
> Men who deeply believe in God wrote the Torah. That doesn't
> mean the Torah is the word of God exactly. It was written by
> man and certain parts should be seen as a product of ancient times
> and rejected or changed and brought up to date. But the Torah
> was still inspired by God. It should be held in high regard.

Survivors who understand God in impersonal terms, as a Power in the Universe, were particularly inclined to speak along these lines concerning the verbal inspiration of the Torah.

Just as there were survivors maintaining that other peoples besides Israel were chosen by God, there are similar shades of meaning associated with the theory of the Torah's divine origin: "I believe the Torah is the word of God. But it is not the only word of God. Shakespeare and Tolstoy and Beethoven and Mozart and all the outpourings of man's creative intellect are also the word of God. All in different gradations. But the Torah is the highest degree."

And another survivor believed that "all peoples have their own Torahs and they are all equally valid and praiseworthy. And they are all inspired by God. Jews don't have a monopoly on Torah." Jewish tradition, however, carefully distinguishes between universal Wisdom, which falls within the province of all mankind, and the Torah, which is exclusively Israel's possession: "If someone shall say to you that there is Wisdom in Edom, believe it; but if he says there is Torah in Edom, do not believe it." [14] Nevertheless, there is no way of ascertaining how many Jews today, survivors among them, have ever reflected upon similarities between their own heritage and the religious legacy of others, that is, between Torah and Wisdom.

The most prevalent view among the Orthodox is, in the words of one such survivor, that "God spoke to Moses on Sinai for forty days and Moses faithfully wrote down all that he learned which was meant to be written down and he memorized everything else and then repeated it perfectly so that it was transmitted in various ways through the ages until our own time." And another said, "I believe the Torah is the word of God. Not only because I have been taught this since I was a child and because it also seems certainly so to me as I study it, but also because the greatest scholarly minds the world has ever known have also said that this is so."

The Torah and the Holocaust

Our research verifies the widely held notion that the Holocaust affected the faith of survivors in various and substantial ways. However, except as a consequence of the general attenuation of religious beliefs, our study provides little hard documentary evidence that the Holocaust experience significantly challenged the idea of the Torah's divine origin. The one survivor statement that comes closest to associating the Holocaust with the rejection of belief in the Torah's divine origin was written by a Czechoslovakian who was among those concentration camp inmates forced-marched from Hungary to Bergen-Belsen:

> The Torah speaks of God's mercy. There was none. The Torah
> speaks of divine justice. Where was it? The Torah speaks of
> God's providence. Where was He? The Torah speaks of faith. But
> I have grave, serious doubts. The Torah speaks of a listening
> God, hearing our prayers. But I experienced Him as unhearing and
> deaf to our shrieks and our outcries. The Torah speaks of man being

created in the image of God. But men are beastly devils, diabolical fiends and evil beings. Does this not mean that God Himself is like these?

As a rule, survivors who discarded the idea that the Torah is His word—and other beliefs as well—came to do so as a concomitant of the loss of faith in God Himself. One survivor of the particularly brutal confinement at Lublin-Maidanek said:

When I became an atheist in the camps like so many others, when I realized no God could possibly exist and allow this horror to continue, I also ceased to believe in everything else I was taught as a child in Heder, the Torah and everything in it except of course the ethical commandments on how to behave morally towards our fellow man. These which help us to become good human beings I accept, but not as coming from God.

And yet, ironically, although no one said that because of the Holocaust "I no longer believe the Torah is divine," there were some who said the converse. For these the experience of brutality and degradation occasioned belief in the divinity of the Torah. One highly observant survivor's remarks are typical:

The Holocaust proved the Torah is true and that all previous events of Jewish destructions such as the two temples, the expulsions and exiles and captivities, all the punishments which the Jews experienced happened just as they are described in the Torah and for the same reasons. If the Holocaust doesn't prove to everyone's complete and final satisfaction that the Torah and commandments are from God, nothing else will.

And another ultra observant survivor spoke in a similar vein:

It is the foundation of our faith that God gave us the Torah through Moses our teacher. When we chose to accept the Torah and live by the commandments we became the chosen people. When we failed to keep them we were punished according to our just deserts by the God who gave them to us. And the proof of its divinity is that even though it was given centuries ago, it teaches us everything we have to know even for today. It knew in advance and anticipated everything—even the Holocaust itself and the creation of Israel—if you know how to read the Torah correctly. And it has been this way for all periods and for all communities of Jews.

Torah as the Word of Man

After the Holocaust, advocacy for the doctrine of the Torah's divinity fell still farther, from 39 percent to 36 percent. Today, perhaps as an aspect of the generally hospitable climate for religious belief in Israel, it has recovered to 41 percent, the same percentage for respondents who claim never to have believed in the Torah's divine authorship. We should now turn our attention to this latter group.

The conception of the Torah's divine origin is usually inculcated during childhood. Similarly, the majority of survivors who see the Torah as a human document have been raised with, or arrived at that persuasion at an age too early to recall. They have had proportionately fewer years of formal Jewish education than those brought up on the idea of its Sinaitic Source, rarely beyond their childhood Heder, and they are not as familiar with the Bible's contents. Proportionately more are of West and Central than of East European origin.

For some of the remaining survivors, particularly the better educated in secular studies, the Torah cannot be of divine authorship for reasons of sociology, history, and comparative literature.

A French-born survivor wrote:

Just study all the other literatures of ancient times. See the parallels in Egypt and Babylonia and elsewhere and you have to conclude that although we revere the Torah and consider it our sacred scripture and take pride in having taught morality to the world through it, it is not the word of God. It was written by man.

A Polish-born Lodz ghetto survivor argued:

I think all people see their holy writ as God-given but much of one contradicts the sacred writings of others in very crucial ways and not in insignificant details of ritual. And I don't believe God would give contradictory commandments to different peoples to confuse us and cause conflict between us.

A survivor from Berlin reasoned as follows:

> To be a Jew you don't have to believe in God or in the Torah as
> His commandments. In fact to say the Jewish people wrote so
> great a masterpiece as the Bible is to be an infinitely better
> Jew than to believe a God gave it and all we Jews had to do was
> to receive it rather than write it ourselves, which is no great
> achievement. I believe we Jews wrote it and gave it to the world
> and should take pride in having done so, and God did not.
> And we have been the most creative people ever since. We are
> chosen people not because we received the Torah but because we
> were privileged and capable enough to write it.

The preceding socioliterary citation was composed by a survivor
whose religious views on Torah correspond to a large extent with those
of a number of contemporary non-Orthodox Jewish theologians whose
creed suggests that all the sacred writings of the Jews, including the
Torah, ensued from God's revelation—others might say inspiration—
but are not identical with it. Rather, according to this view, Torah is
fallible man's record of the divine mortal encounter and as such is
not free of human error and distortion. The sanctity of the Torah,
therefore, lies not in its infallibility, immutability, or absolute finality
but in this encounter or covenant. Moreover, the divine and human are
interwoven and conjoined into the one body so thoroughly that no
instrumentality or strategy, however structured, can be employed to
differentiate between them and disentangle them. Yet, clearly, modernists do continually determine by rational, moral judgments when
human, time-bound Torah laws are to be set aside or abandoned as
false, obsolete, or irrelevant.

A Treblinka internee, who also survived the Kovno blood bath of
June 1941 and is now a kibbutz teacher, spoke these words:

> Torah is the word of God but not every word. Besides the many
> scribal errors of transcription there are so many contradictions:
> Was man created on the sixth day after everything else was
> created or was he created earlier when no shrub existed on earth?
> Then there is the misplaced chronology concerning the reign of
> the kings, not to mention the numerous barbarities such as the
> admonition not to allow a witch to live or the Torah's
> legitimization of slavery or the vengeful command to slaughter a

whole people. But then there are the far, far more numerous truly remarkable uplifting, toweringly great, sublime passages which are without doubt the words of the one living God.

For many respondents, the Torah cannot be the word of God principally because of the internal imperfections and deficiencies they find therein. One survivor maintained:

> I don't believe God spoke such words. I don't believe God spoke to Israel and commanded them to exterminate a whole people, including women and children, the Amalekites, as evil as they might have been, any more than I believe God told the Germans to exterminate the Jews because of *their* shortcomings. I don't hold God responsible for the death of six million and I don't hold Him responsible for all that is terrible and cruel in the Bible.

A Polish-born survivor of more than two years in Auschwitz said:

> Will of God, not word of God. There are things in it God could not have meant for us to do and other things He would have us do as well as instructions as to how He would have us behave towards one another if He *had* written it. But that doesn't mean God actually did. There's also quite a bit in the Torah He'd repudiate himself and expunge if He were rewriting or editing the Torah Himself. And there are many things we humans should do which are not in the Bible, like preserving endangered species and cleaning up the environment and building kibbutzim and fighting inflation.

A Polish-born survivor of Dachau and Auschwitz held a similar opinion:

> There are a great many people who sincerely believe that God spoke to us through the Torah. I cannot. God may indeed speak in various ways to man's conscience but He did not say, regardless of what the Torah says He said, that the adulterer and Sabbath desecrator should be put to death.

A Buchenwald survivor agreed:

There is so much in the Bible that is barbaric and particularistic and there are so many superstitions and outdated commandments like sacrifices which are attributed to God. And I for one cannot believe that God is the source of them.

Devout Survivors and Torah

A high correlation prevails between the belief in God and the idea of the Torah's divine origin. The ultimate reasoning may be that if God exists He most assuredly communicates His will. In our study, 94 percent of the subgroup of survivors who persisted throughout the years in the belief in God's existence affirmed the Torah's divine origin as well during the pre-Holocaust years. Only the idea that Judaism is a true religion consistently enjoyed greater support from this subgroup.

Belief in the Torah's divinity fell to 82 percent at the time of the Holocaust, and still further, to 78 percent, in its aftermath. During and immediately after the Holocaust, when God's presence was experienced as remote, even devout inmates reacted to their isolation by renouncing His foremost tie to them: Torah. Their thinking may have been that God is not after all involved in the affairs of man and is therefore necessarily uncommunicative concerning His will. Apparently, the years living in Israel restored the proximity of God's presence, and the affirmation of His Torah rose to 86 percent, which means that 14 percent of all these devout survivors today hold to the conviction that God exists but the Torah is the work of man.

It was not unforeseen that the correlation of belief in the divine Torah with faith in God would be high, but that it would reach as high as 94 percent before the Holocaust is rather striking: Only 6 percent could believe at once in God and that the Torah is other than His Word—two entirely reconcilable convictions which may certainly be held simultaneously. Several survivors have testified in the previous section how they have fused the two conceptions—belief in God and that the Torah's not His teaching—into a single unity, and the more balanced proportions during and after the Holocaust suggests that others, later, have done the same.

One possible explanation might be that survivors who could depart from traditional Jewish beliefs such as the Torah's divine origin were more likely to allow their faith in God Himself to be temporarily shaken at certain critical times and consequently would not be manifested within the persistently devout subgroup. Just as plausible is the explanation that, for many devout survivors, even if man is responsible for the Torah's composition and writing, God is somehow ultimately connected to it. God is its source or inspiration; although man may have written it, Torah is nevertheless the word of God.

In this respect the following observation by the previously quoted kibbutz teacher–Kovno escapee deserves attention:

> I think that God and man have been in touch—and often. One
> of these times is called Sinai by our people and some of these
> words in the Torah record what God said to us during this meeting,
> however it may have been conducted. But although I believe
> God gave the Torah and it is the word of God, nevertheless I
> also know that man wrote it all and passed it down from
> generation to generation, copied and recopied—we don't have any
> really early copies of the Torah scroll—and each inserted things
> on his own accord consistent with his beliefs about what God
> desired. And so the Torah is not free from inaccuracies and
> exaggerations and the primitive and miraculous and the
> unbelievable.

Devout, Orthodox survivors align themselves with the doctrine that God's Torah was received by Moses along with all the necessary detailed amplifications. Transcribed in the Pentateuch are the verbatim words and expressions, even the precise sentence structure of God's revelation. The written Torah refers to Scripture. And the oral Torah consists of the authorized explanations of biblical ordinances, also divinely revealed to Moses as a teacher instructs a student, and transmitted from him to all Israel by word of mouth. These interpretations are now recorded as sacred Talmudic–Midrashic literature and are as binding as the laws of Scripture themselves. Underscored repeatedly in interviews with these survivors is the view that Jews are not to challenge these postulates: "The Torah was given by God to Moses and through him to all Jews and it is not for us to question this, only to keep His commandments."

Two observations are especially noteworthy and representative. The first survivor, who lost his right eye in a severe beating at the hands of a Nazi storm trooper, said:

> I don't know how it happened or why it happened, which are both
> less important than the fact that it, the giving of the Torah,

actually happened. Jews are not expected to spend time thinking about whether God gave the Torah or if the Torah is or isn't the word of God. That would be apikursish thinking [sinful in itself or provoking sinfulness]. And the question itself is apikursish and should not be answered at all. A Jew believes the Torah is the word of God!

The other survivor spoke even more indignantly:

That's the kind of question a Jew asks when he's beginning to look for reasons and justifications not to have to keep the commandments because they are too difficult or inconvenient or if he has some immoral intention up his sleeve. Then he asks is the Torah after all really the word of God, and he has his answer well in advance. Whenever someone in the camps decided he'd commit whatever act was necessary, even against a fellow Jew or fellow inmate, he first would say to himself, well, the Torah is after all just a piece of paper and not God's own word. Then he'd be free to do whatever he pleased: even kill, or steal, or cheat a fellow inmate out of his bread, or cooperate with the authorities often to the injury or even death of a fellow Jew. When you ask that question, first you give up the mitzvot like kashrut or tephillin, the ritual ones. And then the ethical rules are next to go. And we become beasts who deny God's word. Without Torah anything goes.

A survivor who had been released from the Stutthof Sophienwald Concentration Camp submitted:

The Torah is a matter of faith and intellect. The Holocaust on the other hand deals with experiences, with feelings, with heart—or rather, heartbreak. The two are spheres which in no way may be connected. They do not even overlap. They are two separate matters for Jews to come to grips with: emotion and reason.

These devout survivors argued indefatigably for loyal endorsement and unquestioned, unqualified belief in Jewish doctrine. Others, however, offered various justifications for them.

To the question whether the Torah is of divine origin, one survivor who outlasted *Selektion* upon *Selektion* at Auschwitz offered historical reasons, saying, "of course it is. This was not a private audience with God, a secretive giving of the Torah to some mystical individual. At the foot of Mount Sinai the whole of Israel stood to receive the Torah. Hundreds of thousands of people witnessed and heard and saw the giving of the Torah. The Torah tells us that 'all the people heard and saw and feared not.' No amount of blaming of God for the Holocaust could alter the historical facts."

A survivor whose carpentry skills kept him alive in a half-dozen labor camps said:

> The Torah came from God and we Jews who brought it to mankind have suffered for it ever since. Nobody who cannot behave morally likes to be told to behave morally. What happens is when they fail they then lash out at the Jews for their own failures. Jewish suffering proves the Torah's authenticity. And if we hadn't brought the Torah to mankind we wouldn't have suffered so much.

For another Auschwitz survivor, history proves the Torah's divinity: "The Torah is the word of God which has kept the Jewish people alive and united. Had we not received the Torah we would have long since ceased to exist like the other ancient nations."

And a surviving Hasid admonished:

> The Torah is how God addressed Himself to the Jew. If you reject the Torah as God's word you are rejecting God Himself. Just as your refusal to abide by your parents' wishes is a form of rejecting them. God forbid that Jews should convince themselves not to obey His words.

Atheists and Other Subgroups

Atheists obviously had very little difficulty with the subject of the Torah's origin since, unanimously, in the words of one of them, "there is no God, so there is no Torah from God." Other survivors, non-atheists, were not so certain: 5 percent of the entire survivor community found themselves unable to answer the question. One particularly articulate survivor framed the reasons for his indecision with an especially appropriate metaphor:

Since the Holocaust everything about Judaism—whether the
holidays, the synagogue, Torah, and especially God—is unclear and
shadowy and veiled from before my eyes. It is almost as though
a cloak or some other covering had been hastily thrown over it
after my deportation. I admit that the curtain most probably
can be removed, and it undoubtedly has been for others.
But for me it has not been, as yet. I believe, for the time being,
that covering protects me from the frightening answers that
are to be found behind it, as well as from all the responsibilities
Judaism entails. It in turn is also protected from me and the
violence I am potentially capable of doing to it should it become
revealed to me before I'm ready. So I continue in suspended
judgment—and may continue so for the rest of my life unless
something changes. Until I resolve my problems and raise
the curtain and confront my Jewishness—particularly the matter
of God and His failures—the Torah and the rest of Jewish life
cannot emerge from behind the shadows.

And another survivor felt the same, adding that he would first have to
make up his mind if there is a God, "before," in his words, "I face the
probelm of His communications and commandments as may appear
in the Torah."

Survivors who understood God in impersonal terms proved the most
consistent: Through the years 61 percent rejected the idea of the Torah's
divine origin outright regardless of their inclination to reinterpret religious doctrines. Before the Holocaust, 39 percent affirmed the conviction; during and immediately thereafter, 28 percent did so. And
today one-third of this survivor subgroup associates Torah with God's
reality.

These respondents generally speak of "the universal Spirit infusing
the Torah and other great masterpieces," of "that element of Godli-
ness and sanctity which exists in the world and can be seen with great
abundance and profusion in our Torah." Similarly, "the Spirit of the
Jewish people—which is another way of saying God—is registered in
the pages of the holy Hebrew Bible, the Prayerbook and other sacred
Jewish literature." Finally, "man is the embodiment of the divine and
it was he who composed the Torah. Therefore the Torah, in this sense,
is certainly the word of God as are other celebrated writings of man."

The attenuation of the conviction's acceptance by 11 percent during
the catastrophe may be attributed in large part to the deeply experienced sense of man's betrayal of his Godlike qualities. The disillusion-

ment conduced to the doubt that any of His handiwork, including the Torah, may be considered divine in origin.

The essentially optimistic world view that sees elements of the divine in man's activities was shattered, and in its place arose the pessimistic *Weltanschauung* wherein man constantly proves himself a beast. A Lithuanian survivor spoke of emerging from "the cocoon of Yeshiva life"—with perhaps a somewhat atypical, modernistically inclined theology—only to be cast precipitously headlong from ghetto to death camp. His naive optimism, he explained, was brutally overthrown in the camp—both his naiveté as well as his optimism—and the equation "man-created is God-created" fell along with it. The essentially man-oriented denial of the Torah's divine origin may have been adversely affected by man's inhumanity to man. But these survivors were nevertheless not of a mind to return to the traditional Jewish formula of God's revelation.

A German survivor who fled to Belgium, where he was seized by the Nazis, wrote:

Man has changed in the extreme through the centuries; changed for the worse. It is true that the majority of men were always bloodthirsty and history is the record of a series of pogroms. However, there were always small groupings, a small percentage of men, who were admirably principled and incorruptible regardless of the corruption all around them. Often it was the highly religious who were the worst murderers and some other highly religious people who were the most noble and self-sacrificing. It was these men who were responsible for setting down the Torah in writing. And afterwards, other great works of law and ethics and morality were written—particularly by some Frenchmen and the British and then the American constitutional writers. And others, even Germans. Where have all these God-inspired men been in recent times? Where during the war? And where are they today? All gone! When in the distant and and not too distant past these men who had the spirit of God in them acted or composed or created, God Himself was present. Since they are no longer, I believe it can be said that He too, God Himself, is no longer.

These remarks conduct our attention toward the survivor subgroup that lost faith in God. Before the Holocaust, 68 percent of these survivors in keeping with their faith in Him at the time affirmed the Torah to have been His word. Only 13 percent held to that conviction in the midst of the catastrophe. Afterward, consistent with their total loss of faith in God, none retained the belief in the Torah's divine origin.

True Religions

If religion is a process by which groups of individuals confront problems of the ultimate—the meaning of life; the reality of death; good and evil; one's relationships with others; bringing about a just society; the existence and nature of God; and other fundamental issues touching upon man's presence on earth—then clearly there were a great many religions in the ancient biblical world, as there are in the contemporary world. The adherents of these religions obviously regarded them as true. And indeed they were true in that, at the very least, they fulfilled the requirements of the people at the time. Even if so self-conscious a question could have been posed then, it would have been unthinkable for Jews of the ancient world to reply in the negative to the query, "Is Judaism a true religion?"

At certain times during the biblical period Israel believed that different deities existed, that the gods of the nations were living gods, and that while each people worshiped its god, for a Jew to worship a strange one was apostasy. At other times Israel believed none but its own God existed and no comparison should be drawn between Him, the "living God," and the idols of the surrounding peoples. Undoubtedly, the Israelites would have endeavored to answer the questions as to whether Judaism, that is, the religion of Israel, was a true religion and was Judaism the only true religion with reference to the existence of God and His efficacy. They would not have spoken of true or false religions but of true or false Gods.

The commandment of the Decalogue, "thou shalt have no other gods before Me," is taken by some scholars as expressing the fundamental principle of divine unity and by others as implying the existence of other gods, none of whom is to be held above the God of Israel. And in the Bible no god is ever portrayed as challenging God's sovereignty.

According to a postbiblical Midrashic teaching, an Israelite who professes a false religion—literally, "strange," that is, non-Israelite "worship'" (avoda zara)—denies the Ten Commandments and all that was commanded Moses, the Prophets, and Patriarchs.[15] He who denies all other religions professes the entire Torah.[16] For non-Jews, a prominent Jewish teaching has it that "the righteous of all peoples have a portion in the world to come." And anyone not of the Israelite community who fulfills the seven Noachide commandments has satisfied the minimal requirements of morality, regardless of his beliefs. Maimonides in his fifth principle of faith has observed that the greater part of the Torah is concerned with the prohibition of idol worship. All forms of worship that fell short of absolute monotheism—the worship of heathen deities, images, and other representations of the divine—were each in its time severely censured as idolatrous. In biblical periods the pagan deities of Egypt, Canaan, Babylonia, and Assyria and later, in Rabbinic times, the Greek and Roman pantheon were all so regarded.

Until recently, Christianity's less than perfect monotheism as well as the cultic use of images was also considered by many Jewish thinkers, including Maimonides, who lived in the Moslem world, as idolatrous and not representing a true religion. Islam's God conception, in contrariety, had been generally regarded as far more monotheistic, nonidolatrous, reflective of a true religion. In more modern times, Christianity and Islam and virtually all the major religions of the world are viewed by most Jewish thinkers as nonidolatrous and therefore, along with Judaism itself, true. How do survivors answer the questions "Is Judaism true?" and "Is it the only true religion?"

The conviction that Judaism is true is, upon close scrutiny, nearly tantamount to a profession of belief in all or most Jewish teachings. That it is not precisely so, however, may be seen from the few survivors who accept certain doctrines, such as chosenness and even that catastrophes such as the Holocaust are the will of God, but who still maintain logically that Judaism is not necessarily true: "Many falsehoods abound in Judaism. God exists and can bring on disasters and the Jews are a special, chosen people, but Judaism is not all true and many of its laws should be rescinded and not be obeyed. And its stories like that of creation are entirely inaccurate scientifically."

Since some few survivors maintained that certain Jewish doctrines are true but that generally speaking Judaism is not, it became necessary to distinguish individually among the various most popular and important articles of faith and to list the truth of Judaism as a separate one of them. Most survivors of course equated the various articles of faith taken together with Judaism generally. And the Judaism in "Judaism is true" refers to them all, particularly those not specified elsewhere in the questionnaire.

Throughout the four stages, of the six articles of faith, the one consistently receiving the greatest backing—never less than 10 percent more than any of the others—is the conviction that Judaism is a true religion. Before the Holocaust, 64 percent of the entire survivor community affirmed the tenet. It declined more than any other (by 17 percent) in the midst of the catastrophe—doubtless because it had the farthest to fall. But at 47 percent it still retained its place of primacy among all other doctrines even then. Moreover, this doctrine alone of all the professions of faith of this series began at once to revive in popular acceptance among survivors in the immediate post-Holocaust period. The others, except for belief in the chosen people, which remained constant, declined even further in that time period. Today 61 percent of all survivors believe that Judaism is a true religion. And, demonstrating still further the widespread strength of this conviction, the 22 percent of all survivors who never accepted the principle was less by some 20 percent than those who had never affirmed even the most popular of the other articles of faith. Moreover, not a single survivor suggested that other religions are true though Judaism is not.

The Plurality of True Faith

Turning our attention now to the final article of faith, the tenet that Judaism is the only true religion, we must recognize at once that contradictory metaphysical propositions cannot all be equally true. And indeed, according to Jewish law, a Jew who acknowledges other faiths as equally true is an apostate.[17] Nevertheless, implied in the traditional view that idolatrous faiths are spurious and illegitimate misteachings is the idea that not all non-Jewish faiths are to be so regarded. Nowhere in the mainstream of Judaism is there serious claim to the exclusive possession of all truth. And nowhere among the 613 Commandments for Jews is there to be found a commandment to proselytize to the "true" faith. Rather, the Prophet Micah adjures, "Let all the peoples walk each in the name of its God." [18] God, according to the predominant Jewish view, communicated with non-Israelite peoples and spoke to non-Israelite wise men as well. And there were rabbis of the Talmud who made a point of the teaching that in the eyes of God a virtuous, upright non-Jew finds greater favor than a corrupt high priest.

Unquestionably, although not all religions can be true, and idolatries are certainly false, Judaism respects and dignifies the integrity of every moral faith community and sees fragments of truth in them all. The thesis that Judaism is the only true religion is therefore not strictly speaking a Jewish article of faith as are the others. And 53 percent of the entire survivor community at no time during the years this study covers subscribed to the view. Nevertheless, a substantial segment of the Jewish people have at given times and for various reasons believed it and rendered it sufficient in popularity for the period this study embraces to warrant its inclusion in this chapter along with the five other, more authentic, Jewish teachings.

In the aggregate, before the Holocaust, 41 percent of all survivors affirmed the notion of Judaism's exclusive truth, which percentage fell to one-third of the population during the Holocaust years. Also of importance is the fact that there was considerably more movement than even the 8 percent difference indicates, with scores of survivors shifting and changing their opinions on the subject frequently during the faith-challenging Holocaust period. The diminution of popular support for this thesis too, irrespective of its Jewish validity, is to some extent attributable to the general corrosion and withering away of the strength of belief in Judaism's teachings during this cataclysmic juncture. Any corresponding gain at that time is in large measure to be connected to the view that the various other religions of mankind, seen by Jews as contributory factors in their destruction, failed their supreme test and proved to them altogether sterile and ineffectual—even damnable. And to these survivors Judaism alone appeared good and true by contrast. Concerning the claims they make for their faith: Better to be victim than villain.

Immediately after the war the notion of Judaism's exclusive truth fell another 1 percent, but in the intervening years, for survivors living in Israel, it recovered slightly, to 36 percent. One Maidanek survivor, in business in Jerusalem, thought that the Palestine and Israel years "brought back our memories of the past and how other religious peoples, particularly Christians, caused our suffering and extermination in Europe when we did them no harm at all. And then when we lived here among the Moslems and sought peace with them unsuccessfully, and against our will had to fight the Arabs war after war, it seemed that always, all other religions we had contact with—and these were religions born out of ours—produced murderers, brought misery to themselves and others, had to be false."

It is important to dwell at some length on the view held by half (53 percent) of the survivor aggregate which consistently over the years denied that Judaism is the only true religion. Many of these survivors, as can be seen from the following quotations, understood religious truth as utilitarian and functional: a religion is to be judged true or false according to its effect on its followers. At the same time, for some of these survivors Judaism may be more true than any other religion, but it is not necessarily the only true one:

All religions are true so long as they teach that there is a God and that He commands us to be ethical human beings.

All religions teach ethical behavior and how to reach God.

I don't believe ours is the only true religion because there are other good men in the world besides Jews. And not all Jews, not even all religious Jews, are themselves perfect. Many are liars and cheats and thieves even as they call themselves good Jews and religious men.

That part of religion which is between man and his fellow man [ben adam la-chavero] is true for all religions. But that part which is between man and God [ben adam la-Makom] is false for all faiths except for Judaism because God only chose to reveal Himself to the children of Israel.

We Jews do not go around saving souls because all men have a share in the world to come and our religion is not the only road there. All men can live good lives.

Judaism is a true religion for Jews. Christianity is a true religion for Christians, Mohammedanism for Moslems, Buddhism for Buddhists, and Brahamanism for Brahmans.

When we Jews observe our 613 Commandments for us they are good and our religion is true. When non-Jews keep the seven Noachide laws the same thing holds for them. Their religion is just as true—just a lot less difficult and demanding.

Each religion has its history, its geography and holy places and its heroes and its values and not just its lists of beliefs. There's nothing inherently false about the history of other religious groupings.

Judaism has made a great contribution to the world and so have many other religions. Judaism's contribution has been the greatest of all of them. Therefore it is the most true. But others are also true.

Other peoples have discovered religious truths. We don't have a monopoly on truth. And we're not the only ones to come up with religious ideas and insights.

Was Nazism a true religion? Religions are institutions. They are neither true nor false. It's what they do that counts.

While survivors who believed Judaism to be the *only* true religion were overwhelmingly the devout and ultra observant, survivors who affirmed no more than that Judaism is one of the true faiths ranged from humanists to ultra observant Hasidim. One of the former, a Bucharest survivor of particularly brutal pogroms, spoke for other non-theists in suggesting that all religions "which are man-oriented, which elevate man are true. The religions which elevate God too much or death or the state or one group of society over other groups are untrue because they denigrate man and debase him. Judaism cares more about people than other religions."

Among survivors, humanists far outnumber Hasidim: Many atheists join their ranks in affirming Judaism's truth even without belief in God. Another Rumanian who outlasted various forced labor camps, including Transnistria, declared:

> Judaism is a true religion and I can say that even though I don't
> really believe in God. Judaism is the most true of all the
> religions I have studied—although of course I am aware of the fact
> that I'm not free from some bias since I am a Jew, born a Jew,
> and a proud one at that. I believe also that aspects of
> Christianity and Islam and others are true—and not all of Judaism
> is true. But if there is relevance, if there is life-affirming joy in
> its celebrations, if it makes the people who follow it better human
> beings and happier, then certainly there is truth to be found
> there. In Judaism these and other characteristics of a true
> religion are especially abundant and prominent and substantial.

Few survivors seemed aware of the distinction between the statement that Judaism is true and the view that Judaism contains truth. But almost nearly without exception survivors instinctively interpreted the meaning of truth in its broadest sense. One who did not spoke as follows:

> There is truth to be found everywhere. In Marxism-Leninism,
> Capitalism and Socialism. In the religions of the East and
> West. And in Judaism too. But that doesn't make Judaism true.
> It just means that there is truth and falsity everywhere, Judaism
> included. And I accept certain things in Judaism which seem true
> to me and I reject whatever appears to me as false. But I cannot
> say in a generality that Judaism is entirely true. And I certainly

deny that Judaism is the only true religion. The one question
is complicated; the other is not.

The devout invariably spoke of Judaism's truth in connection with
God's giving the Torah. For many of them, some truth outside of
Judaism *is* to be found. But a typical remark is that "Christianity and
Islam and other religions contain truth in direct proportion to how
much borrowing they did from their Jewish source, our Torah." For
others still, Judaism and religious truths are indeed entirely synonymous,
all of the one being contained in the other. And truth exists nowhere
else except perhaps within the scope of science, which cannot contradict but can supplement the truths of Judaism. These devout survivors
constituted the largest representation of the view that Judaism is the
only true religion.

One ultra observant survivor explained:

Judaism is the one and only true religion. It was revealed by
God to His chosen people as the truth. And it was given in God's
own words and all of God's words are true. Only the Jews
received God's commands and promises, and therefore only Judaism
is true. There is no sense trying to convince everyone of this.
Even some Jews don't accept it due to their own ignorance or evil
nature. And the various other religions are mere copies of ours
made easier for them. But even their copies are false. The Torah
was given to the Jews but meant for all men to keep. Therefore
it is the only true religion.

A devout survivor may hold to the conviction that because other
religions sprung from Judaism some truth may reside in them. Another
equally devout survivor may, as the last citation implies, believe that
precisely because other faiths "borrowed" or "copied" from Judaism,
"they," in the words of another one of them, "do not have the real
authentic thing and are therefore false."
Among the total survivor community the proposition that Judaism
is the only true religion was one of the least popular articles of faith.
Many survivors felt its affirmation smacked of discrimination, even
bigotry, as some of their testimonies reveal:
"It is the Christians and not the Jews who have no belief in the

sanctity of all human life and taught the superiority of one race over
another and the duty of the superior to murder the others."

"We Jews should fight prejudice and teach that all mankind's religions are of worth."

"That is terrible arrogance."

"To say we have all the truth and there is truth nowhere else, invites Holocausts."

It is also being suggested here that many survivors who did affirm
the belief that Judaism is the one true religion were buttressed to a large
extent by their apprehension of the apparent failure of other religions
to prevent their followers from committing the murder of millions.
As such, the avowal is perhaps as much a negation of the validity of
other faiths as it is a ratification of the singular truth of Judaism.

Devout Survivors

All survivors who were consistently devout through the four stages
believed before the deportations began that Judaism is a true religion,
but only 69 percent believed then that it was the only one. During
the faith-impugning Holocaust years, 88 percent continued to believe
in the former principle, a decline of twelve percentage points. And, sustaining a far smaller decline, 67 percent affirmed the latter doctrine,
which percentage remained constant after the Holocaust. The view that
Judaism is true began to climb back toward its near unanimous approbation of 92 percent in the Holocaust's immediate aftermath.

Today, while 71 percent of the devout profess Judaism's sole possession of truth, all believe not less than that it is true for Jews. This may
appear as a self-evident redundancy were it not for the hard evidence
that certain survivors who felt themselves to be pious Jews even in the
camps were sufficiently shaken in their beliefs to doubt the truth of
Judaism, at least temporarily:

> I prayed to God in personal petitions of deliverance and I also
> worshiped in accordance with the prescribed prayers and rituals
> every day whenever I could. And I did believe in God but I
> had very strong doubts as well. I recited the prayers and all,
> but many times I did not believe any of it was true. Yet I kept
> at it.

Just as there were faith-challenging ordeals and impressions, one
devout survivor from Lvov told of his faith-strengthening experience:

We were being forced-marched through a minefield some few
meters ahead of several German vehicles. We were the human
cannon fodder to be blown up rather than damage their precious
machinery and to save German lives. The German commanding
officer was a particularly cruel murderer. For sport he'd have
several of us run and he'd fire from his car and kill. For sport and
target practice. As we walked ahead, some of us hoped that a
mine would explode and end it all quickly and painlessly. But
I always believed God would preserve me. And as I crossed the field
I prayed that we'd get to the other side of the minefield safely.
We did. I then said, dear God, it's his turn. Let him be blown
sky high. At that moment a huge explosion was heard and he was
blown up and killed. And it was in the very row I had walked
myself. I knew then as I had known before but with more
certainty than ever that the Jewish people would always live and
that of all the peoples of the world and all the religions on earth,
ours alone was true. And our God a Jewish God, is a just God,
true to His people. Only we were God's recipient of the truth. That
is why we suffer. But that is also why we will always triumph
in the end.

Nondevout Survivors

As in previous ages, the matter of Judaism's truth is generally connected to the belief in God's existence and providence. As one survivor
observed, "asking whether Judaism is true is really asking if God exists." Nevertheless, a number of survivors, particularly atheists, spoke
not of God's existence but of the "importance" and "necessity" of the
various religions, among them Judaism. They are true, useful in their
salutary effect upon mankind:

"Religion has been good for the world."

"Otherwise man would be an even greater beast had there been no
religion to pacify him and control his murderous instincts. Had there
been no religion there would have been no anti-Nazis and no good
people at all in the camps. These were religious people."

"People should believe in religion and it is better that the average
man believes in God. I do not. But religion, on balance, and despite the
terrible things we all know about, has still been good for the world."

The two doctrines concerning Judaism's truth were of all the six
the only ones which atheist survivors affirmed at various times during

the four stages. Prior to and during the concentration camp period, atheists acknowledged no other article of faith. And even during the time period designated as immediately after the war, except for chosenness, which could lay claim to a mere 3 percent, the twin themes of Judaism's truth and its exclusive truth were the only ones to be avowed by survivors who denied God's existence. The word "truth" is the catchword for atheist survivors.

Before the Holocaust, 12 percent of all atheists considered Judaism to be true; 3 percent the only true religion. During the Holocaust, support by atheists for the former proposition fell by half, to 6 percent, while the latter contention held at its negligible 3 percent. Immediately after the Holocaust, 9 percent believed Judaism to be a true religion and 6 percent that it is the only true one.

The prism of truthfulness refracts various shadings and colors. Atheists and other nontraditional-minded Jews were quite readily able to impose their own interpretations on the conception, apparently even more so than in the case of chosenness. Truth is an exceptionally ambiguous notion offering a multiplicity of interpretations, constructions, and commentaries. A former Betar member—which was the Zionist youth movement of the Revisionist party, later the Herut party of modern Israel—submitted the following:

> When I say Judaism is true I mean it is true as is a poem or a
> song or a dream, all of which are true even if the facts
> surrounding it may not be exact. Truth is broad because there
> are many levels to it. Even legends and myths of the Bible tell
> truths if you know how to read them properly. Judaism is
> true like the stories of the Bible are true. Now, I don't take them
> literally. For example, I don't believe Adam and Eve existed as
> specific people but they represent early humanity after its
> emergence from the caves. And I don't believe in all the myths but
> I do think there is a great truth contained in the biblical stories.

Today, more than three decades after the Holocaust, the doctrine of Judaism's truth apparently has taken on real importance for many atheist survivors. Many more atheist survivors today (35 percent) affirm the doctrine than at the time immediately after liberation (9 percent), a precipitous rise virtually unmatched among other subgroups. Survivors who had been atheists and who gained faith in God at the time of the Holocaust had similar sharp surges of religious belief, but these were predictable concomitants of their newly found faith in God.

For atheists it is another matter altogether. Judaism is a true religion for them in the sense that its "culture is true" and its civilization, grounded in the Jewish state, is tangible, authentic and life enhancing. Some representative atheist remarks:

> You might think that because I do not believe in God I therefore do not believe in anything Jewish. That is not the case at all. God does not exist as far as I can judge, but that doesn't mean that all the rest of Judaism's teachings must be false. I have no problem with saying that Judaism is true—even without God, as I have said before, our culture is true—a great truth from which the whole world can learn and benefit.

> If when you ask whether Judaism is true you mean is it true what the average Orthodox Jew in Israel believes, then I'd have to say that Judaism is not true because it did not happen the way they say. But Judaism is true in the larger sense. It keeps the Jews together. It unites Jews living in the diaspora with Jews living in Israel. It teaches true morality and Judaism tells how human beings really are.

> Judaism is true for us as other religions are true for other people. One man's truth is another man's lie.

> Truth like beauty is in the eye of the beholder.

> I am not sure what you mean by truth, but if there is such a thing as truth then surely Judaism of all the religions of the world must be thought of as true. No other has such great wisdom and insights.

> Each and every fact may not be true but Judaism as a whole is true and it helps us function as a progressive modern state among the nations of the world.

The conception that Judaism is the only true religion also rose sharply among atheist survivors in the time period designated "today," but even though its adherents doubled to 12 percent it still remained overwhelmingly disdained and often derided. Those atheists who did speak of Judaism's exclusive truth often did so in terms of their apprehension of the failure of other faiths during the bloodshed of the war and the responsibility of these faiths for numerous pogroms against Jews and other massacres of history. Further on it will be shown that religion with which Jews had little contact such as Buddhism and Hinduism were rarely discussed. Christianity and Islam, as Judaism's daughter religions and in shared historical experiences, were of special importance among the other religions of mankind.

An Impersonal God and Judaism's Truth

Survivors who understood God as an impersonal Force had less difficulty than atheists reinterpreting the meaning of, and responding affirmatively to, the questions "Is Judaism true?" and "Is it the only true faith?" A great many more did so than atheists, with analogous reasoning. Additionally, their concurrence with the two conceptions was substantial because these survivors were able to speak in terms similar to those spoken by the devout as well as the atheist in an amalgam of opinions.

Just as with the larger community, this subgroup of survivors also preferred the doctrine of Judaism's truth to all other articles of faith, and by a considerable margin. Before the Holocaust, 71 percent endorsed it, whereas the next most popular article for this subgroup, that the Torah is the word of God, could muster only 39 percent support. Belief in Judaism's truth declined to 53 percent during and following the Holocaust and has regained its 71 percent today. Only 29 percent of all who believed in God as Power not Person at no time accepted Judaism as a true religion ("God is not a person despite what Judaism teaches"; "Judaism teaches many false notions and is therefore not true"). Those who accept Judaism as true were apt to agree with the remarks of a Vilna-raised survivor who is highly observant despite her heterodoxy and rationalism:

> God is not a man but man who is capable of being Godlike creates his religions. Judaism was created by the Jewish people for their needs, to express their values and ideas and principles. And to express its own special character. What was created by Jews for Jews is true for Jews.

And she adds on behalf of the two-thirds (67 percent) of her subgroup who never believed Judaism is the only true religion, ". . . just as other religions are true for other men."

As in Pantheistic thought, it may follow from an understanding of God as a cosmic Force that He manifests Himself everywhere, among all people and religions, and therefore all religions possess truth. Nevertheless, as many as one of every three of these survivors, despite the general universalistic ideology of the subgroup, maintained before the Holocaust that Judaism is the only true religion. That percentage fell to 22 during the Holocaust and remained there until today, not necessarily because of an increase in objectivity and broadmindedness but as an aspect of the decline of all religious attitudes then. One who continued in that belief explained that it is Judaism's teachings not the various conceptions of God to which they refer:

> Only Judaism teaches a universalistic God. Other religions teach
> God is Jesus or Allah, a Christian God or a Moslem God or
> Gods of other peoples. Judaism teaches a God of all the world
> which is a true teaching. Other religions want all peoples to convert
> to their faith and believe in their God, but Judaism does not.
> The Jewish idea of God is for all men and that is why Judaism
> is true while other religions are false.

Other Subgroups and Judaism's Truth

Most, but not all survivors who lost faith in God during the Holocaust simultaneously discontinued belief in Judaism's truth. And, as has already been shown, not all of the latter group became atheists. One does not necessarily relinquish belief in God when one ceases to accept other religious doctrines. Before the Holocaust, three-quarters of all survivors (77 percent) who lost faith in God believed Judaism to be a true religion. (By contrast, 100 percent of all survivors who retained their faith in God had before the Holocaust believed Judaism to be true.)

Half the population of former believers posited Judaism as the only true faith before the Holocaust. During the Holocaust, only 13 percent continued in that partisan conviction, and immediately afterward only 7 percent. Today a tenth of this subgroup currently living in Israel professes Judaism as the true religion. Also during the Holocaust years, although belief in God was lost for them, 23 percent continued to affirm Judaism as true—however it may be defined without the deity. "In Auschwitz," a Polish survivor explained, "I came to doubt the existence of God, as did many others in that death house. I've never had any reason to change my mind with the possible exception of the Six Day War. When my son returned, I blessed God. I have to consider myself an atheist. No God, if He exists, could allow such suffering. But Judaism's teachings and commandments are true." That is, 54 percent of all survivors who discontinued their faith in God during the catastrophe simultaneously ceased to believe that Judaism is true. And immediately after the Holocaust and today, 19 percent of these survivors persevered in that conviction for a total loss of 58 percent.

However small a subgroup they may form in the aggregate, survivors who gained faith in God during the Holocaust years also began to believe, to a greater or lesser degree, in all corollary articles of faith as well. The final two propositions each won the approval of half their population. Before the Holocaust this subgroup had believed in neither proposition, consistent with their denial of God's existence. After the Holocaust, whereas the final proposition on Judaism's exclusive truth remained to this day with the same 50 percent support, the basic idea of Judaism's truth continued to win adherents, mounting to two-thirds after the Holocaust and to near unanimity at the time of the survey for these few former atheists.

A former atheist whose Holocaust experience was seen as proof of Judaism's exclusive truth relates a particularly interesting and relevant episode in her Holocaust career:

> There was a young man in his early twenties who found us in hiding
> in a barn at the edge of the forest. There were four of us in all
> and we all liked him instantly and adopted him. We had been
> hiding there for only a few short weeks when he found us and we
> all remained about a month or so longer. We soon met one
> of the village priests—I really don't think I ever knew his precise
> title or even his exact religious denomination. I do know that he
> appeared at first very good-hearted and generous and he brought
> or sent along to us many things which helped keep us alive:
> food and clothing items and occasionally even small amounts of
> money. He wanted us to stay on there in safety as long as we
> could. A nice young Jewish boy shortly afterwards came to take
> away one of the young women of our small group and I never
> learned what happened to them. The priest was very upset at her
> absence and began to proselytize very strenuously among the
> remaining three of us. We knew we couldn't stay long and he felt
> he was working against time. The young boy, who was very
> sweet and simple and immature, fell victim to the priest's words and
> promises. Some time later, it may have been only a matter of a
> few days, the boy returned and passionately tried to convert me
> and the other young man with me. He was abusive. Words
> were exchanged and that night we left because he hinted that
> he'd not hesitate to let the authorities know where we were. He

had no concern for his own welfare or safety. He must have
been led to believe that the priest could save him and that his
conversion would matter to the Nazis and protect him. Or I
don't know what. Perhaps the belief that Jesus would protect
him? But I felt he no longer could be trusted, that he wouldn't
hesitate to betray us, that this was precisely what he wished to
do if we too would not follow him into the arms of Christ.
We left that night and it was wise that we did because I had no
doubt that he intended to find a way to betray us. He had become
even more rabid an anti-Semite than his mentor and friend,
the priest. I heard he ended up in Auschwitz himself and rose
to the rank of Kapo. No doubt protesting all along that he was not
a Jew—which couldn't have helped him survive in the slightest.

I tell you about him because any religion that could do this—
prey upon a gullible, weak-willed child and turn a nice boy
into a hate-filled would-be murderer—such a religion is false, a
malicious lie and a fraud. And by contrast Judaism, none of
whose converts ever became murderers of their former coreligionists,
is credible and trustworthy.

Christianity and Islam

Today, when survivors are asked to contrast Judaism's truth with that
of other faiths, it appears that despite the immediate proximity of millions of surrounding Arab Moslems it is still Christianity and not Islam
that provides the major point of religious reference and controversy
for these former Europeans. Islam is simply not looked upon as a
significant religious rival to Judaism in the same way as is Christianity
regardless of their awareness that the world war into which these survivors had been swept and the attendant tumult and stress of that
convulsive period were launched and conducted primarily by Christians
and not Moslems.

Several obvious explanations may be suggested: First, the survivors'
upbringing in yesterday's Europe and the relatively deeper contact
they had with their non-Jewish countrymen there has made them culturally people of the West, where Christianity predominates; a second
explanation might be the entirely different attitudes of the Moslem
Middle East. Perhaps the present hostility of their Arab neighbors plays
a part as well.

A German Jew who fled to several East European countries before being seized by the Nazis dismissed both Islam and Christianity simultaneously with the opinion that

> . . . they have each in their own way at different times proven
> to be savage, barbarian, and base. They are bent more on the
> destruction of nonbelievers and infidels than on improving the lot
> of their own. They're more interested in murdering us Jews who
> gave them their religion than with effecting their followers
> with morality and decency. Christianity and Islam are both equally
> false and Judaism by contrast—having never treated the
> followers of the daughter religions in the awful way they treated
> the followers of the mother religion—has been shown to be true.

To like-minded survivors, repeatedly, here and elsewhere in this study, Islam and especially Christianity, which receives the greater attention, have revealed themselves to be false by the behavior rather than the beliefs of their devotees. But theology was not overlooked.

Nondevout survivors in their comments on Judaism, truth, and Christianity tended to speak of the improbability of the Christian Godhood and the messiahship of Jesus: "How can you believe that God divided Himself into three equal parts and one part became a man who died."

And another survivor: "If Jesus was the messiah, he was a terrible flop. Anyone who believes in him in accordance with their teachings is a very gullible fool. We Jews have known the likes of them in our own history from time to time."

A Belgian survivor who has spoken about Christianity in an earlier section is in agreement with the foregoing:

> At least to be a Jew you don't have to accept nonsensical miracles
> and supernatural wonders. And you can deny all the wonder
> workings of the Bible and still be a Jew. But you can't deny the
> absurdities of Christianity like the virgin birth and resurrection
> and God becoming man and the like and still remain a
> Christian. All you'd have left is Judaism. Christianity teaches you
> to believe in nonsense. Small wonder German Christians could
> believe in the absurdities of Hitler's teachings. They were
> trained to believe in ridiculous things by their Christian upbringing.

A survivor of a number of camps whose academic career at the Sorbonne was cut short by the Nazi occupation said:

I'll tell you how the Nazis are like Christians. The Christians try to level all distinctions and so do the Nazis. In the early years, they would reach a region whose people had a perfectly appropriate and valid cultural tradition and outlook on the world and they would convert everyone in sight, undermining their own tradition and stealing their culture. And the world is a poorer place, not as rich in the varieties of cultural expression as before the proselytizing Christians preaching the Gospel came their way. Often the Christians superimposed an inferior Christian religion upon them and nothing was left of their own culture and religion. Christianity did it subtly and by stealth. They even told some of them to keep their Gods but to gain immortality and salvation they must take on one additional God, Jesus, and put him at the top. Now the world has lost all of these beautiful traditions. The Nazis did the same but weren't as subtle; they tried to do the same thing to the various races, wiping them all off the face of the earth, so that there would be only one left—so boring and tedious. And they very nearly succeeded, particularly with the gypsies and Jews. What a great theft from the world it might have been.

Devout survivors spoke occasionally of the contrast between "the Torah's truth and the New Testament's obvious falsity":

The Five Books of Moses are clearly the work of God's genius whereas the sayings and parables of Jesus—when they are not outright copies and rewritings and imitations of Jewish sacred writings—are simply ridiculous imbecilities and the mutterings of idiots, a travesty on what a Bible should be like, if you read objectively as I have.

And from devout survivors, constantly, "the Torah is a book of truth beyond doubt and so Judaism is true. . . . Other religions are false except where they are duplications and reproductions of Judaism's truth."

"Christianity and Islam are true to the extent they follow Judaism and are false wherever they depart from Judaism."

"The Torah was given to Jews, God's people, and not to others regardless of the reasons why. There is no way Catholicism or Protestantism or Buddhism or Hinduism or any of them can be true. God did not reveal Himself to them, only to His chosen people."

To Jewish survivors, Christian religious beliefs fall short of the truth. And in terms of Christian behavior, civilization is no closer to the millennium.

Jewish Doctrines and the Retention of Faith

A child is exposed to religious practices long before he hears talk of God or is instructed in principles of religious ideology. Then, when religious ideas are finally spoken of, the child is taught to believe in God before instruction begins on other doctrines of religious faith. Not only chronologically but in emphasis and importance as well, belief in God's existence precedes the various supplementary religious doctrines including the character of the Jewish people, the significance of the Torah, the coming of the messiah and the rest. The belief in God conduces to other religious doctrines; they are all grounded in belief in Him. It would be difficult to make a case for an article of faith having precedence over faith in God Himself; rather, faith in God adumbrates and reinforces other religious doctrines. But can it be shown that there are religious doctrines that in turn reinforce belief in God and enable one to uphold one's faith in Him through periods of crisis?

It is particularly important to examine how a survivor's acceptance of Jewish doctrines influences his faith in God Himself. Will a survivor who held to no or few ancillary articles be more likely to lose faith in God than another, more "religious" survivor who affirms many of them? And are certain doctrines predictive of retention of faith in God as others are not?

The statement that Judaism is true, as has already been pointed out, can be thought of as an abridged designation for a profession of most articles of Jewish faith. It is also the most popular, least demanding principle affirmed by survivors. We find that survivors who before the Holocaust accepted the principle that Judaism is true were far more likely (68 percent to 12 percent) to retain their faith in God.

The three least popular articles of faith were belief that catastrophes like the Holocaust are God's will (26 percent), the coming of the messiah (35 percent), and that Judaism is the only true religion (41 percent). Were survivors who accepted these more likely to retain their faith in God than survivors who affirmed only the three more popular, "less demanding" ones, namely, chosenness (49 percent), that the Torah is the word of God (54 percent), and that Judaism is true (64 percent)? We cannot contrast survivors who believed in all six religious doctrines with those who believed in none at all, inasmuch as the latter group was virtually nonexistent. But our findings are that survivors who affirmed the three least popular religious doctrines before the Holocaust would be more likely (83 percent to 66 percent) to retain their faith than those who affirmed only the three more popular articles. We do not mean to imply that their faith in God was necessarily stronger at that time by virtue of these other beliefs, for there is no way of knowing this, but clearly the more beliefs one holds the greater the likelihood of the retention of faith in God despite faith-challenging experiences. There is evidence to suggest, therefore, that faith in God is strengthened by other religious teachings.

As has been shown previously, this study divides and designates observant survivors in accordance with the number of commandments they perform or "keep." A nonobservant survivor is one who keeps fewer than six. An observant survivor keeps six or more, a moderately observant survivor more than ten, and an ultra or highly observant survivor fourteen or more. Will a devout survivor who was ultra observant before the Holocaust be more likely to retain his faith in God through the Holocaust ordeal than an equally devout but less observant survivor?

Chronologically, religious practices become part of a child's life somewhat before, or virtually simultaneous with, belief in God, although the former are rooted in the latter. Even if the obligation of the commandments first devolves upon a child at the age of thirteen—or twelve for girls—the child has nevertheless long previously been performing, not merely "practicing," religious observances. We have just shown that the more religious doctrines one accepts, the greater the likelihood of the retention of faith in God. May we also assert the more observances a survivor kept, the more predictive for his retention of faith in God? Here we may contrast the two opposable subgroups of survivors who kept virtually all the commandments before the Holocaust and survivors who kept five or fewer. Ultra observant survivors retained their faith in God by 78 percent to 22 percent (virtually the same proportions as survivors who believed in God and affirmed all religious principles), but nonobservant survivors were nearly as likely to lose their faith as retain it: 55 percent retained faith and 45 percent lost faith in God. And survivors who were "merely" observant, keeping between six and nine of the commandments, were at 67 percent also somewhat less likely to retain their faith than ultra observant survivors.

Clearly for survivors, and doubtless for others as well, the greater the number of observances kept and the more religious doctrines one believed in, the stronger the reinforcement of faith in God.

In conclusion, it should be noted that not one of the six articles of faith ever recovered to its pre-Holocaust level. Our findings seem to refute the popular wisdom that one who has had a religious upbringing and who relinquishes his faith at some later time tends to return to it in advanced years. And although one may argue that a slow recovery process is still in operation following the immediate post-Holocaust period, and that the years ahead may yet see a full restoration of pre-Holocaust faith, such a likelihood appears remote indeed. The leveling-off effect appears to have been reached and passed during the intervening years and is well behind us. Nor is there evidence that there could ever be a full and permanent recovery for survivors in the intensity and certainty of their various previously held convictions. However, it is not merely that popular wisdom is here inexact. Rather, the Holocaust may have been too jarringly singular an experience for the expected, "conventional" processes to resume.

FIVE

Seven Theological Questions

On Sensitive Questions

THE HOLOCAUST, even for non-Europeans and non-Jews, can hardly be the subject of superficial, casual conversation. For the survivors them-selves, deep emotions are almost always aroused when the Holocaust is discussed. That respondents consented to be interviewed and to offer answers on critical questions touching upon the depths of the meaning of their Holocaust experience is rather remarkable. Their willingness is largely attributable to the study's support and endorsement, however unofficial, by Yad Vashem, Israel's renowned and prestigious agency for Holocaust research. A number of survivors remarked that had the sur-vey been without the Yad Vashem imprimatur, "I would not have forced myself to endure it," so painful, apparently, was the prospect of the inquiry for many survivors. And parts of the study were indeed emotionally provocative and agitating, stirring nearly dormant feelings.

However, after the interview a number of the survivors spoke of the welcome catharsis it provided. They expressed their thanks to the re-searchers and Yad Vashem for the emotional release it furnished as well as for the opportunity of making their token contribution to the corpus of Holocaust research, a contribution they had long wished to make. Many even acknowledged subsequently that although some questions were painful, "it was good that they were finally being asked." A sur-vivor whose knowledge of languages helped keep her alive as interpreter and typist said:

> I forced myself to answer these questions because they originated from Yad Vashem. Some of the questions caused me to feel ill and

become upset and some of them at first glance even appeared offensive to my religious beliefs. But I quickly saw their wisdom and understood their necessity. I understood the importance of answering the questions seeing that the opportunity of asking them may never arise again. And the future generations are entitled to know what is in our hearts and minds. I was grateful, ultimately, to have been selected to answer the questions, and I hope I contributed to the knowledge. And I hope that the testimony I gave as a survivor helped provide a better understanding of what we went through.

In the questionnaire's cover letter, and here again, immediately preceding the next seven highly sensitive questions, survivors were forewarned of their unsparing and provocative nature and were advised of their option to skip over them (an approach that was felt preferable to the risk of incurring the anger of respondents):

The next seven questions, however necessary and important for the study of survivor attitudes, may cause you to be upset, or perhaps injure your religious sensibilities. We ask in advance for your indulgence, your understanding, and your cooperation; and please be reminded that you may choose to answer them or skip over them entirely, whichever you prefer.

For the overall study, one thousand randomly chosen survivors were contacted for either personal interviews or for mail completions, and 70 percent (708) responded. Of the 70 percent only 4 percent refrained from answering all seven religiously or emotionally "sensitive questions." In all, 33 percent answered all seven questions of the series with no skipping at all. Virtually the same percentage obtained for concentration camp survivors and non–concentration camp survivors (34 percent and 32 percent respectively), which may mean that the former were no more or no less likely to feel discomfited or threatened by religiously provocative questions than other survivors; it may also mean that whether within or without the camps, survivors were just as likely to be affected by their ordeal, at least to the extent of their willingness to answer potentially disquieting questions.

The first question of the series was the most frequently avoided question, skipped over by 31 percent of all respondents. It was formulated as follows:

Theologians hold various views concerning God's role and the Holocaust. With which of the following do you most closely identify?

a. God causes or allows tragedies like the Holocaust to test man's faith and to teach him to keep the Torah.

b. The suffering that God brings or permits in this world is compensated for in the world to come.

c. Both of these views.

d. Neither of these views.

Perhaps it was not the nature of the question itself but, rather, the fact that this question immediately followed the warning and the reminder that the series may be skipped encouraged the largest number to leave out the first question of the series. Moreover, lending credence to this view, the next two questions were respectively the second and third most frequently omitted. But the last of the series was the fourth most frequently omitted.

It is the subjective judgment of the researcher, based on the impressions gained at interviews, that survivors seemed to feel most assailed and ill at ease facing the final two questions of the series, which dealt with the connection between the Holocaust and the creation of the State of Israel. The final question evidently was particularly threatening. It asked if the State of Israel could have been established only as a direct outcome of the Holocaust, was it worth the sacrifice of six million Jews? Among the respondents, 20 percent chose not to answer the question. Even for those who answered it in the course of the interview, many did so with evident reluctance and with considerable misgivings. In advance of the study it was anticipated that the issue of the connection between the death of the Six Million and the establishment of the State would prove difficult for survivors to deal with. Accordingly, respondents were given the option of choosing "I don't know" for the two questions touching upon the subject.

Since 24 percent more chose "I don't know" in answer to the final question of the series, a total of 44 percent preferred to avoid the question of the connection between the State of Israel and the death of the Six Million. And a total of 35 percent (21 percent choosing "I don't know") elected to keep distant from the preceding question, which asked whether:

a. the Six Million died that the State of Israel be established

b. the Six Million died to teach Jews to keep the commandments

c. both of these reasons

d. neither of these reasons

e. I don't know

As noted, the final two questions were probably the most trouble-some and difficult ones for survivors to answer. It may well be that the connection between the Six Million and the State of Israel presents a dilemma for a more widespread population than other "religious ques-tions," more far-reaching even than vexing questions concerning God's role in the Holocaust. Religious questions may tend to assail pious and religiously committed survivors alone and leave the nonreligious rela-tively unaffected, whereas religious and nonreligious survivors may be similarly assailed by the intractable connection between the Holocaust and the establishment of the State. The statistics appear to justify this line of reasoning since observant survivors were just as likely to sidestep the question as nonobservant survivors (51 percent and 53 percent respectively).

Faith-testing, Discipline, and Afterlife

Throughout the course of the development of the Jewish system of thought, the suffering of the innocent has often been attributed to God's unchallenged prerogative of putting the pious to the supreme test of faith as in the biblical Book of Job—regardless of the question of the justice of the evil unleashed.

Nearly always linked to God's test of man's faith in Jewish tradition is His wish to instruct and discipline man to follow His Toraitic teach-ings. To the pious survivor, then, perhaps this reasoning may be attri-butable to God and provide explanation for His bringing about or allowing the Holocaust to have happened.

Moreover, Jewish tradition has at various periods offered a way out of the dilemma of the innocent suffering in this world by positing a recompensing world-to-come, a solution conspicuously absent from the Book of Job.

Significantly, among these 708 twentieth-century Jewish victims not one thought the world-to-come—whether as afterlife, heaven, messianic future, resurrection, or whatever a survivor may conceive—was suffi-cient alone to make sense out of the Holocaust. Some, however, believed in a world-to-come when linked with other principles of faith.

One concentration camp survivor spoke about an afterlife in these words:

Most people simply do not believe in Heaven and Hell any more—if they ever did. Surely except for the extremely religious no Jew I ever met during the war believed in it or that there is any kind of life after death even if we were all rather vague about it. I have heard that some non-Jewish groups in the camps like the Jehovah Witnesses believed in Heaven. And that's what kept some of them alive. They reasoned that since this world is evil and far from God's presence, how can anyone expect anything other than the horrors of ovens and crematoria and lingering death. Because, after all, this world is only a vestibule of pain leading to the bliss of Paradise. The Jehovah Witnesses got just what they expected of this world. And they kept their sanity. But no Jew I knew, not even Hasidim, believed the world insane or that it is merely an interlude of terror and evil culminating in an Eden after death. Jews live in this world. And the next world, if there is any, will take care of itself. Besides, nothing, no possible reward however great which we may be entitled to and which we may receive in a world-to-come can ever compensate for the suffering which we endured in this world. Ten more wives and a hundred more children will never replace the one beloved wife and the two precious children I lost to the Nazis.

Although never offering the suggestion by itself in explanation of God's will, 7 percent of all survivors answered Question 1 by declaring that they did believe in a world-to-come where "the sufferings which God brings or allows in this world will be compensated for with good things." Invariably these survivors at the same time expressed the belief that "God brings or allows catastrophes like the Holocaust to teach faith in God and to instruct men to keep the Torah."

No survivor expressed belief in the former without the latter, but an additional 7 percent accepted the latter alone. Survivors were able to view the Holocaust as God's instrument for instruction with greater equanimity than as linked with a potentially reassuring afterlife or world-to-come. That is, 14 percent of all survivors, and these were almost without exception ultra observant Jews, saw God's role in the Holocaust as one of chastisement with the intention of promoting faith in Him and correcting man's behavior. One of these suggested that

. . . we mortals *can* understand God's ways; God smites His people but gives them the strength and the courage to endure it. When they are punished they are also being helped to understand what the punishment is for. The Jewish people are an eternal people but their mission and purpose is to keep the commandments. And they will suffer greatly in proportion to their trespasses (although we cannot always comprehend God's calculations) when they fail to conduct their lives according to His Torah teachings. The prophet Amos said that God explained His motivations, "You alone have I known of all the families of the earth; therefore I will visit upon you all your sins!"

Included among these are survivors who blackened out "God causes" in Question 1, leaving only "God allows catastrophes like the Holocaust." Others eliminated the second half of the sentence, which suggested reasons for the Holocaust, explaining that there is no way of knowing why God brought it about or allowed it to happen. And still others did both of these, adding that they believed strongly that in the world-to-come there will be justice and recompense and perhaps even understanding of the event.

For observant survivors answering Question 1, 60 percent believed the Holocaust was God's way of teaching faith in Him and instructing Jews to keep the Torah. Half of these survivors at the same time believed that the world-to-come would offset the suffering of the Holocaust. Among all other survivors answering Question 1, only 10 percent saw the Holocaust as God's severe exercise in guidance and discipline. And fewer than half of these expressed belief in the recompense of a world beyond this one.

Survivors were hardly expected to be consistent or uniform in their views on this or on any subject. There is one survivor, for example, highly observant in his religious practices throughout his life and learned in Jewish tradition, who nevertheless commented on the question by saying that "God could not have existed then. For if He had existed . . . . and if the Holocaust was His way of punishment, He would Himself have said 'enough!' and would have been full of remorse and regrets. For He would Himself have had to stand in judgment after the war. Perhaps He was off creating other worlds because God could not have been around at the time."

Most observant survivors simply answered along with the one who said, "naturally, God does everything, and is responsible for everything good as well as evil, but why and what for? This only He Himself knows." Or as another put it: "God's ways are mysterious. He is the Author of good and evil but His ways are unfathomable." And, "God's ways are hidden. Who are we mortals to inquire of His ways?" And, "I don't know the ways of God. No doubt there is meaning to the Holocaust but it is hidden from me." Or, avoiding the issue altogether, "I have no firm idea on the subject." And another, quoting the Psalms:

> How enormous are Thy deeds!
> Thy Thoughts are so unfathomable.
> The ignorant man can never know
> Neither can the fool comprehend it.
> The wicked may shoot up as the grass
> And all the workers of evil may thrive
> Only to be destroyed at the end.

Many other observant Jews said firmly, "I refuse to answer this question," and others, "the question is too disturbing to me."

Numerous observant as well as nonobservant survivors answered the question by insisting that there was no connection at all between God and the Holocaust. Others, almost invariably nonobservant survivors, answered that from their own religious frame of reference they simply "could not relate to the issue of an afterlife or to a concept of God which suggests that He might bring about destruction and death to teach faith in Himself." Other nonobservant survivors also acknowledged that the question was "too deep, delicate, and difficult to answer." And still another responded that "they are indeed happy who can lean on a belief in God so simple and pure as to offer a Heaven as a way out of the dilemma of the death of the Six Million." One nonobservant survivor pointed out in response to the question that "other nations also suffered from holocausts—*lehavdil* (granted the enormous differences)—were they also being tried by God? Were they also being taught to obey the words of the Torah?" And atheists often responded with the comment that "for an atheist there can be no connection between a God whose existence is denied and what happened in Europe to the Jews. So the answers were omitted from this question."

To students of Martin Buber, the Jewish existentialist philosopher, God is "in eclipse." To more radical theologians, Jewish and Christian, God is dead. Rabbi Richard Rubenstein, who is also mentioned among the atheologians, prefers to speak of the "time of the death of God," rather than "God is dead." Many survivors speak of themselves as having experienced the total absence of God at a time when He was most needed and sought. But no survivor spoke of God's death. And not even those who were—but would have rather not been—moved to renounce their conception of the loving Father God could hold out for themselves the possibility of His resurrection or reappearance. They and others rather preferred to articulate the charge expressed wistfully and earnestly that now that He was gone or now that we know for certain He never was, man must become God in place of God.

Beliefs Not Held

To gain an adequate understanding of the Holocaust community it is as essential to survey the beliefs *not* held by survivors as to examine the theological views they expressed relative to the meaning and origin of good and evil and the prospects of their reconciliation in a hereafter.

Among the views not offered by survivors, and quite prominent in its absence, is that the evil of the Holocaust is illusory, an unreal manifestation, merely an opposite reflection of good. The ideas of Maimonides, who saw evil as the absence of good, as sickness in the absence of health; and those of the authors of the mystical Jewish tract, the Zohar, who taught that evil consists of the husks of things, not the real things, were decisively rejected by Holocaust survivors. Even ultra observant Hasidim, whose philosophy stresses the essential goodness of the universe, for whom evil is but "the vase containing the good," were not of a mind to subscribe to the Hasidic proposition that "in the upper world the lower world's bad is seen as good." No one who had experienced the daily lashings from the whip of starvation and the terror of death's imminence in the ovens of Auschwitz could suggest that what appeared to be evil was really good in disguise "if viewed from the proper perspective." One survivor in connection with the question of the creation of the State of Israel out of the ashes of the crematoria quoted Isaiah's admonition, "Woe unto them that call evil good and good evil."

Another theological posture without representative survivor spokesmen is the Mishnaic dictum that the sufferings of the righteous are real enough but they are "trials of Divine Love." It is one thing for some pious survivors to accept the notion that God often tests man's faith. And the Holocaust may have been the severest test of all. But it is quite another matter to appraise the Holocaust in terms of Divine Love. Or as one survivor put it, "there is an old Jewish joke concerning the statement of faith that the Jews are the chosen people of God. The punch line has the old bearded learned Jew throw his arms heavenward pleading with God in a huge voice to go choose someone else for a change. Such love we can do without."

Similarly, the Holocaust was too severe for any adherents of the Hermann Cohen view of suffering: It is God's way of strengthening us and He inflicts some pains on man to refine his nature or to purify his moral character. Or, in Alshekh's symbolism, "Man can become a lamp of pure gold only through the cleaning and polishing effect of suffering."

One Maidanek survivor who currently holds a high government post and contributes to scientific journals addressed himself to this subject:

> I don't believe I am a better person because of what I went through.
> It is more likely I am less the person, inferior to the person I was
> or might have become had I not gone through the camps. But even
> if I could be persuaded to admit that I'm somehow without fully
> realizing it better, maybe more sensitive or compassionate, more
> understanding of the suffering of others than I would have been had
> I not been the subject of Nazi persecution, I still would ask, did
> God use the death of the Six Million for whom there was no future
> as a sacrifice for my improvement? A suffering for the benefit of
> those that lived? That's insane. It means that people die for others
> to live "improved lives." What a great injustice to the dead that
> would be even if it were so. Sounds like a terrible evolutionary
> theory; the fittest survive because God wanted them to survive so
> that they will be better humans morally. But the deaths themselves
> are immoral. The immoral means of their death—brought about by
> God who, therefore, must be immoral Himself—for the purpose of
> refining our moral sense? An immoral God trains His children in
> morality? That sounds like nonsense. I cannot believe that.
>
> Besides, the improvement of my moral sense certainly is no sav-
> ing grace for those that perished. And I cannot believe that the
> dead were intended to be the moral cannon fodder of the living.
> Surely their moral sense was in no way improved. They're dead.

Nor was there support from survivors of the view that God causes or permits suffering to reveal His enormous power to mortal man. For Holocaust survivors God could have found other ways of demonstrating His might.

Certain notable exceptions were cited earlier in this chapter with reference to the belief in God as an impersonal Force in the universe. Nevertheless, Holocaust survivors, despite the enormity of the evil they experienced, were in no way estranged from the timeless view held by Jews that, regardless of the issue of the nature of God, no devil, demi-god, or demon coexists with Him to whom the Holocaust can be attri-buted. Evil, whatever its ultimate source or explanation, does not come about from a malevolent God. God may or may not be the source of evil as He assuredly is of good, but to all Jews, including survivors, no other Godlike being exists.

Holocaust survivors had no difficulty relating to the idea that in Europe they had been "in the land of their enemies." Many survivors articulated this thought in passing. The full biblical passage, Leviticus 26:44, that provides the sources for this quotation expresses an important religious corollary concept which few if any doubted: "Nevertheless, even when they are in the land of their enemies, I will not discard them, or cast them aside to annihilate them completely." At no time, not even at the threshold of the crematoria—if we are to judge from the paltry numbers who were themselves "brands snatched from the flame"—was the view held that the war's conclusion would see the end of world Jewry or that God was bringing about the destruction of the entire people. Some may have believed that European Jewry would be destroyed utterly but Jews in other places would endure: in Palestine, in the Soviet Union, in the United States, Canada, and elsewhere. Even among survivors who believed that the Holocaust was the will of God, none thought that the final retribution awaiting a rebellious Israel was at hand or that the imminent destruction they faced, along with so many others, would usher in the millenium or the end of the world. However, some, particularly among the ultra orthodox, may have felt that God, for reasons of His own, intended to destroy a particular portion of world Jewry completely, as in the case of the ten tribes exiled by Assyria to Lachlach and Chabor.

One survivor who claims that his vow never to fail to study the weekly biblical reading is rooted in the Holocaust—another Holocaust mitzvah—spoke of Jacob's conduct in preparing for his encounter with his brother Esau. The patriarch, anticipating the possibility of the destruction of his entire tribe, divided his camp into two parts so that were one attacked the other might flee and remain alive. Indeed that stratagem became a symbol for the fortunes of the Jewish Diaspora in later times (when one Jewish community was annihilated or uprooted, another thrived and welcomed escapees). Furthermore, survivors often found some measure of consolation, even as they faced the likelihood of their own deaths, that the Jewish people would go on and would incorporate the stories of their own lives and martyred deaths into the memory and history of the people.

Resurrection and Suicide

Turning to the theological views of the hereafter denied by survivors, the doctrine of the resurrection of the dead is undoubtedly the most prominent. In Jewish thought the doctrine of resurrection held so important a place that, although not taught explicitly in the Torah, it become expressed as one of Maimonides's Thirteen Principles or Articles of Faith. It is also the theme of one of the Eighteen Benedictions, which forms part of the daily prayer service:

> Thou sustainest the living with faithfulness, and revivest the dead with great mercy; Thou supportest all who fall, and healest the sick; Thou freest the captives, and justifiest the fidelity of those who sleep in the dust. Who is like Thee, Lord of Power? Who resembles Thee, O King? Thou bringest death and restorest to life, and causest deliverance to flourish.

The Talmud upheld the prominence of the doctrine with this rather extreme pronouncement: "since a person repudiated belief in the doctrine of the resurrection of the dead, he will have no share in the resurrection."[1]

But if the survivors of Nazi terror in any way reflect the current status of contemporary Jewish theology, then it can be said that, except as an aspect of the coming of the messiah for a small portion of ultra observant survivors, the doctrine has now been abandoned with the same zest and alacrity as it had been championed by some in previous periods. Despite their experiences in this life, *Holocaust survivors with near unanimity did not feel compelled to postulate a return to this world after their deaths when the iniquities would be released and Divine Justice made evident.*

Our study has already shown that the doctrine of the coming of the messiah has not sustained the same overwhelming rejection as the doctrine of the resurrection of the dead.

The subject of suicide arose too frequently in interviews in this context to ignore. The taking of one's life is made comprehensible even under certain circumstances justifiable when there is a belief in resurrection or the world to come. But it was never really a serious stratagem for those Jews who lived in the midst of calamity. Although many wished it in moments of hopelessness and desperation, or joked about it in the camps as when black humor and dark quips were exchanged (for example: "Don't drink that soup; it's only wasted on you and you'll be too heavy for me to carry tomorrow to the furnace. Have a heart and give it here." Or another: "Q. What is a protected list? A. A collection of the names of the Jews who will be deported next."), even survivors who believed in an afterlife never really considered suicide, despite the fact that the attitudes "if I die, I die" or "If I am selected, so be it—it's God's will" were rather commonplace. Perhaps it may be suggested that suicide was so rare in the camps because so few believed in an afterlife. It would be more correct to assume that few concentration camp internees chose suicide, with the notable exception of those who volunteered to be taken next to the furnaces when they had nearly reached the stage of the musselmen, or the walking dead, or when they knew death was imminent or inevitable, or when they were about to die by torture or degradation. But suicide, when yet there remained a single sheaf of hope to be gleaned, was not a frequent occurrence.

In those instances when suicide was turned to, mortification was a frequent reason, as when hunger drove one to steal the food ration of a loved one or a friend in a bunker, and the "thief" in remorse would take his own life, or arrange the circumstances leading to his death. And within the privation of the ghettos, there were "hardly any suicides . . . the beaten down, shamed, broken Jews of Poland . . . love life, and they do not wish to disappear from the earth before their time." [2]

The sacrifice of one's life for another occurred with great frequency in the midst of the ineffable horror of the camps. To suggest that such an act was a form of suicide, which to a certain extent it may have been, explains little and deprecates the courage of those who sacrificed. Too many other motivations converge when one human being forfeits his life for another. We must not necessarily dismiss or categorize as a suicide a death that appears to have been brought upon oneself or even when self-inflicted.

Emile Durkheim's research classic, which presents us with the categories of self-inflicted death, reflects his difficulty with the definition of suicide. Ruling out motivation as too subjective for his scientific inquiry, suicide, for Durkheim, applies to "all cases of death resulting directly or indirectly from a positive or negative act of the victim himself, which he knows will produce this result." [3] Suicide, however, has generally been understood as the *intentional* taking of one's life. For example, the death resulting when a nonswimming parent leaps into deep water to save a child is not usually classified as suicide, even if Durkheim would have it so.[4] The life-jeopardizing behavior of Jews in the ghettos and death camps, which frequently paralleled this example, confounds the issue and Durkheim's thesis still further. But clearly suicide was a rare occurrence for Jews trapped in the Nazi web.

The account of the ninety-three girls of the Beth Jacob School in Warsaw, who, rather than submit sexually to the Nazis, took poison, may be, like Massada, an entirely apocryphal episode. Regardless of whether or not the event occurred, Jewish tradition neither honors nor condemns such actions. "Leave them in silence," is Rabbi Akiba's advice.[5]

The Holocaust and God's Role

Atheists, in consequence of their disbelief, are exempt from an entire catalogue of questions concerning God's withdrawn presence which believers, according to the same logic, are obliged to confront. Thus, 26 percent of all survivors were nonbelievers who felt the second question of the series, on God's comportment, to be inapplicable to them. However, since survivors generally claimed no rigorous theological consistency, and many often held to a thesis and its antithesis simultaneously, not every atheist judged the question's irrelevancy as quite so self-evident. Some survivors spoke of God's nonexistence and His unforgivable abandonment quite in the same breath. Question 2 was formulated as follows:

> With regard to the destruction of the Six Million which one of these responses is the most acceptable to you.
> a. It is inappropriate to blame God for the acts of man (man may decide to kill or not to kill).
> b. It is not for us to judge the ways of God.
> c. God was unable to prevent the destruction.
> d. The Holocaust was the will of God (it was part of His divine plan).
> e. Nothing can excuse God for not having saved them.

The selection by survivors of one of the five answers to the question by no means precluded concurrence with one or several of the others. And various survivors indicated their second preference as well; only the first choice, however, has been computed statistically here.

Man May Not Judge God

It follows from a professed belief in God that an explanation of His whereabouts and comportment during the Holocaust years should be offered even if only to suggest that "it is not meant for man to judge

God" (answer b). This attitude, while providing no resolution to the dilemma, at least acknowledges it. About one of every three survivors responding to Question 2, or 34 percent, chose this answer. Half were observant survivors who had retained their religious practices throughout the years, and the remaining half were distributed rather evenly among all other categories of observant and nonobservant survivors.

One observant survivor articulated a frequently expressed religious affirmation:

> I remained an observant Jew all my life and never questioned God's wisdom or God's actions. Man is an insignificant creature who is mortal living only a brief span of years and then is gone. The Psalms teach us that
>
>> Man is like vanity
>> His days pass away as a shadow
>> In the morning he flourishes
>> And grows up
>> In the evening he is cut down
>> And dries up . . .
>> For in his death he carries nothing away.
>
> God is eternal and sees far into the future and back into the distant past. He sees all and knows all. It would be folly for man to imagine that he could begin to know God's purpose and plan for mankind. God governs not only this world, but the entire universe and the cosmos. He doesn't owe man an accounting. We are His creatures and we owe accounting of our behavior to God. And we plead for forgiveness for our wrongdoings on the Day of Atonement. He is of a different realm from man. He is Master of the World.
>
> When I was in Auschwitz I prayed to God for deliverance but never blamed God for neglecting me or for being responsible for my presence there. Jews have faith in God; they do not judge Him.

Another observant survivor of seven different work camps in Eastern Europe said that he did not "believe the Holocaust was part of God's plan for mankind but rather that God granted man the freedom to be righteous or wicked, to destroy or create, to follow his evil inclinations or his good inclinations. But," the survivor went on to say, "I did not choose answer (a) because far more important to the Jew than finding reasons to vindicate God and to recognize man for what he is, is the need to be reminded that the pious Jew does not judge God. That is the worst sin of hubris [chutzpa]. That implies that man knows as much as

God and is as great as He is. So, although I believe in (a) as well as (b), (b) is the more religious answer . . . it is the only religious answer."

Blame Man, Not God

Again on Question 2, 27 percent resolved the problem of God's whereabouts by contending that God had nothing to do with the destruction of the Six Million (answer a): It is inappropriate to blame God for the acts of man (man may decide to kill or not to kill). One survivor spoke movingly of the vision he had while in the camps, of God, in sorrow, weeping for His people and at man's inhumanity to man. These survivors were generally of one mind in their view except for the few, as reflected in the second quotation below, whose religious coloration suggests a modern deist as much as a pious Jew.

One traditional-minded pious Jew, a Bergen-Belsen survivor, maintained that

> . . . God gave man free will. God did not create man a robot but rather capable of making decisions and free choices. He can be barbaric and bloodthirsty or kind-hearted and humane. If every time man was about to do evil God intervened and prevented it, man would not have been created free to act as he wished and would in fact have been an entirely different creature than God intended him to be. He would not have been man. This way man can do as he will but he is also responsible for his actions and I will not allow the Nazis off the hook by saying they were not responsible for what they did. So they had to be free—just as God made all men free. Some kill, others do not.

The survivor quoted previously, representing contemporary deist philosophy, said:

> I believe that God created man then left him on his own. That is why He created us in His own image to give the job of running the world to us to succeed with or fail. So far we're failing. Proof— Auschwitz. God set it all in motion, man and the world, but then had nothing else to do with it . . . and doesn't even become involved—as we would understand that—with man's calamities on earth. The universe is a rather large place to occupy God's attention. Scientists tell us that worlds are being created and destroyed all the time.

Of those preferring to stress man's role in the destruction, 84 percent were nonobservant survivors, and the remaining 16 percent observant survivors. Concentrating on the consistently observant survivors alone, in the previous section it was pointed out that fully 60 percent preferred not to judge God with regard to the death of the Six Million (answer b); 14 percent preferred to judge man (answer a), an answer well in conformity with traditional Judaism. And 16 percent, the second largest subgroup, attributed the Holocaust to God's will (answer d).

The Holocaust as God's Will

Our attention should be drawn to the fact that the second most frequently selected answer of survivors who remained observant was that the Holocaust was the will of God. That is, 30 percent of all Jews who remained observant throughout the years were divided between the view that man alone can be held responsible for the Holocaust since he is free to kill, and the view that the Holocaust was God's will, part of His divine plan for the Jewish people, with the latter group slightly larger.

These two apparently antithetical positions were reconciled with little difficulty in the minds of survivors by the contention that while the Holocaust was God's will, man himself must be held responsible for bringing it about. (Our survey, however, sought to urge survivors to declare themselves as preferring to stress one aspect over the other aspect of otherwise reconcilable convictions.) It is also undeniable that the attitudes that man must not judge God and that the Holocaust was God's will may be looked upon as not only eminently reconcilable but as sides of the same theological coin: We must not judge God for allowing the Holocaust or for bringing it about. The unwillingness to judge God is an aspect of pious resignation reflected in rabbinic Judaism's view that He, in His perfect wisdom and goodness, knows best. And His visitations and dispensations must be accepted without complaint and without murmuring.

As has already been indicated, the second most preferred response among consistently observant survivors was the view that the Holocaust was God's will. But this view was next to the least favored, preferred by 9 percent, among the entire survivor community. Only the view that God could not prevent the Holocaust found fewer proponents.

Of all survivors responding to the question with an expression of the belief that the Holocaust was the will of God, three-fourths were observant Jews. And yet fewer than 4 percent of them were former concentration camp inmates. Perhaps, although little else indicates it, the actual experience of the camps was too radically Godless for even observant survivors to allow the possibility that it may have been a facet of God's agendum.

The ancient, "all but obsolete" [6] view apparently still persists among pious modern Jews and Holocaust survivors that suffering implies previous sin. An observant survivor seeing the hand of God in the catastrophe spoke for many others in his recognition that afflictions which befell the Six Million were retributive, the penalty of transgression or neglect of God's holy will:

It's not difficult to come up with very suitable and acceptable reasons for God having brought about the Holocaust. Any really religious Jew who has studied Torah can give you the reasons why God permits tragedies like the destruction of the Temple in Jerusalem, the Inquisitions, Crusades and pogroms to engulf His chosen people. The Talmud, too, can be consulted for explanations of God's punishment of the people Israel.

Of course there are members of the Jewish people who even if they heard a *bat kol*, a heavenly voice, would not believe they heard it. They'd look for scientific explanations. And they certainly would not believe what the voice said. They could not accept the content of the message. They would not become *baalai tshuvah*, penitents, turning to God. So why should we expect they'd understand the Holocaust which is somewhat less obvious, but not terribly less obvious? Not unclear to really good Jews. You have to first be conditioned to God's Torah to understand God's ways and to understand why and when Jews suffer.

The concentration camp was a kind of *bat kol* announcing to the Jewish people to keep the Torah, to observe the commandments, to remember the Sabbath, and so forth. But look at Jews living in Israel today, even survivors, it's as though they didn't hear God's voice at all, it's like they buried their heads in the ground and pretended not to have seen or heard or witnessed God's punishment. What a terrible waste. The tragedy is compounded by the failure of Jews today to heed the message of the Holocaust and begin to keep the Torah according to God's bidding.

Whenever a Jew dies the observant mourner acknowledges God's righteousness and submits to the justice of the divine dispensation with

the recitation of a series of prayers at the burial service. Quoting from
these verses, one ultra observant survivor, an ordained rabbi from Poland, expressed his belief that "God brought about the Holocaust to
even the scales of justice. God's purpose in the Holocaust was to punish
the guilty."

> He is the Rock. His every deed is perfect for all His ways are
> justice; a faithful God without wrong. He is just and right. He
> is the Rock. His every deed is perfect. Who can say to Him, "What
> doest Thou?" He rules below and above. . . . Thou art just O
> Lord in causing death and life; Thou in whose hand all souls
> are kept. Whether man lives a year or a millennium of what benefit
> is it to him; he will be as though he had never been. Blessed be the
> true Judge, who causes death and life. Blessed be He for His
> judgment is true; His eye ranges over all and He punishes and
> rewards man according to strict account. All must render ac-
> knowledgment of His name.

Nonobservant survivors who viewed the Holocaust as the fulfillment
of the divine will were naturally not as inclined to link the destruction
with the Jewish people's failure to "keep the Torah according to God's
bidding." For example, one nonobservant survivor, an especially ardent
Zionist in his youth in Poland, claimed to "understand God's larger
plan for the Jewish people" in another way:

> We must not look at the single Jew, the individual Jewish victim,
> and fail thereby to see the total picture. For the individual Jew
> there is no justice nor has there ever been justice. But that would
> be looking only at the shadowy surface of the destruction and no
> deeper. We have to see beyond the individual to the larger group—
> the whole people. For the whole people there is justice and for the
> individual as part of the whole people there is justice. For example,
> the State of Israel is the compensatory justice for each Holocaust
> victim even though each Jew who died has not experienced the
> justice personally. The people have experienced the justice. Each
> Holocaust victim sacrificed himself knowingly or unknowingly
> for it.
>   It is similar to a war fought against a tyrant; the young men
> who are killed defending their homeland may not personally enjoy
> the victory but his country makes use of his sacrifice and his suf-
> fering, so that the nation to which he belongs may be free.

Ardent Zionists such as the one whose convictions are here expressed, seeing in the Holocaust God's calculated, programmed vehicle leading to the creation of the State, were almost as likely to be nonobservant as observant Jews. Their convictions will be studied in greater detail in the forthcoming section on the survivors' view of the relationship between the Holocaust and the State of Israel rather than here as a dimension of the Holocaust and God's will. In this section it remains necessary to delineate the views of nonobservant survivors who found justification for the Holocaust other than, or in addition to, the creation of the State of Israel. A particularly interesting view was expressed by a totally nonobservant survivor who saw in the Holocaust

. . . God's means of bringing about the end of the world as we know it, the demise of Western society and the inauguration of a new era which may be viewed as the beginning of redemption. The Holocaust was the low point, the nadir, of Western civilization, the trauma of the Western history of man from which there is no recovery. The war was the beginning of the death throes and the concentration camp symbolized the final death gasp and expiration. It proved that Christianity was a failure, morally bankrupt—a proven failure in that it could not prevent its followers from murdering their fellow men, including helpless women and children and the defenseless and the aged. All religions failed but especially Christianity and the Christians. The Christians, ignoring, or perhaps fulfilling, their religion sought to kill all the Jews in a fight to the death. The Christians were unsuccessful, they lost the battle, they failed because Jews survived and more so, rose up again in the new State of Israel. Israel symbolized the death of Christianity and the birth of the new world. This is how God works in the world and how He brought about the end of Christianity and the end of Western civilization by the sacrifice of the Six Million.

Another nonobservant survivor understood the Holocaust in diametrically antithetical terms. She saw the purpose of the destruction of the Jews of Europe as God's way of saving, not destroying, Western civilization:

Hitler lost the war because of his obsession with the Jews. Had he been able to overcome his compulsion to destroy the Jews and conquer his need to expend his Nazi army's energies in searching for Jews, rounding them up, guarding them, in concentration camps, supervising their work parties and labor camps and finally exterminating them—so many able-bodied soldiers wasted and misused, not to speak of machinery and material and arms of war—I believe the Germans would have won the war and changed the course of history, our culture and civilization. God's plan was for Hitler's destruction and to accomplish that He offered His people, we Jews, as His sacrifice. God's plan was a kind of bargain: I'll permit the Jews to be killed, slow down Hitler's war machine and defeat him by means of his Jewish obsession and then compensate the Jews with Israel. That's exactly how it happened.

Denial of God's Omnipotence

Far from conceiving of the universe as indifferent toward human destiny—a neutrality which may be implied in attributing to man sole responsibility for the Holocaust and in the refusal to judge God—these and similar survivors, totaling nearly one of every ten, actually discovered providential value in the destruction ("the Holocaust is the will of God"). Another small group of survivors, also eschewing the proposition that there is no personal God concerned with justice, morality, and human suffering believed that "God could not prevent the Holocaust." Not that He *would* not prevent it, having granted man freedom of the will to do good or evil, but rather that "God is not all-powerful."

Misgivings concerning God's omnipotence may seem to most Jews a substantial stride toward thorough nonbelief. For if one strips away so essential an attribute of God, His very existence is impugned. Omniscience, benevolence, omnipotence, these are fundamentals touching upon His very definition, without which there is no God. Or so it may appear to most modern Jews as well as most survivors.

However, the God of the rabbis of the Midrash—and some contemporary Jewish theologians would include the God of the Bible and the God of the founders of Hasidism, as well—is a God-formulation

> . . . profoundly at variance with that of the official pronouncements of the synagogue. That God of the Midrash is not an infinite God; He is not omnipotent. He is one among many powers; He is the power for good, among the other, indifferent and dark, forces of the universe . . . a confession of impotency is very often on His lips: "What can I do?" is an expression quite frequently put into His mouth. God can forgive; but the silly omnipotence which can

play fast and loose with the laws of truth and morality, or which can pretend to undo the effects of evil once these have been launched upon the world, is denied Him.[7]

What is more, a finite God-conception was thought to be far less radical and more admissible today after the Holocaust for some survivors. Still, asking survivors in an interview about a limited God was seen as rather vague; about an "all-knowing" God as not especially pertinent; about a "nonbenevolent" God (and much more so a "malevolent" God) as almost entirely inadmissible for God-believers. Survivors were therefore surveyed concerning their belief in God's "omnipotence" alone. *And one of every twenty survivors responding to the question expressed the view that God is not omnipotent and could not have prevented the Holocaust.* Their reasoning paused and turned at the religious crossroads they saw laid out before them which required a choice between a God who is all-powerful and a God who is all-good. Or as one such survivor put it:

> You can't have both, a God who is good and cares about His creatures and a God who is able to do everything, a God who is perfect. God cannot be both and still have allowed so many millions of us to have been murdered. No, God is either evil or weak. I can't believe in the former at all but it is possible that God tries His best but has a lot to contend with. He does the best He can to control the destructive forces in the universe, not the least of which is man. God is great and powerful but not all-powerful or He would have stopped the Nazis then and the Arab terrorists today.

The Holocaust brought these few survivors to a view of God approaching that of the Midrash: God is imperfect and could not forestall the Holocaust. Moreover, as another survivor indicated, "we must make allowances for God; He is to be forgiven His inadequacies. I forgive Him His failings, His ineptitude, His imperfections." And still another suggested that "God redeemed Himself and regained His strength with the creation of the State of Israel and the miraculous victories against the Arabs."

Nothing Can Excuse God

In the course of administering the questionnaire there emerged among certain survivors the attitude of indignation and rage directed at God for not having interceded to save the Six Million. Forgiveness of God's inadequacies was hardly the disposition of this final subgroup of survivors responding to the question. One of every four, far from forgiveness, convicted God for not having prevented the calamity. The formulation of the question accurately reflected their resentment and indignation: "Nothing can excuse God for not having saved them."

The high frequency with which self-professed nonbelievers selected this response reaffirms the findings that the narrow borderline between atheism and anger pursues a jagged course and is at times entirely indiscernible. And a considerable number of survivors straddled and intercrossed it repeatedly.

For the most part, however, these are survivors who in their indignation do not deny that God exists; rather they are determined to renounce Him for not intervening in the Holocaust. Not denied but denounced is He. God is not to be disavowed, declared untrue, or disclaimed, but He is to be accused publicly in a solemn, formal charge. He is then to be cast off, repudiated, and rejected, for by His inaction He Himself became party to the cruel injustice of the indiscriminate bloodshed, a God who failed and who is not to be forgiven His failing. One such survivor said, "I refuse to make allowances for Him or exonerate Him for not acting to save the Jews."

Fully 80 percent of the survivors who expressed this attitude were either always nonobservant or became nonobservant after the Holocaust. But one consistently observant survivor's opinion is of special interest:

> There have been miracles performed by God for the Jewish people throughout history saving Jews from destruction. Why were there no miracles this time?
>
> Israel was a form of compensation after the fact, but not a miracle of salvation. It happened too late to save us.
>
> Religious Jews looked for a miracle because no other time warranted it and no other people merited it quite as much, but none was forthcoming.
>
> If there had never been any miracles before, we would not have come to expect any, but we Jews know otherwise. We have had them in the past. Why did not God perform a miracle and put a stop to it?

The attitude of most of the 25 percent of the survivors selecting this response was reflected by the following view expressed by a formerly observant survivor:

If God exists, where was He? This is posed in the form of a question. And I would like to know the answer to the question: How could He possibly have allowed it to have happened, innocent men, women and a million and a half unfortunate children who had harmed no one in their lives and who deserved no such sentence of death. God is supposed to be Providence who governs all things according to objective standards of equality and righteousness and justice; who cares beneficiently for His creatures. But instead guiltless, pure, incorruptible, blameless souls went up in a Holocaust of fire, with almighty God nowhere in evidence. What do we need a God for if not to deter the wholesale slaughter of the innocent? I do not care for any of the philosophical and pious reasons and contrived explanations of the rabbis which are mere bromides and clichés. There is and can never be any acceptable excuse for God.

Sin and the Six Million

With Question 3, survivors were confronted by the unambiguous choice between man's sinfulness and man's proven capacity to destroy his fellow man; that is, by "religious reasons" or "secular reasons" as explanation for the Holocaust. Their responses produced a disproportionate and uneven polarity. And whichever their persuasion, whether temporal or devout, survivors appeared to react tenaciously doctrinaire and assertative in their contradictory views. The question asked:

With which of the following propositions do you agree most:
  A. The Six Million were destroyed not because of sin but only because of man's relationship to man; with no connection whatever to God.
  B. The Six Million who were destroyed were sinners and were punished for their sins; otherwise God would not have allowed them to die.
  C. The Six Million were destroyed because the entire Jewish people sinned and they were the sacrifice.
  D. The Six Million were destroyed because of the sins of the entire world and God chose them as a sacrifice.

Taking B, C, and D together, 21 percent of all survivors responding to the question saw man's sinful behavior coupled with God's requiting wrath as explanation for the Holocaust, whereas 72 percent preferred the thesis that the Six Million were destroyed entirely due to the relationship between man and man, with no connection to God or to sin.

Sinfulness of the Six Million

There are, however, various ways of understanding and accounting for sinfulness and retribution. For example, to whom should the sinfulness be attributed? When provided with the choices of the sinfulness of all mankind, the sinfulness of world Jewry, or the sinfulness of the Six Million, a mere 2 percent of the survivors selected the latter. While a representative of such an opinion has already been furnished in another connection, a fellow highly observant survivor, who writes religious treatises on the subject of the Holocaust, reflected as follows:

> God is not unjust and He is not a Christian God who can offer some third party, Jesus or the Jews of Europe, to die for the sins of others. If a man commits a crime he goes to jail for it, not someone else; that is justice. Christianity is not just and the idea or notion that the Six Million died but were blameless and righteous is also unjust and unacceptable to me.
>
> I may not be able to comprehend the sins of the Six Million and understand what they did wrong. No man may ever know. But one thing I do know: there is no vicarious atonement in Judaism in a way which would have God sacrifice six million of the innocent for the guilty, nor were they sacrificial lambs, or goats dispatched to the wilderness to absolve the sins of others. The Six Million died for themselves alone, for whatever sins for which they were culpable.

Sacrificed for Mankind's Sins

Another highly observant Jew, a devoted student of the Bible, representing 11 percent of his fellow survivors, cited the book of Isaiah for his rebuttal in support of the view that God indeed sacrificed the Six Million because of the sinfulness of the world:

> Isaiah teaches that the Jews are the suffering servant. This means that it is they who bear the pain and endure the misery of the world even to death, generation after generation throughout history, because of their special nature and unique relationship with God.

That is one of the roles ordained by God and meant for the Jewish people. The Six Million were the suffering servants who died for the sins of mankind. Whenever the world sins the Jews suffer.

This selection garnered the greatest number of survivors who accounted for the Holocaust by sinfulness and retribution. One reason may have been that by a particular misreading of the statement the survivor could "blame the world" for its sins especially of "not lifting a little finger to help the Jews of Europe." This, of course, is a major distortion of the statement since it emphasizes the misbehavior of the world and studiously avoids the argument that "they were chosen by God as sacrifice." Another 8 percent were of the opinion that the destruction took place because the entire Jewish people sinned and the Six Million were sacrificed for them. One of these survivors explained his views as follows:

These [the Six Million] were without question the best Jews in the world, the most observant and pious and good. They were the cream of world Jewry. It would have made much more sense if the Jews of America suffered the pogrom instead of the orthodox and Hasidic Jews of Eastern Europe because American Jews are irreligious and assimilated and marrying out of the faith, and they do not care about being Jews and they certainly do not concern themselves with Halacha, Jewish law. So the good and the best Jews died and the worst live on. The only way you can make sense out of that is to assume that the one was sacrificed for the other—not only for the Jews of America but for all Westernized, secular Jewish communities—Europe, Israel, Russia. All over, wherever Jews ceased being true Jews.

The judgment that the Six Million died exclusively due to man's inhumanity to man (selection a) runs through the pages of this study as a persistent theme. A representative advocate expanding upon this proposition asked:

How is it when a man murders another man you never hear that God is at fault? No magazine or newspaper articles or religious tracts are composed attributing the killing of an individual to God when analyzing the manner of the death and the nature of the victim and the villain. Why? Because it is only one single person? Somehow when it is translated into the millions, the very same kind of murder committed a million times over, then is God brought into the picture to explain and account for it. And to judge God by it. A political assassination? Not a word about God. A terrorist attack killing a number of people? The terrorists are blamed, not God. But somehow with regard to the death of the Six Million European Jews, God has to be dragged in to explain what ought to be explained simply by the fact recurring again and again of the mistreatment by one portion of humanity of another portion of humanity, especially the mistreatment of Jews by others.

Nazi Anti-Semitism

To some survivors, man's inhumanity to man referred to Nazi anti-Semitism, which may be explained by either of two coexisting but conflicting theories preserved in the minds of survivors three decades after the destruction. The one holds that the Jew was held in contempt by the Nazis as an inferior being, a subhuman species, or, to use Hitler's own last words dictated in the Reich Chancellory Bunker on April 30, 1945, "The World-Poisoner of All Nations." The Jew therefore was unworthy, at first of toleration on European soil, and then ultimately of life itself. And as one survivor suggested, "To the Nazi mentality, the Jewish masses, potentially capable of contaminating the pure Aryan blood of its youth, stood directly in the eastern path of German territorial expansion, ambition, and conquest. We had to be eliminated; Europe had to be Judenrein."

A corollary of this first theory, which even some Jews believed at the time,[8] suggests that the Germans were *ubermenschen*, civilization's supermen destined for dominion: "The Germans believed that the Jew was the lowest creature on the face of the earth whereas he himself was the highest being on earth. And the highest would eliminate the lowest. . . . It was a consequence of the natural order, native to the species of man, an evolutionary principle on the same scale as the survival of the fittest."

The second theory of the etiology of Nazi anti-Semitism repeated frequently in the camps and elsewhere contradicts the first with regard to the nature of the Jew. According to it, as one survivor explained,

The Germans believed that the Jews were in the highest positions of power everywhere on earth, in politics, medicine, business, law, and especially finance. And wherever he turned, his most capable competitor was a Jew, shrewder, wiser, more successful than he. And, according to this bizarre notion, each and every Jew was backed up by the conspiracy of international Jewry, a powerful force capable of bringing down nations and governments, a cabal of Jewish capitalists aided by Jewish communists.

For some survivors, then, the subject of man's inhumanity occasioned reference to "the hate of the Nazis for the Jewish people," and the assumption that "the war provided the opportunity to translate that hate into action." For others, it referred to "the envy and enmity of Jews by Christians together with the Church sermons to simple-minded people that Jews were Christ killers."

Another illustration of man's inhumanity concerns "the blaming and accusing of Jews by falling, failing governments that held the Jews at fault whenever political or economic crises arose." And another survivor commented that "it happened because we were spread out, scattered without a state of our own plus the fact of our upbringing in obedience and submission which taught us to bow our head to the goy. We believed we'd survive that way, a very costly mistake." And another survivor asked:

What had God to do with the Six Million or for that matter with millions of Russians or millions of Polish children? Or what has God to do with Genghis Khan or Nero or the Napoleonic Wars? If we suppose these have to do with something other than man it would look like a constant punishment for all of mankind. Is God also punishing man with earthquakes and floods? Is everything a punishment of God's?

Divine Judgment Rejected

Surely one of the more impressive findings of this study is the virtual absence, despite the prominent and dramatic exceptions already cited, of advocacy among survivors for the proposal, supported often with considerable enthusiasm in nonsurvivor circles, that God was scourging transgressors and that the Holocaust was literally a burnt offering, a sacrifice for the atonement of the sins of the Six Million. *The theory that Jewish martyrdom in our time must be explained as divine judgment has been overwhelmingly rejected by 98 percent of those who very nearly experienced it themselves.*

It has sometimes been suggested that it is precisely because the survivors very nearly experienced martyrdom themselves and do not believe themselves to be very different morally or religiously from the Six Million whose lives were lost that they reject the idea of sinfulness; that if the Six Million were sinners then they themselves must be similarly categorized. But the converse has also been offered and held up as true: Precisely the fact that these survived and those did not proves their fundamentally different natures; the sinners perished, the virtuous did not. The two propositions cancel one another, and neither proposition finds appreciable corroboration within the survivor community, regardless of what others may think.

In fact, it is only among the consistently observant survivors that the twin concepts of sinfulness and retribution—even at their broadest definitions—register at all beyond the very minimum. Explanations of the Holocaust by 93 percent of survivors who were consistently non-observant throughout the years were disposed toward man's relationships rather than retribution; and 89 percent of survivors who had been observant but are no longer so today were so inclined. Only the consistently observant spoke more of sin and retribution (55 percent) than of the relationship between man and man (32 percent) in their explanation of the Holocaust.

An Omnipotent and/or Benevolent God?

Accordingly, if nearly three of every four survivors were of the conviction that the Six Million were destroyed only as a consequence of man's inhumanity to man and with no connection whatever to God, how is God to be understood and what *is* His relationship to man? Question 4 of the series asks:

a) Is He a benevolent, omnipotent God except that He does not interfere in the area where man's will prevails?

b) Or is it that while He is benevolent and omnipotent, His ways are simply incomprehensible to and hidden from man?

c) Or while it may be inconceivable to believe that God is not all-good, perhaps, as has already been represented, God is not all powerful?

d) Or is it simply that God does not exist at all?

Given these choices (as well as "I don't know"), which do survivors prefer?

Clearly the various propositions or statements are related to the subject matter of the discipline of theology, hardly the superficial, cursory, public opinion gathering of the routine questionnaire. And while there may be some truth to the maxim that "every survivor is perforce a philosopher, for by experience alone he so qualifies," nevertheless considerable, earnest reflection is required here, if not the rigors of an education in metaphysics and philosophy. Small wonder that 17 percent elected not to answer the question altogether and of the remainder another 17 percent selected "I don't know" as their answer. The other responses to Question 4 have already arisen in previous questions—with the exception of the nuances of selection (a)—although they have not been advanced previously as contending theories.

In the present context a number of previous findings appear to be corroborated and validated, leading to the conclusion that, throughout, survivors pondered their answers with considerable diligence and treated their deliberations quite seriously. Survivor consistency from question to question suggests as much. For example, omnipotence and benevolence as attributes of God are taken as almost axiomatic except for some 4 percent of the survivor population responding to Question 4 who believe that God is all-good but not all-powerful. For "if He were all-powerful He would have put a stop to it." Previously in Question 2 we had found that a similar small segment of the survivor community, 5 percent, were of the conviction that "God could not have prevented the Holocaust." For these few survivors, although God is all good and would have wished to forestall the destruction, it was beyond His powers to do so. For most other survivors, "a God who is not all-powerful is no God at all." It is significant, however, to take note of the small, consistent number of survivors who prefer to have a somewhat diminished God, in power if not in goodness, to reconcile His existence with His seeming inaction.

In response to Queston 4, 26 percent of the survivors selected the proposition "God does not exist," which corresponds reasonably well, when taking into account those who did not answer, with the findings of a previous chapter that 31 percent of all survivors living in Israel today consider themselves to be atheists. For those, obviously, there is no dilemma concerning His goodness or power or whereabouts during the course of the destruction. God is not.

The largest grouping of survivors, 35 percent, reverted to the standard response recurring throughout this study, which avers that God is everything that Jewish tradition claims for Him—omnipotent, benevolent, undoubtedly omniscient, and loving as well—except that

His ways are incomprehensible and hidden from man. The Jobian answer: He is a great God, beyond our mortal minds; His actions are a mystery.

The final grouping, 17 percent, singled out the belief that God is benevolent and omnipotent but does not interfere where man's will prevails. One survivor explained:

> I used to think if God exists and is good, that means that if He cares
> for the good people on the earth and punishes the evil people and
> if He can do everything and know everything and He listens to
> my prayers and knows what is in my heart, then such a thing
> cannot happen. But it did happen. So at first while I nearly died at
> Auschwitz and along the march to other camps during which time
> I gave up prayer, I was positive that God could not exist for if
> He is God then He is good and couldn't let me suffer so and allow
> us all to die. But we were dying . . . but I also understood that it
> wasn't God who was doing it. He wasn't killing us; the Germans
> were. In the Bible whenever the Jews were attacked the reasons
> given were that we suffered because we deserved it, as a punish-
> ment . . . but I think that was primitive thinking; convincing
> then but unconvincing now, today.
>
> For a long time I thought that if God was good then He
> would take care of the good people—that God couldn't be good
> otherwise. But I also understand His plan in creating man was to
> give him dominion over this world to do good or bad. God is good
> but man can do as he sees fit. The Nazis could just as well have won
> the war and ruled the world today. God would not have prevented
> it. Goodness may have ultimately triumphed in this instance but not
> because God helped goodness along. Might does not make right, but
> right does not necessarily emerge victorious. Might emerges victori-
> ous. The Allies were the mightier. God lets man do what he will. He
> is good but does not constrain man's action.

This answer to some extent attracted survivors from various points along the theological spectrum. Those survivors who understood God as an impersonal Force (24 percent of all survivors) were especially drawn to it for His noninvolvement in man's activities. It was also preferred by others who believe in God in more traditional terms as a personal God, not indifferent to man's ways ("keeping watch upon man"), but by self-limitation, leaving the contours of man's personal freedom, be-stowed by God upon man and fundamental to his makeup, as beyond

His reach. They often spoke of God as having fashioned man "not as a puppet on a string or a pawn on the chess board, but created with a good inclination and bad, responsible for his own behavior." God is both omnipotent and benevolent but, as explanation of His noninvolvement in the Holocaust, He is distant, remote, transcendental.

The Six Million: Ordinary or Holy

The memorial service of the Jewish liturgy conducted during festivals and Holy Days recalls the lives of the departed relations of the worshipers. In most synagogues the service also includes a prayer recited by the entire congregation in memory of Jewish martyrs. The Birnbaum Prayerbook asks that "God remember the souls of the saintly martyrs [hakedoshim vehatehorim] who have been slaughtered, burned, drowned or strangled for their loyalty to God [kiddush hashem]." And from the Rabbinical Assembly of America Sabbath and Festival Prayer Book:

> May God be mindful of the souls of all our brothers, departed members of the house of Israel who sacrificed their lives for the sanctification of the Holy Name [kiddush hashem] and the honor of Israel. Grant that their heroism and self-sacrificing devotion find response in our hearts and the purity of their souls be reflected in our lives. . . . Grant [the deceased] perfect rest beneath the shelter of Thy divine presence among the holy and pure [hakedoshim vehatehorim] who shine as the brightness of the firmament.

For world Jewry of the post-Holocaust era the Six Million are nearly universally regarded as having joined history's legion of martyrs. But, Question 5 asks, for the survivors who knew them personally and not as an abstraction, who witnessed their death and were near to them in life, were they "holy and pure"? Were they for the most part good people? Or were they average individuals with no special claims of distinction apart from the fact of their deaths during wartime?

The majority of survivors (59 percent) looked upon the Six Million as ordinary men and women, in keeping with the following view expressed by a survivor from Warsaw:

> I knew personally hundreds of the dead from my own town and others I met during those years. They were like people everywhere, some good, some scoundrels, some a little of both. There was the

dishonest butcher of our town, a crass, shamefully wicked man who suffered very greatly and lost his life and his family in the gas chambers. And there was a neighbor's immoral wife who, with no concern for what others might think, had her clutches out for every man she saw, who disgraced her fine family repeatedly. These and others were hardly righteous and pure and they didn't die for the sanctification of God's holy name. Neither did the many other low and unprincipled scoundrels who preyed on others in the camps, most of whom died and some of whom lived. One I see all the time on the street even though I try to avoid him and he tries to avoid me. Usually the more unprincipled and corrupt they were, the greater their chance for survival. They didn't volunteer their lives for the sake of God's name like the Jews of Spain and other places for example. Some would have committed any despicable act to remain alive even though others would suffer and die because of them. No, very few saints were among the Six Million.

And yet, another survivor, holding the same view, averred that he recognized that

. . . time, the passage of the years, changes our perspective and our opinions of the dead. As time goes by we tend more and more to elevate them in our estimation. Probably in a few years, I am sure others as well will forget their flaws, defects, and blemishes and we will become less fault-finding. And in years to come they will become like the other sainted martyrs in previous centuries who probably were not that much holier in their own lives than the people we knew personally. That's what happens. And future generations will overlook entirely the imperfections in their lives and will see them as paragons of sainthood. Future history will probably record them as entirely virtuous. I'm simply not yet prepared to do that. I knew them, the good and the bad, too well.

Increasingly, survivors have begun to regard the Six Million paradigmatically and as ranked collectively, rather than individually. As an abstraction, or as a class, their personal differences are being disregarded in favor of collective sainthood. It may be that before this takes place, those who viewed the Six Million as "for the most part good people" will dissipate and diminish still further from its 21 percent in favor of either contrast, sainthood, or commonness. There is little evidence that survivor attitudes regarding the Six Million are progressing straightforwardly from average to good to sainthood. More likely the above-mentioned polarity will develop still further, later to be resolved when survivors more and more will hold to the consideration—now at 28 percent—of the Six Million as "saintly martyrs." And this projected development may be seen as a dimension of the larger process whereby all victims of Nazism begin to blend into the corporate memory of future Jewry.

Survivors espousing the intermediate opinion that the Holocaust victims were "for the most part good people" were to a certain extent caught up in the uncertainty of the two alternative propositions—as is reflected by the remarks of one survivor of the camp Dora Mittelbau, who said:

> I can't make up my mind about them. Sometimes I think they
> were just plain people murdered arbitrarily for no reason that makes
> sense, just people who were not special: men and women and
> children, cobblers and teachers and laborers and artisans, young
> and old, important and unimportant, religious and irreligious, from
> the villages and towns and cities, and you cannot generalize
> about them. But at other times, I feel they were all sainted martyrs,
> special and holy and privileged to give their lives as Jews. Not being
> able to make up my mind and at the same time convinced anyway
> that these were for the most part good and innocent individuals
> who were unlucky to have been where they were, caught up in a war
> waged by a madman, I won't be wrong to say along with answer b
> simply that they were good people.

There were some survivors who refrained from answering the question altogether because "there were kapos who died in the camps and members of the Judenrat and Jewish policemen and collaborators also. Most of the Six Million were 'holy and pure sainted martyrs,' but not all." And some survivors suggested "all three, that is, there were holy people, good people, and plain people, and we cannot generalize." Because of vigorously negative reaction during the questionnaire's pretesting, two additional selections were dropped entirely from the final version of this question. The options, "The Six Million were for the most part base individuals" and "The Six Million were wicked evildoers who deserved the punishment they received" not only found virtually no support, but what little there was surfaced elsewhere in this study— such a belief being difficult to suppress—leaving little justification for having to place so sensitive and unfortunate a formulation before the eyes of surviving families of those so characterized. Although certain ultra observant and highly devout survivors cited earlier believed that God could not have allowed the undeserved death of the Six Million, these are clearly the exceptions to the otherwise universally held survivor opinion of the essential goodness of the victims. Yet, one nonobservant survivor did say in what may be the closest parallel view of the Six Million's various faults and imperfections, "it's a wonder how attractive people become once they are safely dead."

The findings on this aspect of the study must be considered tentative and subject to change many times before the status of the victim is settled and resolved in the minds of most survivors. Only the opinion of survivors who maintain that the Six Million were holy and pure sainted martyrs may be considered well-established and final. There is nothing undecided about the following view, repeated over and over again by 28 percent of the respondents:

> Every single Jew who died during the war, who was killed by the Nazis and their henchmen in every country of Europe gave his life, willingly or unwillingly, consciously or unconsciously, *al kiddush hashem*, for the sanctification of the great name of God. Whenever a Jew dies because he is a Jew, whether in life he was a good person or a bad person, he is elevated immediately to the special category of martyr and saint. Their very death, by definition, raised and exalted them to that great role—and it can never be taken away from them. They join the ranks of the self-sacrificing, virtuous Jews from the beginning of history until our day who forfeited their lives for a noble purpose, for God and for the Jewish people. All murder victims of tyrants (harugai malchut) are sainted martyrs at the very moment of their deaths.

Nevertheless, notwithstanding this ardor and certitude and despite our speculation on the tentativeness of other views, it must be borne in mind that *survivors by a margin of more than two to one demur from characterizing the Six Million as sainted martyrs who shine as the brightness of the firmament. And overwhelmingly those who hold to that conviction do so primarily because of the manner in which they lost, rather than the conduct by which they lived, their lives.*

In this connection, the comparison of the consistently observant with the consistently nonobservant is especially illuminating: 50 percent of the former regard Holocaust victims as "holy and pure," as opposed to only 9 percent of the nonobservant. A full 83 percent of the latter felt that they are ordinary men and women, whereas 31 percent of the observant felt that way. We are inevitably drawn to the quite logical conclusion that the more observant the survivor the more likely would he be to regard the Six Million as falling into what is manifestly a religious category: sainted martyrs of the Jewish people.

Did They Die for Some Purpose?

Among survivors who reflect upon such matters, it is a controverted question whether the Six Million died for any "purpose" or "design" or to accomplish any "objective" however interpreted, secularly or spiritually. It has already been shown how disturbingly enigmatic is the subject of the Holocaust's connection to the creation of the State of Israel—so many survivors recoiled from or circumvented considering it. It has also already been shown that for some 15 percent, mostly observant survivors, the Holocaust can be understood as having had a disciplinary and faith-testing, or other "religious" purpose or objective.

Question 6 brought these two elements together by asking survivors (a) whether the Six Million died that the State of Israel might arise; (b) whether the Six Million died to teach Jews to keep the commandments; (c) both of these; (d) neither of these; or (e) I don't know.

Israel and/or the Commandments

The alternative selections (a) and (b) were not intended to create specious intellectual tensions between advocates of "secularist" and "religious" opinion. No strict secularist–religious dichotomy obtains in the survivor community; nor is any suggested by the question. Although the keeping of the commandments must certainly be regarded as exclusively a religious category, the creation of the State of Israel, as several survivors pointed out, is not necessarily a secularist's department alone. In fact, 9 percent of all survivors answering Question 6 saw as the dual purpose of the Holocaust *both* the establishment of the State and instructing Jews to keep the commandments. And 61 percent of these were observant survivors. For the most part, they understood the rebirth of the State in religious terms as connected with an age-old divine promise to the descendants of Abraham and as indemnification for the near-destruction of the people.

While it is true that certain secularist Zionists may regard the State nonreligiously, for most observant and nonobservant Jews alike the Torah, the Jewish people, and the Land of Israel are religious categories inextricably intertwined. In Jewish religious literature there is frequent reference to exile from the land and the regathering to the land.

The assiduously observant, for example, will be of a mind, along with the traditional prayer book, to believe that "because of our sins we were exiled from the land." And at virtually all synagogues, in Israel as well as the Diaspora, worshipers recite each day at the morning service, "O gather us peacefully from the four corners of the earth and cause us to walk uprightly to our land for You are a God who works for redemption," an ancient prayer probably instituted by the rabbis of the Talmud in the early second temple period. And again in the Jewish prayer par excellence, The Eighteen Benedictions (nineteen in present form), the fourteenth is a blessing for a restored Jerusalem. And the tenth reads:

> Sound the great horn for our freedom. Raise up the standard to gather our exiles together and assemble us from the four corners of the earth. Praised are You O Lord who gathers together the dispersed of His people Israel.

The prayer for the new moon, chanted with great solemnity by the cantor as the Torah is held aloft and the congregation rises to its feet, contains the paragraph:

> May He who performed miracles for our fathers and delivered them from servitude to freedom, shortly deliver us and gather our scattered people from the four corners of the earth that all Israel may be comrades and let us say, Amen.

The ingathering of the exiles, then, may be understood as a corollary of the rebirth of Zion, and both are regarded by Jewish tradition as religious concepts. They are therefore not to be juxtaposed against observing the commandments. For the return to Zion is itself one of the most important commandments.

Attention must also be paid to the rather extreme proposition that the recreation of the State is so decidedly a religious category that the present commonwealth, having come about by political expediencies rather than by divine intervention manifested by the arrival of the messiah, is a sacrilege, "a wicked entity," to be vigorously opposed. The purpose of the Holocaust for these survivors, who are a negligible but outspoken and prominent 1 percent of the total, was not to bring about the State but solely to teach Jews to observe the tenets of their religion. For them there is an overriding religious distinction between the land of Israel and the State of Israel: the first sacrosanct and hallowed, the latter an unsanctified desecration and profanation—at least in its present composition. One such ultra observant Hasid cited the commentary on the Talmud by the eighteenth-century Rabbi Jacob Enden, as a prophecy for our time: "Before the messiah is dispatched there will first be a Jewish government composed of nonbelievers." [9]

Another equally extreme and outspoken survivor put it in a lengthy denunciation:

> How can anyone believe that Ben Gurion and Levi Eshkol and Moshe Dayan, who *are* the State of Israel, were meant to be the successors to the priests and the prophets, the judges and David and Solomon? The State of Israel should not even be named Israel because Israel was to be governed and ruled by the Torah, both the written and the oral law, and not by man-made laws taken from the goyim of the world and not by those who deny God's law who run today's Israel government, who are depraved and Godless transgressors, who set bad examples for the youth of our people and drive them from the Torah, who should resign and do penitence and contrition and acknowledge their sins and make atonement for having led so many thousands astray. These were not meant to be the "greats" of our people and this government is not what God intended.
>
> If the State was what God wanted, then part of the answer to this question would be fulfilled already and Jews would be observing the Torah and its commandments. But the opposite has happened because of the new State. Jews living here, and others living elsewhere in the Diaspora following their examples, are now being steered even further away from keeping the Torah and from faith in Him. The Zionist "redemption" has brought about the destruction of the Torah.

And another survivor said that "Israel has done even more harm than good because Jews are now actually hostile to the Torah, not any longer simply neutral or ambivalent; and not simply incapable of observing the Torah due to lack of inner strength. There are now heretics preaching disbelief because of the State."

Not quite on the opposite extreme are the few survivors, surely not much more than the 1 percent of their counterparts, who view the state "as a necessary evil not as an ultimate good." These are the anti-nationalists whose philosophy looks forward to the dissolution of *all* independent nation-states:

> As a religious principle, religious in its truest sense, I would do away
> entirely with all the governments and nations of the world and I
> hope that day will come. If there had been no super-nationalism
> in Germany, had there been no Germany at all as a political entity,
> it is doubtful that there would have been any racism or any Holo-
> caust or any Six Million dead. There also would be no Egypt or
> Syria to war against my children today.
>
> Of course, this hope of mine is unrealizable in the immediate
> future and perhaps the distant future as well. And the Jews who
> had been the only true international people, maintaining their
> identity in all parts of the world without a state, today need a
> state to protect them and to assure their survival, to reach the
> day when Utopia will arrive. The world is simply not ready for
> it yet.
>
> I am a socialist and a communist but for the meantime a
> capitalist as well, so that Israel may survive. Anti-Semitism in its
> modern and in its ancient forms is the justifiable reason for the
> existence of the State of Israel in modern times.

Ironically, both antinationalist survivors and the ultra Orthodox quoted previously are united in declaring that the prayers for the return to Zion transcribed above refer to post-messianic Utopian times.

A full 24 percent of all respondents to Question 6 asserted that the Six Million died that the State of Israel might be established: 15 percent selected answer (a) that that was the sole "reason" for the Holocaust, and nine percent chose answer (c) which encompassed both (a) and (b).

Significantly more (27 percent to 19 percent) consistently observant survivors believed in the proposition that the Six Million died that the State of Israel may be created than in the twin propositions (a) and (b) combined. One survivor explained why:

> It is not inconceivable to me that God could have fixed upon the
> death of six million to give birth to the State of Israel. Historical
> mountain peaks must emerge alongside historical valley-rifts.
> The one may come about as a consequence of the other. But it is not

possible for me to believe that God could not have found a method or object lesson other than the death of six million to teach Jews to keep the commandments—a hillock and not a mountain peak event at all like the creation of Israel.

For observant and nonobservant Jews alike, the Holocaust is more acceptable as having as its purpose the creation of the State than that it brought some purely religious message, such as the keeping of the commandments, to the Jews of the world.

Taken together, a high proportion, 25 percent of all respondents to question 6 ascribed meaning (a) or (b) or both to the Holocaust. But 49 percent chose answer (d), denying that the Six Million died for the creation of the State or to teach Jews to keep the Torah. It must be borne in mind that these survivors, only half of all who held any opinion at all on the subject of Question 6, may not have believed that the Holocaust had a purpose. They may, however, view the State as having come about as a political *consequence* of the Holocaust.

Several survivors spoke to this distinction. One said: "Israel is the outcome of the Holocaust but not the reason for it." Another said: "There was not any philosophical purpose or a fulfillment of the will of God. It was the result of the war and politics and the United Nations and the United States and the Soviet Union and Jews fighting . . . all these are reasons, but the Six Million did not die for it." And others said: "This much is certain. The Holocaust is the main reason we got this State of ours. The world became ready for the notion of a Jewish State because of the destruction of the Six Million."

Of the survivors who deny seeing religious purpose in the Holocaust, only 4 percent were consistently observant survivors. But half of all who chose "I do not know" as their answer were of this same category of consistently observant survivors. For the pious the actual denial of religious meaning for the Holocaust in a world overshadowed by God is exceptionally difficult.

Was Israel Worth the Price?

The seventh and final question of the series asks survivors: If the Holocaust was the only way for the State of Israel to have been reborn, was the sacrifice of the Six Million worth the price?

Any serious student of the laws of Judaism and the history of the Jewish people will eventually come upon the doctrine that the preservation of life is emphatically of the foremost priority, perhaps the overriding commandment. The verse in Leviticus 18, "that a man shall live by them," is amplified by the Talmud to mean and not die by them or for them.[10] That is, one must choose to live even if it entails the violation of virtually all other Jewish commandments.[11] Only to avoid incest, idolatry, or murder may a Jew willingly sacrifice his own life, and these are to be interpreted quite narrowly. Moreover, Maimonides teaches that it is laudatory but not compulsory or expected to forfeit one's life even for the avoidance of these three egregious transgressions.

According to G. F. Moore, circumcision and the Sabbath are Judaism's two fundamental observances.[12] Nevertheless, the Talmud teaches that the circumcision of a sickly infant is always deferred until after his recovery.[13] And if two sons have already lost their lives by fever due to, or subsequent to, circumcision, the surgery on the third is put off indefinitely or until he has grown strong.[14] For a frightened child accidentally locked up in a room on the Sabbath, the door may be broken through lest he die of panic.

In defiance of the unbending Sabbatarians who chose to be killed rather than violate the Sabbath by fighting in defense of their lives, the Maccabees, in the second century before the common era, took up arms when attacked by their enemies on the Sabbath day in keeping with the general principle that all the laws of Judaism are subservient to the one enjoining the preservation of life lest the Jew not remain alive to fulfill the others. In the Talmudic discussions of saving a man from danger, one scholar says, "violate one Sabbath for him that he may live to observe many Sabbaths." [15]

Given this Jewish disposition concerning the preservation and safekeeping of human life and despite the indispensable paramountcy of the land of Israel to the Jew, it is not astonishing for our research to disclose that only 6 percent of all survivors could bring themselves to say that if the sacrifice of the Six Million was the only way for Israel to have come about, it was worth it. And these often with reservations:

We can't continue to suffer devastation every generation through history and still survive. The machinery of destruction has become too all-encompassing and efficient. There is no escape from ruthless tyrants of modern times, like Hitler and Stalin, when they are bent upon Jewish slaughter. It used to be we could sustain a pogrom and still survive because Jews would escape to the neighboring town or village, but now the neighboring town is no longer exempt because the tyrant's net is so wide and tightly woven. Today there is no escape. There is no haven. Better to lose the Six Million all at once and secure a refuge for the rest for now and for the future.

The wife of the survivor who made this statement, herself a survivor, although not appearing in our statistics, picked up the analogy in agreement with her husband:

> I believe we could have lost the Six Million by smaller massacres, which would not have resulted in the return to Zion. But the one huge explosion was better than smaller periodic outbreaks which would have occurred throughout the twentieth century and later centuries to the Jew. Without the Holocaust the fate of the Jew would have been to continue in exile and to sustain eruptions with the same end results, the loss of millions, perhaps more than even the Six Million. But the point is, there would have been nothing to show for it. In the long run it was worth it. We could just as easily have had the sacrifice without the compensation.

There are survivors, of course, among the 6 percent who mention simply that "it was worth the sacrifice. If God ordained it that way." And others said, "It was a high price but anything good requires a high price. It was bought and paid for and delivered with Jewish blood, but it was worth it and we must make it worth it." And, "It was worth it for the sake of future generations." Still another said:

> On balance it was worth it but too many died. And yet millions of people from other lands also were killed defending their own countries. The survivors would have to say they paid the necessary price. There is always a huge price to pay. In a way they, the Six Million, sacrificed their lives for our land that it be re-established. Other countries are different in that they never have to lose even a fraction as many as the Jews lost, three times as many dead as are now living in the land. But the Jews were different because they did not have the land as their own state in the first place, so their sacrifice had to be so much greater than the sacrifices made for other lands. They were not defending a land, they were fighting for it. In a way, the first war for the State of Israel was not the war of 1947–1948. But rather the Holocaust itself was the first war fought for the establishment of the State. It was worth it because it had to be.

And another survivor who was wounded severely by Nazi Stuka
dive bombers said:

> It was worth it because at the very least the establishment of the
> State of Israel gives us the feeling of security that more mis-
> fortune will not happen again. At least not without a fight. Israel
> is now like all other nations. No longer shall we say, "We are
> chosen," or "You have chosen us from all the people." Israel is now
> able to stand strong with the power to defend herself. That in
> itself is worth any sacrifice.

Another who miraculously survived the firing squad suggested, "Each
one of the Six Million would have said it was worth sacrificing my life
that the State be born. The great tragedy is that it took so many." And
another, "I believe it was worth it or will be worth it in the long run if
the State grows strong and secure and survives, and that in centuries to
come we will look back and say it was worth it, but until then it may be
too soon to tell." And still another, a metalworker employed in several
labor camp workshops, said: "I have become a fatalist during the Holocaust. Whatever is, is for the best. Because it has to be. There is nothing
to be done to change it or prevent it. So one is forced to say it is worth
it because it could not have been otherwise."

Although a full 29 percent said they did not know if the sacrifice
was worth it, the greater majority of survivors, 64 percent, adhered to
the Jewish thesis that the preservation of life is the more overarching
consideration even above that of the age-old dream of the resurrection
of the Jewish homeland. Only the opinion in Question 3 of this series
that the Six Million died not because of God's doings but because
of man's relationship to man marshaled greater assent among survivors
than the view that the State of Israel was not worth the cost of the
death of the Six Million, 72 percent to 64 percent.

Numerous survivors repeated the statement, which proved more
rhetorical than substantial when pressed in the dialectic of discussion,
that "the land was not worth the hair of a single child." One survivor
self-consciously reminded himself that "altogether we with reluctant
willingness gave up our children in defense of Israel in war after war
with the Arabs, the difference is that if we don't sacrifice some of our
youth in battle, all will be gone in a defeat and destruction similar to
the Holocaust. But if one has the choice of the children or the State, we
would all take the children."

Or as another has said: "A sacrifice of smaller proportions may have been worth it, but not so great as the one we made. The children, one and a half million children, that is too great a loss."

And another survivor maintained: "It was not worth it because we could have lived on in exile each one with his family. And the pioneers would have continued to redeem the land for the rest of the Jews. And it would have brought about the same objective eventually without such a great cost."

In fact, numerous survivors insisted that "the sacrifice was not worth it because the State would have come about anyway, a little later. The Holocaust was entirely unnecessary from the point of view of the establishment of the State." "But the Holocaust was not the only way to have brought the State about . . . better to have waited even years because the sacrifice was too great. Remember the surviving victims of the Holocaust were not the first to arrive here."

There was much agreement with the following sentiments: "I alone remained alive of all my family and I believe it was too costly even though I myself and all others such as I may have been willing to sacrifice our own lives for the creation of the State if necessary." And repeatedly: "One dead child was not worth it. If I had to choose between the Six Million or the existence of the State of Israel, I would choose the Six Million." And one survivor, tersely, "It is forbidden for us to offer human sacrifices."

And another survivor agreeing with these expressed his thoughts in the following words:

I think that each one of the Six Million would have said he would have gladly sacrificed his life, but if he knew how many others would have to sacrifice their lives along with his, how great the price was, I believe he would have said too much! Take my life and others as well but not all the Jews of Europe. That is not worth it. The cost is too great; the Jewish people itself may not survive it. They may not now have the numbers to do so.

And another survivor astutely observed:

I would not be surprised if most survivors, by a great majority, said the price was not worth it, but I would be interested to know how the ratio would compare to the general population of non-survivors, your average Israelis and especially the younger generation. They may have another opinion entirely. They would be more likely to say it was worth it, that any price was worth the winning of the State.

If you ask the average young Sabra, wouldn't he reflect upon the question and say I bet the survivors themselves, because they lost so many dear ones and beloved family, don't think it was worth it, if Israel could only have come about that way, while we Israeli-born would be more inclined to believe it was worth it!

When a war, fought between two countries, is over, doesn't the family of those who lost their lives experience grave doubts, years later, when a son is dead and the country is back to normal, having even re-entered into normal relationships with yesterday's enemies? Do they not say my son is dead, for what real purpose? I guess it is more worth it when the suffering happens to others. Who knows.

Nearly 30 percent chose "I do not know" as their answer, but perhaps as often as it is an expression of uncertainty this choice served to indicate a reluctance to ratify one or the other view:

How can I bring myself to say it was worth it when Six Million Jews lost their lives? I am not so unfeeling to suggest so great a loss can be condoned. On the other hand, I feel in my bones that no sacrifice is too great for the homeland. It is not that I don't know. I thought about it a great deal. And I do not wish not to answer the question and appear uncooperative. It is just that I refuse to, or can't come down on either side.

And a less mild-mannered survivor, in the tradition of the great Rabbi Shamai who drove away a heathen desiring to be taught the entirety of Judaism quickly ("while I stand on one foot") said, "I don't know but I do know the question is impertinent and scandalous. I refuse either answer."

The Holocaust and the establishment of the State of Israel are the two predominant events of Jewish life in the twentieth century. Whether viewed historically or spiritually, they are so inexorably inter-twined it is impossible to pull them apart. Nevertheless, based on this research, it is reasonable to conclude that to the frequently framed question occupying the minds of modern post-Holocaust Jews living in Israel and elsewhere—Was the State worth the price of the Holocaust?—the answer survivors provide is, if not a resounding and thunderous no, then certainly an emphatic no, a declination with little hesitation or uncertainty.

One survivor said:

It most probably is true that many of us survivors feel that the world owes the Jewish people generally, and the survivors particularly, a debt for its treatment of us by aggression or indifference. And Israel is thought to be a kind of small repayment of the enormous debt, but it is even more certainly true to say that if it were possible to "return the goods for the purchase price," we would gladly do so.

An Afterword

THE MOST MONSTROUS TRAGEDY OF HISTORY befell the Jews of our time. The Jews of Europe sustained and absorbed it upon their persons corporeally. And the entire body of the Jewish people, still staggering from the blow, tries to come to terms with it, endeavors to understand it and integrate its meaning into its scarred consciousness. Three decades have elapsed since the Holocaust was doused by the Allied forces and its charred embers swept away and gathered in other parts of the world. But survivors continue to reel from the shock waves bearing off the continent of Europe whose widening orbits reach every Jewish community of the world and virtually every Jew within them.

It is still disputable among Jewish thinkers whether the Holocaust is different in kind as well as in degree from previous Jewish calamities. And this research in no way sought to take sides or settle the controversy. Jewish history has shown that previous disasters affected both Judaism and the Jewish people. Jean-Paul Sartre has suggested that the effects of these disasters upon the people were salutary—refining and sensitizing the character of the Jew and, hence, the Jewish character. Even if someone dare suggest such a thought in connection with the Holocaust of our time, it is surely premature for such a verdict. But it is not too soon to insist that the price was too great for such a relatively small return, particularly since, surely, that "character refinement" had long previously passed the point of diminishing return. And the Jew hardly needed a third of his people destroyed for further character refinement. Most survivors maintain that the annihilation of the Six Million was too great a price even for the re-establishment of the Jewish state.

248

Previous disasters—crusades, inquisitions, pogroms—brought forth changes in the Jew of course, although at those times there were no instrumentalities to measure precisely how survivors then were affected and how their thinking changed. Nor can we know how the entire people scattered elsewhere were affected. We can at best study the nature of Jewish fast days and festivals to learn how Judaism has been recast by these previous tragedies. And we can study the diverse personal memoirs written then to see how certain individual Jews were affected by their survival of disasters of generations and centuries ago, how their religious sensibilities were conditioned and their theology qualified.

In our own time we have no concrete evidence as to how the rest of world Jewry, non-European Jews, those individuals who fortunately never knew the inner workings of the camps and the up-close experience of atrocity, were affected religiously in their behavior and beliefs by the Holocaust. It is not too late to conduct such an inquiry, one which would essentially ask, "Are you in any way different, and if so, in what way are you a different kind of Jew today because of the Holocaust?" It will not do to dismiss the matter by merely joining in the recitation of the cliché, however true, that, as for world Jewry in the aggregate, we know how it has been changed: The light of the great European Jewish diaspora has been extinguished.

In the absence of studies on general Jewish attitudes, the thoughtful and often deeply moving testimonies of survivors provide us with important insights into the nature of Judaism in the post-Holocaust world. And until careful surveys are conducted, survivors will not be speaking for themselves alone: They represent a sensitive barometer of contemporary Jewish beliefs and behavior, not only concerning the Holocaust but on a wide variety of issues. Here is telling proof that the terrible experiences of Auschwitz made victims of the Holocaust acutely aware of the existential condition of man in general and the Jew in particular.

This research has sought to answer the question: How have the survivors of the Nazi Holocaust been affected in religious ideas, beliefs, and practices by the experience they underwent and endured? A qualitative study such as this must be seen as invaluable because it offers an objective look at survivor attitudes, at times corroborating commonly held assumptions, at times refuting them. It is apparent that the research has revealed certain typical forms of religious thinking. It has also borne out the expectations that survivor testimonies and transcripts would transcend mere reporting: They translate a particular hell into a cosmic one.

To know what practices a Jew should perform, tradition teaches that we are to go about and observe what the Jews are in fact doing. And to know what a Jew should believe? For this there are no such similar instructions. Moreover, Judaism, unlike Christianity, has no prescribed creed. We do nevertheless wish to know what Jews believe even if these beliefs are not necessarily compelling for others. They are compelling in another sense: In previous ages certain thinkers rose from the midst of the people to interpret for all the Jewish world the meaning of the tragedies sustained. Our age is no exception: Fackenheim, Berkowitz, Frankl, Rubenstein, Borowitz and numerous other Jewish teachers and rabbis have helped us in important ways to understand the catastrophe of our times. They are our credible guides whose written and spoken words must be returned to again and again, but we, and they as well, must pay even closer and more careful attention to what the others who have undergone the experience being interpreted have to say: the thinking by survivors in these pages and elsewhere.

In short, we can know how Judaism has been modified but we cannot know how Jews were affected by previous Jewish calamities. Today it may be too soon to say we know how Judaism has been recast by the most recent, most devastating Jewish calamity. And we may not yet be able to say, if we ever will be able to say, how average Jews have become different—stirred, changed, or transformed—by the Holocaust, but we at least can now speak with some measure of assurance about how survivors of that catastrophe were affected religiously by it.

Notes

Chapter One. Introduction

1. Zorach Warhaftig, *Uprooted: Jewish Refugees and Displaced Persons After Liberation* (New York: Institute of Jewish Affairs of the American Jewish Congress and World Jewish Congress, November 1946). Warhaftig cites the statement made by Herbert Lehman, former Director General of the United Nations Relief and Rehabilitation Administration (UNRRA), printed in the *New York Times*, August 4, 1946, to the effect that there "will undoubtedly remain a hard core of much more than 500,000 people who have been displaced from their homes and who are not repatriable." For a more recent estimate of the number of Jewish Holocaust survivors, see Jacob Robinson's article entitled "Holocaust" in the *Encyclopedia Judaica*.

2. Elie Wiesel, *One Generation After* (New York: Random House, 1970), pp. 7–8.

3. Terrence Des Pres, *The Survivor* (New York: Oxford University Press, 1976), pp. 29–30.

4. Simon N. Herman, *Israelis and Jews* (Philadelphia: Jewish Publication Society of America, 1971), p. 182.

5. Shabtai Teveth, *The Tanks of Tammuz* (London: Weidenfeld & Nicholson, 1968, pp. 35–36.

6. Arthur Hertzberg, "The American Jew and His Religion," in Oscar I. Janowski, ed., *The American Jew: A Reappraisal* (Philadelphia: Jewish Publication Society of America, 1967 [5727]), p. 118.

7. Gerhard Lenski, *The Religious Factor* (Garden City, N.Y.: Doubleday, 1961), pp. 45–46.

8. Hertzberg, "American Jew and His Religion," p. 118.

251

9. Georges Friedmann, *The End of the Jewish People?* (Garden City, N.Y.: Doubleday, 1967), p. 176.

10. *Ibid.*, p. 216.

11. Moses Cyrus Weiler, "The Commandments in Modern Times," *CCAR Journal* (Central Conference of American Rabbis, Houston), June 1970, p. 44.

12. *Ibid.*

13. Hannah Arendt, *The Life of the Mind, I: Thinking* (New York and London: Harcourt Brace Jovanovich, 1971), pp. 15 ff.

14. Gerald Reitlinger, *The Final Solution* (New York: Beechhurst Press, 1953).

15. Lawrence L. Langer, *The Holocaust and the Literary Imagination* (New Haven: Yale University Press, 1975), p. xii.

Chapter Two. The Religious Behavior of Holocaust Survivors

1. Philip S. Bernstein, in *CCAR Yearbook* 79 (Central Conference of American Rabbis, Houston, 1969): 227.

2. Michael M. Bernet, "Unknown Diarist of the Lodz Ghetto," *Hadassah Magazine* 51, No. 2 (October 1969): 6.

3. David P. Boder, "The Impact of Catastrophe," *Journal of Psychology*, 1954, p. 1.

4. Mishna, Pirke Avot 2:1.

5. Case studies have shown that many observant Jews conducted their lives, even in the camps, according to Jewish religious laws, depending upon the particular camp and the strength of will of the inmates.

6. Given the universal assumptions concerning survivor attitudes and behavior, our findings on their relative unchanging nature for half the population are significant in themselves, regardless of the reasons they offer.

7. David P. Boder, *I Did Not Interview the Dead* (Urbana: University of Illinois Press, 1949), p. 220.

8. The 4 percent of nonobservant survivors who claimed to have had their religious practices weakened points to the fact that even minimal observances could be still further reduced.

9. Terrence Des Pres, *The Survivor* (New York: Oxford University Press, 1976), p. 29.

10. Jack Kuper, *Child of the Holocaust* (Garden City, N.Y.: Doubleday, 1968). Alexander Donat, in *The Holocaust Kingdom* (New York: Holt, Rinehart & Winston, 1963), identifies the anguish as well as the war years'

circumstances that brought a Jewish youngster, the author's own son, to the temporary abandonment of Jewish identity in the church. The son, William Donat, now lectures on the Holocaust in America to Jewish and Christian audiences.

11. David P. Boder, "Topical Autobiographies of Displaced People," manuscript, Yivo Library.

12. Jerzy Kosinski, *The Painted Bird* (New York: Modern Library, 1970).

13. Ka-tzetnik 135633 (pseud. for Yehiel De-Nur) *Sunrise Over Hell* (London: Corgi Books, Transworld Publishers, 1978), pp. 187–188.

14. Alexander I. Solzhenitsyn, *The Gulag Archipelago, Three* (New York: Harper and Row, 1977).

15. Des Pres, *The Survivor,* p. 42.

16. *Ibid.,* p. 20.

17. Mishna, Pirke Avot.

Chapter Three. The Faith of Holocaust Survivors

1. Rashi, the eleventh-century commentator, offers in his notes on Deut. 11:16 the corresponding proposition: In good times one forgets God.

2. Richard Rubenstein, *After Auschwitz* (Indianapolis: Bobbs-Merrill Co., 1966), pp. 69–70.

3. Terrence Des Pres, *The Survivor* (New York: Oxford University Press, 1976), p. 44.

4. *Ibid.,* p. 49.

5. Leon W. Wells, *The Death Brigade* (New York: Holocaust Library, 1978; first published by Macmillan as *The Janowska Road*), p. 201.

6. *Ibid.,* pp. 201–202.

Chapter Four. The Meaning of the Holocaust

1. Talmud Sanhedrin 90a.

2. Leviticus 26.

3. Moses Maimonides, *Kings and Their Wars,* 12:4.

4. Talmud Sanhedrin, 97a.

5. Gen. R. XLII:4.

6. Deut. 7:6–7.

7. Exodus 19:6.

8. Midrash Ex. 29:4.

9. John Hospers, "Implied Truths in Literature," in Joseph Margolis, ed., *Philosophy Looks at the Arts* (New York: Scribner's, 1962), p. 212.

10. Deut. 14:2.

11. Talmud Sanhedrin 10(11):1.

12. Sifrei Num. 15:31 and elsewhere.

13. Talmud Meg. 31b.

14. Lamentations Rabbah 2.

15. Sifre (ed. Friedmann, b. 31b–32a).

16. Horaiyot 8a.

17. Talmud Sanhedrin 63a (based on Ex. 22:19).

18. Micah 4:5.

Chapter Five. Seven Theological Questions

1. Talmud Sanhedrin 90a.

2. Chaim Aron Kaplan, *Scroll of Agony* (New York: Macmillan, 1965), p. 131.

3. Emile Durkheim, *Suicide* (New York: Free Press, 1957), p. 44.

4. Whitney Pope, *Durkheim's Suicide: A Classic Analyzed* (Chicago and London: University of Chicago Press, 1976), p. 10.

5. Semahot 2:1.

6. C. G. Montefiore and H. Lowe, eds., *A Rabbinic Anthology* (New York: Schocken; Philadelphia: The Jewish Publication Society of America, 1970), p. 541.

7. Henry Slonimsky, *Essays* (Cincinnatti: Hebrew Union College Press, 1967), pp. 7–8.

8. Moshe Flinker, *Young Moshe's Diary* (Jerusalem: Yad Vashem, 1965).

9. Talmud Baba Mazia 86.

10. Talmud Yoma 85b.

11. Deut. 33:15–19.

12. George Foot Moore, *Judaism* (Cambridge, Mass.: Harvard University Press, 1958), Vol. 2: p. 16.

13. Talmud Shabbat 134a.

14. Talmud Yebamot 64b.

15. Talmud Yoma 85b.

Selected Bibliography

Survivor Accounts and Testimony

Bettelheim, Bruno. *The Informed Heart*. New York: Free Press, 1960; London: Thames & Hudson, 1961.

Birenbaum, Halina. *Hope Is the Last To Die*, tr. David Welsh. New York: Twayne, 1971.

Borzykowski, Tuvia. *Between Falling Walls*. Beit Lohamei Hagetaot, Israel: Ghetto Fighters House, 1972.

Brand, Sandra. *I Dared to Live*. New York: Shengold Publishers, 1978.

Donat, Alexander. *The Holocaust Kingdom*. New York: Holt, Rinehart and Winston, 1965; London: Corgi, 1967.

Flinker, Moshe. *Young Moshe's Diary*. Jerusalem: Yad Vashem, 1965.

Frank, Anne. *Diary of a Young Girl*. New York: Pocket Books, 1965.

Frankl, Viktor E. *From Death-Camp to Existentialism*, tr. Ilse Lasch. Boston: Beacon, 1959.

Hart, Kitty. *I Am Alive*. London and New York: Abelard-Schuman, 1962.

Kaplan, Chaim A. *The Warsaw Diary of Chaim A. Kaplan*, tr. Abraham I. Katsh. New York: Collier, 1973. Under the title *Scroll of Agony*. New York: Macmillan, 1965; London: Hamish Hamilton, 1966.

Ka-tzetnik 135633 (pseud. for Yehiel De-Nur). *House of Dolls*. New York: Simon and Schuster, 1955.

———. *Atrocity*. New York: Lyle Stuart, 1963.

——. *Sunrise Over Hell*. London: Corgi (Transworld Publishers), 1978.

Klein, Gerda Weissman. *All But My Life*. New York: Hill & Wang, 1957; London: Elek, 1958.

Kuper, Jack. *Child of the Holocaust*. London: Routledge & Kegan Paul, 1967.

Lengyel, Olga. *Five Chimneys: The Story of Auschwitz*, tr. Paul P. Weiss. Chicago: Ziff-Davis, 1947; London: Mayflower, 1972.

Levi, Primo. *Survival in Auschwitz*, tr. Stuart Woolf. New York: Collier, 1969. Under the title *If This Man Is a Man*. New York: Orion, 1959; London: Orion, 1960.

Lewinska, Pelagia. *Twenty Months at Auschwitz*, tr. Albert Teichner. New York: Lyle Stuart, 1968.

Mandelstam, Nadezhda. *Hope Against Hope*, tr. Max Hayward. New York: Atheneum, 1970; London: Harvill, 1971.

Maurel, Micheline. *An Ordinary Camp*, tr. Margaret S. Summers. New York: Simon & Schuster, 1958. Under the title *Ravensbruck*. London: Blond, 1958.

Mechanicus, Philip. *Year of Fear*. New York: Hawthorn Books, Inc., 1968.

Meed, Vladka. *On Both Sides of the Wall: Memoirs from the Warsaw Ghetto*. Beit Lohamei Hagetaot, Israel: Ghetto Fighters House, 1972.

Newman, Judith Sternberg. *In the Hell of Auschwitz*. New York: Exposition, 1964.

Nyiszli, Miklos. *Auschwitz: A Doctor's Eyewitness Account*, tr. Tibere Kremer and Richard Seaver, with "Foreword" by Bruno Bettelheim. New York: Frederick Fell, 1960; London: Panther, 1967.

Pawlowicz, Sala. *I Will Survive*. New York: Norton; London: Muller,

Perl, Gisella. *I Was a Doctor in Auschwitz*. New York: International Universities Press, 1948.

Ringelblum, Emmanuel. *Notes from the Warsaw Ghetto*, tr. Jacob Sloan. New York: McGraw-Hill, 1958.

Rousset, David. *The Other Kingdom*, tr. Ramon Guthrie. New York: Reynal and Hitchcock, 1947.

Sereny, Gitta. *Into That Darkness*. New York: McGraw-Hill, 1974; London: Deutsch, 1974.

Vrba, Rudolf. *I Cannot Forgive*. New York: Grove; London: Sidgwick & Jackson, 1964.

Wdowinski, David. *And We Are Not Saved*. New York: Philosophical Library, 1963; London: W. H. Allen, 1964.

Wells, Leon W. *The Janowska Road*. New York: Macmillan, 1963; London: Jonathan Cape, 1966.

Wiesel, Elie. *Night*, tr. Stella Rodway. New York: Avon, 1969; London: Fontana, 1973.

Zylberg, Michael. *A Warsaw Diary: 1939–1945*. London: Valentine, Mitchell, 1969.

Zywulska, Krystyna. *I Came Back*, tr. Krystyna Cenkalska. London: Dennis Dobson, 1951.

The Holocaust and Religious Thought

Berkowitz, Eliezer. *Faith After the Holocaust*. New York: Ktav Publishing House, 1973.

Borowitz, Eugene B. *How Can a Jew Speak of Faith Today?* Philadelphia: The Westminster Press, 1969.

———. *Modern Theories of Judaism*. New York: Behrman House, 1980.

Fackenheim, Emil L. *Quest for Past and Future*. Bloomington: Indiana University Press, 1968.

———. *Encounters between Judaism and Modern Philosophy*. New York: Basic Books, 1973.

———. *The Jewish Return into History*. New York: Schocken Books, 1978.

Maybaum, Ignaz. *The Face of God After Auschwitz*. Amsterdam: Polak and Van Gennep Ltd., 1965.

Rubenstein, Richard L. *After Auschwitz: Radical Theology and Contemporary Judaism*. Indianapolis: Bobbs-Merrill Co., 1966.

INDEX

Index